Qualitative Interviewing

Qualitative Interviewing

The Art Of Hearing Data

Herbert J. Rubin
Irene S. Rubin

SAGE Publications
International Educational and Professional Publisher
Thousand Oaks   London   New Delhi

For information address:

SAGE Publications, Inc.
2455 Teller Road
Thousand Oaks, California 91320
E-mail: order@sagepub.com

SAGE Publications Ltd.
6 Bonhill Street
London EC2A 4PU
United Kingdom

SAGE Publications India Pvt. Ltd.
M-32 Market
Greater Kailash I
New Delhi 110 048 India

Printed in the United States of America

Library of Congress Cataloging-in-Publication Data

Rubin, Herbert J.
    Qualitative interviewing: the art of hearing data / Herbert J.
Rubin and Irene S. Rubin.
        p. cm.
    Includes bibliographical references and index.
    ISBN 0-8039-5095-0 (alk. paper). — ISBN 0-8039-5096-9 (pbk.:
alk. paper)
    1. Interviewing. 2. Interviewing in sociology. I. Rubin, Irene.
II. Title.
    H62.R737   1995
    001.4′222—dc20   95-9036

This book is printed on acid-free paper.

        98 99 10 9 8 7 6

Sage Project Editor: Susan McElroy

H
62
,R737
1995

Contents

Preface

Qualitative interviewing has filled our lives with adventure. This incredibly powerful research tool has extended our intellectual and emotional reach and has kept our work fresh and useful over several decades. We wrote *Qualitative Interviewing* to share our excitement with our own students. We wanted to communicate to our students in political science and sociology not only the techniques of interviewing, but also the exhilaration we have experienced, to reignite the excitement of learning where it may have begun to fade. Qualitative interviewing opens broader worlds to study; it is exciting and enriching as well as rigorous. This book is our response to our students' complaints that they cannot research what interests them using quantitative techniques alone.

Our approach to interviewing also speaks to those in many other fields who need to acquire a rich understanding of other peoples' lives and experiences. Practitioners and students in education, counseling, and law and other professionals, from nurses and doctors to police, from managers to union organizers, need to be able to find out what happened; what goes on here; and how their clients, their students, their customers, their patients, or their suspects view their worlds and their experiences.

The book was also motivated by a desire to respond to colleagues who believe that only statistical analysis can be rigorous, and who think that the investigation of causes requires quantitative data. These colleagues have little idea of the standards, the checks, the systematic nature of collecting data through qualitative interviewing. They needlessly reduce people to numbers and lose the richness of context because they do not understand the qualitative research model. These colleagues may never read *Qualitative Interviewing,* but they should.

Qualitative Interviewing merges our experiences from many projects with our reading of the literature on interviewing. We know that our approach to qualitative interviewing is not the only one available, but we feel that *Qualitative Interviewing* offers a good place to start in learning how to hear others. After reading this book, the student should have sufficient understanding of the philosophy and techniques of qualitative interviewing to continue to learn more about interviewing and define his or her own style of questioning. This book does not propose a new orthodoxy that must be practiced exactly as we present it; rather, it opens up an exciting—and rigorous—way of learning, intended to be personalized and adapted in use.

We would like to thank Jim Thomas, our colleague in sociology at Northern Illinois University, for sharing so much of his field experience with us for this book, and Mitch Allen, our acquisitions editor at Sage, whose continual (polite) nagging pushed up the date of completion of the manuscript. We would also like to thank the anonymous reviewers of the book for their excellent and constructive comments. They know who they are, even if we don't. Finally, we would like to thank all of our conversational partners over a lifetime of research for all that they have taught us.

1

Listening, Hearing, and
Sharing Social Experiences

I'll tell you one thing. It has been a very interesting conversation with you because I think in the course of conversation it's given me the time . . . to reflect . . . on what we are doing and how we are doing it. . . . It has given me a good opportunity.

An interviewee

ualitative interviewing is a great adventure; every step of an interview brings new information and opens windows into the experiences of the people you meet. Qualitative interviewing is a way of finding out what others feel and think about their worlds. Through qualitative interviews you can understand experiences and reconstruct events in which you did not participate. Through what you hear and learn, you can extend your intellectual and emotional reach across time, class, race, sex, and geographical divisions.

Qualitative interviewing builds on the conversational skills that you already have. In ordinary conversations, people routinely ask questions and listen to the answers. "These pills are 2 years old—are they still good?" "I am lost, where is Alden Place?" Such conversations follow well-known rules. People know whose turn it is to talk and that it is impolite to interrupt. Everyone knows when to talk at length and when to answer briefly. People know it is okay to change the subject and how to do it with grace. And speakers know that it usually doesn't matter exactly what they say, because ordinary conversations are as much about being in a relationship as they are a means of sharing information.

Qualitative interviewing builds on these rules, but differs from ordinary conversations in important ways. A key dissimilarity is that qualitative interviews are a tool of research, an intentional way of learning about people's feelings, thoughts, and experiences. Interviews provide the information that the researcher later analyzes and shares with others through books, reports, and articles. A second distinction is that qualitative interviews are held between strangers as well as among acquaintances. A third difference from ordinary conversations is that qualitative interviews are guided by the researcher, who intentionally introduces a limited number of questions and requests the interviewee to explore these questions in depth. The researcher encourages the interviewees to reflect, in detail, on events they have experienced.

To conduct a qualitative interview and truly hear what people say requires skills beyond those of ordinary conversation and takes considerable practice. How do you think of questions for a topic that you have chosen? How do you get people to stay focused on what you want to hear about? Whom do you interview and why? How can you trust what people are telling you?

On a more technical level, how do you persuade a person to become an interviewee? How specific should a question be? Is the wording too biased? How do you get people to elaborate on what they say? How do you put together different tellings of the same event? When do you take on-scene notes and when should you rely on memory? Do you use a tape recorder or a camcorder? In *Qualitative Interviewing* we offer some practical guidelines to help develop the technical skills of qualitative interviewing.

But qualitative interviewing is more than a set of skills, it is also a philosophy, an approach to learning. One element of this philosophy is that understanding is achieved by encouraging people to describe their worlds in their own terms. A second component of this philosophy is that interviewing involves a relationship between the interviewer and interviewee that imposes obligations on both sides. Third, this philosophy helps define what is interesting and what is ethical and helps provide standards to judge the quality of the research, the humanity of the interviewing relationship, and the completeness and accuracy of the write-up. *Qualitative Interviewing* describes this philosophy of qualitative research to provide the underpinning for the more technical skills of interviewing.

THE WHAT AND WHY OF
QUALITATIVE INTERVIEWING

Qualitative interviewing is an extremely versatile approach to doing research. Students and scholars interview to learn about customs in a Caribbean island or neighborhoods in Detroit (Mast, 1994). They can do interviews to ferret out how members of Congress relate to their constituents (Fenno, 1978), to understand the rites of passage in a college dormitory (Moffatt, 1989), or to share the stories of those dying from AIDS. The qualitative interview is a principle research tool for the sociologist, educator, political scientist, criminologist, public administrator, social worker, anthropologist, and historian. It is how people in health care, social agencies, and the police learn about the problems their clients face. It is the basic tool for investigative reporters and an important technique for evaluating a program or project.

Qualitative interviewers listen to people as they describe how they understand the worlds in which they live and work. What are the differences in what success means to a poor farmer, a Wall Street lawyer, a teenager in love, or a deaf student? One person may view it as extortion when a youth offers to guard a car in the inner city, but how does the youth who makes the offer understand the encounter? Do students see college as an experience to be endured or a chance to develop and satisfy intellectual curiosity? Or does college represent something else, such as independence or maturity? What do people intend to communicate when they dye their hair pink, wear three earrings in one ear, or wear gray, double-breasted, pin-striped suits?

People who live or work together or have similar racial, ethnic, or religious backgrounds develop shared understandings that are communicated to others in their group and constitute their culture. In-depth qualitative interviewing helps explain how and why culture is created, evolves, and is maintained. Qualitative interviews also explore specific topics, events, or happenings. Interviewers can solicit personal histories to examine social and political phenomena. How were people changed by war? What motivates a person to become a rebel or a whistle-blower? How do families adapt as an increasing number of women share time between home and job? How do bureaucrats balance equity and humanity in service delivery?

Qualitative interviewers explore social, political, and economic changes. A rural area is transformed into suburban sprawl, malls replace farmlands, and open space becomes clogged with traffic. How did this happen? What were the interests of the land developers, future homeowners, and farmers? Did the environmentalists have a say? What role did politicians play? A city passes a budget disproportionately targeting services to downtown and all but neglecting the poorer neighborhoods. Why is there an imbalance of power and how do big businesses persuade those in office to focus on business needs rather than those of the poor?

Through qualitative interviews, researchers evaluate all kinds of projects and programs, whether for social reform or managerial improvement. Interviewers talk to people who are trying to solve social problems and examine their successes and failures. Are inner-city adults more empowered by community literacy programs or by better homes? Why did penitentiaries become such brutal and unconstructive places? What were the impacts of the reform agenda in the National Performance Report issued under the guidance of Vice President Albert Gore in 1993? How is the new fee structure at the day care center working out?

Researchers put together the information they find from qualitative interviews to form explanations and theories that are grounded in the details, evidence, and examples of the interviews. Such *grounded theories* (Glaser & Strauss, 1967) explain what is happening in the terms of those involved in a situation. Grounded theory is based on exchanges in which the interviewees can talk back, clarify, and explain their points. These explanations and theories are not just of academic interest, they can have practical implications.

Suppose your goal was to improve reading scores of children in inner-city schools through a peer-tutoring program. A paper-and-pen test of reading scores showed no improvement and you wonder why. If you try to get into the world of the children through interviewing, you may learn that they cannot pay attention because they are hungry. Or that there is no quiet time or place for the child to practice reading, and little brothers and sisters tear up books. Or you may find out there is a gang culture that argues against doing well in school. Depending on what you find out, you know where to concentrate your efforts to solve the problem.

Or suppose you have become the head of an agency and find to your dismay that errors are slipping through that cost both time and money, yet people appear to be working hard and have good qualifications for their jobs. By interviewing your employees, you can learn which events in the company's history contributed to the problem. It may be that everyone repeats to new employees the story about a worker who was fired for catching an error made by a boss. The employees learn quickly not to report mistakes. From these depth interviews, you learn that you have to make employees feel secure enough to call attention to mistakes.

Qualitative interviewing is both an academic and a practical tool. It allows us to share the world of others to find out what is going on, why people do what they do, and how they understand their worlds. With such knowledge you can help solve a variety of problems.

THE FAMILY OF
QUALITATIVE INTERVIEWS

To elicit in-depth answers about culture, meanings, processes, and problems, you can choose from a family of closely related types of qualitative interviews. Though each of these approaches to interviewing differs somewhat, each reflects the same philosophy of qualitative research: Find out what others think and know, and avoid dominating your interviewees by imposing your world on theirs.

Within this gentle approach to interviewing, there is some variation in the degree to which the researcher directs the conversational agenda. With an *unstructured* format, the researcher suggests the subject for discussion but has few specific questions in mind. For instance, the interviewer might suggest, "Let's talk about how it feels to be a graduate student" and let the interviewee answer any way he or she wishes (Douglas, 1985). When researchers want more specific information, they use a *semistructured* (also called *focused*) format (Merton, Fiske, & Kendall, 1990). The interviewer introduces the topic, then guides the discussion by asking specific questions. You might ask the graduate student, "What happened when you discussed your thesis with your adviser?" or "Are you prepared to do qualitative research?"

Many qualitative interviews have both more structured and less structured parts but vary in the balance between them. In the less structured parts, the interviewee does most of the talking, perhaps explaining what an idea, event, or bit of background means; in the more structured portions of the interview, the interviewer poses specific questions to get detail, example, and context. Regardless of the balance between more and less structured questions, qualitative interviewers do not impose a set of answer categories, such as "agree" or "disagree." If they did, they would not be able to find out what the interviewees actually think.

Another way qualitative interviews are distinguished is through the kind of information that they seek. With *cultural* interviews, researchers ask about shared understandings, taken-for-granted rules of behavior and standards of value, and mutual expectations. Cultural interviewers are looking for what people have learned through experience and passed on to the next generation. To learn about particular events or processes, researchers use *topical* interviews; thus they can find out, for instance, how an antidrug program is run. With *oral histories,* the researcher chooses a period of time, such as the Roaring 20s, or a crucial event, such as the making of the atomic bomb, and asks those involved to describe what happened. In *life histories,* what is being studied is the major life events of those being interviewed. With qualitative *evaluation* interviews, the researcher learns in depth and detail how those involved view the successes and failures of a program or project.

Though the approaches to different kinds of qualitative interviews differ slightly, what they share in common is far more important.

SHARED CHARACTERISTICS
OF QUALITATIVE INTERVIEWS

All qualitative interviews share three pivotal characteristics that distinguish them from other forms of data gathering in social and political research. First, qualitative interviews are modifications or extensions of ordinary conversations, but with important distinctions. Second, qualitative interviewers are more interested in the understanding, knowledge, and insights of the interviewees than in categorizing people or events in terms of academic theories. Third, the content of the interview, as well as the flow and choice of topics, changes to match what the individual interviewee knows and feels.

Interviews as Conversations

Qualitative interviews and ordinary conversations share much in common. As in normal conversations, questions and answers follow each other in a logical fashion as people take turns talking. Researchers listen to each answer and determine the next question based on what was said. Interviewers don't work out three or four questions in advance and ask them regardless of the answers to earlier questions. The interview, like an ordinary conversation, is invented anew each time it occurs.

Because interviews are invented anew each time, they can be wonderfully unpredictable. The person being interviewed may take control of the interview and change the subject, guide the tempo, or indicate the interviewer was asking the wrong questions. Sometimes interviewees become hostile; sometimes they become overly friendly, threatening, or flirtatious. Occasionally, bizarre events occur such as getting to an appointment and finding the interviewee sitting in the middle of the room with a shotgun in his lap. Part of the skill of the qualitative researcher is in being able to adapt quickly to a situation that did not go as expected.

Although qualitative interviews are similar in key ways to ordinary conversations, they differ in the intensity of listening to the content of what is being said. The qualitative interviewer listens intently to pick up on key words and ideas and to mark important omissions. The researcher listens to the words actually said and to the nonverbal cues that indicate emphasis and emotional tone. Sometimes you follow up with questions about the emotional tone you observed rather than the content of the answer. If in describing a marriage, the interviewee skips from the courtship, to having children, to the horrors of a divorce, you might want to follow up with questions about the events that led to the divorce. Qualitative interviewers develop listening skills that point out what ideas, themes, or issues to pursue in later questioning.

In qualitative interviews you listen so as to *hear the meaning* of what is being said. You develop skills to listen carefully, sentence by sentence, and word by word. Qualitative interviewing requires listening carefully enough to hear the meanings, interpretations, and understandings that give shape to the worlds of the interviewees. You listen

to many responses from teenagers and hear that the change from childhood to adulthood is a time of confusion. You ask about what goes on
in a marriage and hear how people feel about and understand an insti-
tution that uncomfortably combines sex, gender-role definitions, child
rearing, and economic interdependence.

To get beyond ordinary listening and hear meanings, you have to
focus the discussion to obtain more depth and detail on a narrower range
of topics than you would in ordinary conversations. You encourage
people to elaborate, provide incidents and clarifications, and discuss
events at length. The depth, detail, and richness we seek in interviews
is what Clifford Geertz (1973) has called *thick description*. Thick
description, rooted in the interviewees' firsthand experience, forms the
material that researchers gather up, synthesize, and analyze as part of
hearing the meaning of data.

Discovering the World of the Interviewee

Qualitative interviewing explores the shared meanings that people
develop in work groups, ethnic neighborhoods, recreational centers,
hospitals, churches, and any other place where people interact. The
researcher has to figure out the special new vocabulary and the taken-
for-granted understandings (Schutz, 1967, p. 74) within the setting.
These understandings might be expressed through symbols and metaphors that suggest how people interpret their experiences and how they
deal with others. To understand what people say, interviewers need to
pay attention to the symbols and metaphors with which people describe
their worlds.

For example, in a topical interview study, Irene Rubin was trying to
learn how a city's budget process changed. She had asked a fire chief
to describe how his department viewed the budget office. The chief
replied, "We view them as suits, and they view us as unable to see the
whole picture."

"Suits?" Irene thought, "What does 'suits' mean?" Irene had to puzzle
out the taken-for-granted meaning of the word *suits*. She listened to find
out how other people used this word and deduced its meaning from
examples. Those in the budget office acted like executives, dressing up
like bankers and telling everyone what to do, whereas the people in the

fire department wore hard hats and blue-collar shirts and got things done. The clothes symbolized a class gulf, but with a twist. In different contexts, a term can take on different meanings. As a result, you cannot take for granted that you understand a term when you enter a new setting. When Herbert Rubin was doing cultural research on community developers, he also heard the term "suits," this time contrasted with the word "jeans." Herb's interviewees described bankers as routinely dressing in suits, whereas community developers wore jeans. When community developers visited the banks, the developers had to wear a suit, but bankers, even when they came to the neighborhoods, never put on jeans. To the community developers, suits are clothes that you put on to impress someone—a phony thing. Moreover, the clothes became symbols of the lack of social equality between the bankers and the developers.

Listen to how the words were used when Herb asked a community developer to describe a meeting with a banker:

Herb: Who dressed for whom?

Community Developer: I'm trying to remember. They didn't dress for us. I know that much. They never do. I can't remember a circumstance when a banker did dress for us. And I used to be very uptight about that subject, and always wear a suit and tie when I met with bankers. Until I discovered, I don't have to do that. If I am in the position of power in negotiations, I dress just like I am dressed right now [jeans]. But if I am in a very weak position, I put on a suit and tie, a power suit, red tie, you know, the works, and go into the meeting.

In both these situations, the word *suit* was symbolic of assumptions about control, accomplishment, and pretense. The use of the terms overlapped, but the nuances differed.

To understand what people are saying, interviewers learn to hear the taken-for-granted assumptions of the interviewees and try hard to understand the experiences that have shaped these assumptions. A white, middle-class researcher interviewing in a minority neighborhood learns that community members are reluctant to report a crime to the police and wonders why. Further inquiry will show that people in minority

communities, regardless of their status and accomplishments, are frequently stopped by police on suspicion and often know someone who
was beaten by the police. The taken-for-granted assumption here is that
police are to be feared and are not helpful. Interviewers cannot change
their own experiences with police, but they can learn to recognize the
legitimacy of another perspective based on very different experiences.

Qualitative interviewers understand that one person's experiences are
not intrinsically more true than another's. If the interviewer discovers
four different versions of the same event, it doesn't necessarily mean
that one of interviewees is right and the other three are wrong. They
may all be right, reflecting different perspectives on what happened or
observations of different parts of an event. People looking at the same
events may understand them differently. After all, to a banker, a suit is
just clothes. Jeans may mean something entirely different to the banker
than to the community developer.

Conversational Partners

Unlike survey interviews, in which those giving information are
relatively passive and are not allowed the opportunity to elaborate,
interviewees in qualitative interviews share in the work of the interview,
sometimes guiding it in channels of their own choosing. They are
treated as *partners* rather than as objects of research.

Questions are asked that tap the interviewee's experiences. We can
ask a young resident in a crime-ridden area how he feels as he walks
home from school at night or ask the middle-aged librarian how she is
dealing with the fatal illness of her husband. We can ask health professionals how they react to patients in pain. From the resident of the
housing project, we can begin to learn what it means to be young, afraid,
and vulnerable, and what the appeal of street gangs might be. From the
librarian, we can begin to understand the extent to which middle-aged
women rely on family, friends, and neighbors during a prolonged
illness. From the health professionals, we can begin to understand how
society deals with pain and painkillers, and what unintentional or
well-meaning cruelty is.

In this book we sometimes call those who respond to interview
questions *interviewees*, sometimes we call them *informants*, and some-

times *conversational partners*. Interviewee is a relatively neutral word. Informant usually means someone who is telling us about the research setting, about how things work in that setting, not just about his or her own experiences. In some cases, however, informant means someone who tells police about another person's crime, so this term has to be used with caution. The term *conversational partner* has the advantage of emphasizing the link between interviewing and conversation, and the active role of the interviewee in shaping the discussion. Moreover, the term suggests a congenial and cooperative experience, as both interviewer and interviewee work together to achieve the shared goal of understanding.

Researchers and conversational partners share the task of maintaining the flow of dialogue, creating the frame in which discussion takes place and creating a setting (both symbolic and physical) in which communication is relatively easy. Thinking of the interviewee as a conversational partner reminds the researcher that the person being interviewed can legitimately take over the direction and flow of the interview. Together the researcher and conversational partner decide what issues to explore, suggest what remains to be said, and work to provide the thick description that builds toward an overall picture.

Each conversational partner is an individual who has concerns and interests of his or her own and responds in a distinct manner to the researcher. Some conversational partners are self-revelatory, others more restrained and formalistic. Some need prodding to elaborate; others won't stop talking. Some are well informed, and others know little on the topic. The researcher has to customize what is asked to each interviewee. This approach contrasts with that of the survey researchers, who to find out how widely held some small bit of opinion data is, must ask the same question of everyone.

Asking everyone the same questions makes little sense in qualitative interviewing where the goal is to find out what happened and why, in rich and individualistic terms. An interview is a window on a time and a social world that is experienced one person at a time, one incident at a time. If you want to know how women coped with household tasks before electricity, you let elderly people describe what they did, what they remember, and what it felt like; you don't try to find out how many of them did their wash on Monday.

The image of a partnership with the interviewee does not always work, but it represents the goal of integrating those who give us information into our research. If the partners can direct the conversation to matters that interest them and that they think are important, interviews gain depth and reality. If you impose on them what you think is important, you may miss important insights about the subject you are investigating and you may substitute your ill-informed view of the field for their experienced and knowledgeable one.

TO HEAR DATA, KNOW YOURSELF

In qualitative interviewing, the researcher is not neutral, distant, or emotionally uninvolved. He or she forms a relationship with the interviewee, and that relationship is likely to be involving. The researcher's empathy, sensitivity, humor, and sincerity are important tools for the research. The researcher is asking for a lot of openness from the interviewees; he or she is unlikely to get that openness by being closed and impersonal.

The interview is affected by the researcher's personality, moods, interests, experiences, and biases. How the researcher asks questions changes depending on how he or she feels about the topic or the interviewee. And what the researcher hears from the answer may depend on his or her mood and prior experiences. Some interviewers are not comfortable with people who expose their vulnerabilities or talk about their unhappiness, and therefore cut short answers that reveal such weaknesses. Some researchers get angry during the interview if an interviewee lies to them. Some get so enthralled with what they are learning that they forget to ask about the downside of the topic.

The depth of understanding required to do qualitative interviewing makes it difficult for qualitative researchers to remain value free or neutral toward the issues raised (Bowman, Bowman, & Resch, 1984). Doing in-depth interviewing encourages researchers to develop a strong empathy for the interviewees. Talking with people living in the worst public housing, you learn about teenage pregnancies, substance abuse, and gang fighting. But you also learn about toilets that don't work, schools without books or heating, and lack of meaningful job opportunities. Qualitative research blurs easily into advocacy and efforts to find solutions to problems (Forester, 1993; Thomas, 1993).

How objective does the researcher need to be to do good research? A bias against the group or person being interviewed may block access or distort the results, but too much sympathy can also be blinding. On the other hand, neutrality is probably not a legitimate goal in qualitative research. For one thing, it is impossible to attain. Even if a neutral role were possible, it is not desirable, because it does not equip the researcher with enough empathy to elicit personal stories or in-depth description. Once researchers recognize that neutrality is neither possible nor useful in the research, they have to learn to handle emotion so that it does not hurt the research.

The goal is to achieve some empathy, but not so much involvement that you cannot see the negative things, or if you see them, feel that you cannot report them. A second goal is to learn to go for balance rather than neutrality, that is, you should ask about multiple sides of a story, questioning each interviewee with intensity and empathy. That means that you may have to learn to empathize with different and conflicting points of view, a task that is not always easy.

If you find yourself sympathizing with interviewees who are killers, racists, or religiously intolerant, or who are abusing public trust, you might begin to have questions about yourself. The interviewer might wonder, who am I really? Is there a "me" apart from the research roles I assume? Another problem occurs if researchers feel that they have abused a friendship by getting information to use in research and writing (Adler, Adler, Rochford, & Burke, 1986).

These are real problems and they must be dealt with one way or another. There is a "you" that remains constant, even when you have to change your research role or empathize with people on opposite sides of a spectrum. Interviewing roles and questioning styles are not like masks that can be easily put on and taken off. Instead, they reflect the researcher's own personality. All the research roles that you assume are you, unless you intentionally try to deceive, which is generally not a good strategy. If empathizing with opposite views or with views you disagree with makes you feel too hypocritical to function well, then you may have to redraw the boundaries of your research to avoid topics that you cannot research. If you cannot empathize with both management and labor, then study just management or just labor.

Part of the philosophy of qualitative interviewing is that interviewees and interviewers are both individuals, with emotions and interests and biases that affect how the research is done. Personal involvement is a great strength of the methodology, but it also creates problems that must be addressed. An interviewer has to be sensitive to his or her own biases, to the social and intellectual baggage he or she brings to the interview.

THE AUTHORS

In *Qualitative Interviewing,* the two of us, Irene Rubin, a public administrator, and Herb Rubin, an urbanologist, share with you the excitement of our own interviewing projects. Our experiences include formal interviews with high-ranking government officials, casual conversations in rice paddies with peasant farmers, and informal interviews in retirement homes. We have had interviews with those who have put one over on us and we have had interviews whose depth and frankness have embarrassed us. On occasion, we have had to act aggressively, like an investigative reporter; more often we have listened in a less directive way to what our conversational partners wanted to communicate.

We supplement what we have learned with some of the experiences of Jim Thomas, a criminologist. As we were working on this book, we noticed that most of our conversational partners were in mainstream professions and usually on the right side of the law. Jim generously shared with us his experiences with people in jail and others that the mainstream labels as *deviant.*

In our most recent projects, Irene has been interviewing city officials on how they make budget decisions, Herb has been examining how community organizations work to renew desolated urban areas, and Jim has been studying the culture of computer "hackers." Years ago, Herb and Irene lived among the rural poor in Thailand to explore how government affects the lives of farmers. In a former project, Irene interviewed federal employees who were affected by budget cutbacks in Washington. Herb has examined the rape of suburbia through too-rapid development and talked with those whose job it is to promote economic growth. Many of our examples are taken from these experiences. In teaching, as in interviewing, biography affects what is shared.

THE FLOW OF THE BOOK

Interviewing is both art and science. As with all science, there are normative standards that the researcher must follow. As with all arts, general principles and techniques are invariably modified to fit the individual style of the artist. The experiences we share in *Qualitative Interviewing* should help you develop your own style and confidence as a qualitative interviewer.

To develop your own style, practice interviewing. To help you get the most out of these practice sessions, read the techniques and philosophies presented in this book, try them out, and incorporate the parts that work for you and find substitutes for the rest. Though none of what we write is meant to be followed mechanically, you need to pay particular attention to the materials on normative standards and ethics, as here your responsibility is broad.

In Chapter 2, we explore the theories that underlie qualitative interviewing. These theories argue that knowledge is contextual and that it often doesn't make sense to look for abstract rules of behavior that are not grounded in the context in which they occur. Stripping away context is stripping away meaning. Moreover, facts, statistics, and summary data by themselves tend to be dry.

Chapters 3 and 4 describe how to design the research so when you are finished analyzing the interviews what you have found is both meaningful and convincing. How do we figure out what to ask and of whom? How do we adjust what we are asking as we learn more about what we are researching?

In Chapter 5 we explore how conversational relationships are formed and maintained. We discuss how the interviewer and interviewee become comfortable with one another during the discussion. We also cover the pragmatics of forming a conversational relationship, such as how to set up an appointment for an interview. We include in this chapter a discussion of research ethics. Research ethics involve a careful balancing of the obligations owed to the conversational partner with the researcher's desire to obtain a deep understanding of the topic or culture.

Chapters 6 and 7 provide an overall introduction to the techniques of interviewing. In Chapter 6, we discuss how to encourage people to talk and how to guide the flow of conversation. Chapter 7 covers the types of questions that guide a qualitative interview and ways to maintain structure in an interview while adjusting what you ask next to what conversational partners have just told you. In Chapters 8 and 9, we describe how to carry out the two major types of interviews, cultural and topical.

In Chapter 10, we describe how to analyze interview data, and in Chapter 11, how to share what conversational partners have taught you by writing up the research in a vivid and convincing manner for others to read.

2

Foundations of Qualitative Interviewing

ualitative interviewing requires intense listening, a respect for and curiosity about what people say, and a systematic effort to really hear and understand what people tell you. You don't need the detail of qualitative interviews to find out how frequently people wash their hair, watch a television program, or buy a particular product, but if you want to know what people think about personal hygiene, why they watch so much television, or whether people feel that they gain status by buying a particular product, qualitative interviewing is the right approach.

To understand complicated problems, such as how people deal with a poor self-image or why health care costs are increasing so much, you must be able to explore the topic with your interviewees. To learn about how people lived through historical events, such as wars or embargoes or rapid inflation or depression, or how people adapted to downward social mobility, you have to let them describe their experiences in their own terms.

Armed with an openness to new meanings and perspectives, researchers can confidently interview in many different domains—about religious values or criminals' codes of honor, about family life or fraternity behavior. Interviews range in scope from trying to understand national cultures—why are Americans so concerned with wealth—to focusing in on narrower topics—how did a new computer change teaching methods in one school.

Through qualitative interviews, you set out to learn about the world of others, but real understanding may be elusive. Even when the interviewer and interviewee seem to be speaking the same language, the words they use may have different cultural connotations. Communication may be even more difficult when you are interviewing people very different from yourself.

In recent interviews, Herb asked leaders of community development organizations about their advocacy campaigns. Based on his own youthful experiences, Herb thought *advocacy* meant demonstrating and leading protest marches, but as he later learned, the development leaders with whom he was talking defined advocacy as lobbying for financial resources. Herb was asking about rebellious and demanding actions, but his conversational partners answered by describing conference-room deals. For a while neither understood the other.

To improve communication and increase the chance of real understanding, researchers encourage the interviewees to teach them about the meanings of words that are distinctive in that research setting. If you are talking to congressional staffers and they start describing a reconciliation bill, your ears might go up; you don't know what the word *reconciliation* means in this context, so you ask. Or if you are interviewing people about how they feel about First Lady Hillary Rodham Clinton, and they tell you that she is aggressive and pushy, you would probably want to know what they meant by those terms—whether they mean that she seems ambitious or tenacious, or that she has a policy agenda, or is smart and doesn't hide it, or is looking for and provokes controversy.

In addition to learning more about what the interviewees are trying to communicate, the researcher must listen to him- or herself and learn what he or she is conveying to the interviewee. Researchers' biases, angers, fears, and enthusiasms influence their questioning style and how they interpret what they hear. An older male interviewer, for example, may assume that women should be home raising children and thoughtlessly begin a discussion by asking a female interviewee why she is working. She may find the question threatening and judgmental because of the implication that she is doing something wrong. Her reaction may be to respond briefly and without depth.

By being aware of your own specialized vocabulary and cultural assumptions, you are less likely to impose your own opinions on the interviewees. It is the interviewee's ideas you want to hear, and you don't want to block that communication by putting your own assumptions in the way. Underlying our approach to qualitative interviews are three guiding themes. First, successful qualitative interviewing requires an understanding of culture. Culture affects what is said and how the interview is heard and understood. Second, interviewers are not neutral actors, but participants in an interviewing relationship. Their emotions and cultural understandings have an impact on the interview. Third, the purpose of qualitative interviewing is to hear and understand what the interviewees think and to give them public voice. Qualitative interviewers try to avoid dominating the interview relationship, so the voice and thoughts of the conversational partner can come through. To do this successfully, the interviewer must learn the interviewees' cultural definitions and ensure that both interviewer and interviewee can understand one another.

In this chapter we provide the background for how we do qualitative interviewing. After defining key terms such as *culture* and *research arena*, we discuss the types of information presented in qualitative interviews and the variety of interviewing forms. Qualitative interviewers hear about culture or learn about a specific topic by listening to examples, narratives, stories, fronts, accounts, and myths. How qualitative interviewers listen is shaped by their philosophy about social data and social interaction. We conclude the chapter by examining our philosophy of qualitative research by contrasting it with three other outlooks toward gathering data: the positivist approach, the interpretive approach, and feminist critical social research.

BASIC DEFINITIONS

Qualitative interviewing encompasses a variety of ways of questioning. The family of qualitative interviews differ in the degree of emphasis on culture, in the choice of the arena or boundaries of the study, and in the specific forms of information that are sought. How we interview depends, in part, on what it is we are trying to hear.

Culture in Interviews

Culture is about how people interpret the world around them by developing shared understandings. People learn collectively how to interpret what is important and unimportant and how to behave in specific circumstances. Culture provides people with rules about how to operate in the world in which they live and work.

In interviews, we are often trying to figure out the rules of the culture we are studying, whether we are looking at norms of budget presentation or the development of an economy inside prison walls. But asking directly about the rules that structure behavior can be difficult, because for those who share a culture, these understandings and interpretations constitute what Schutz (1967, p. 74) calls a "taken-for-granted" reality. In asking about culture, interviewers are often asking fish to describe the water in which they swim. They cannot see it, and even if they could, they cannot describe it because they have nothing to compare it to.

Unlike the water in which fish swim, however, culture changes. Culture is created and evolves to solve shared problems.

> Culture can be understood as a set of solutions devised by a group of people to meet specific problems posed by situations they face in common. . . . This notion of culture as a living, historical product of group problem solving allows an approach to cultural study that is applicable to any group, be it a society, a neighborhood, a family, a dance band, or an organization and its segments. (Van Maanen & Barley, 1985, p. 33)

These learned solutions are then passed on from one generation to the next. Researchers can ask new members of a cultural group to describe what they learned as they became part of the group. The answers provide a pretty good idea of what the culture is all about.

Another way of learning about culture is to ask about the meaning of particular words and phrases. Cultural assumptions are embedded in the language that people use. A "pig" is not just a barnyard animal. In some cultures, it represents unclean or forbidden food; in some subcultures, pig means police, with a negative and insulting spin. In addition to these meanings, the word can convey the idea of someone who eats too much or takes too large a share of the roadway.

Sometimes words become broader symbols that communicate cultural content. Symbols are simply things that stand for something else.

A flag, for example, can be a symbol of nationality, patriotism, or rebellion; a t-shirt or an earring or a cap can convey membership in a group or a choice of lifestyle. Words can be complicated symbols loaded with cultural meaning. The word *girls* in the phrase "girls' night out," when the "girls" are in their 60s and 70s, is loaded with cultural freight; so is the old expression "boy" when used as a term of address from a white adult male to a black one. In neither case does the term mean a male or female child under 14 years of age. The "girls are going out together" reflects a continuing longing for youth and belief that women are of value only as long as they are young. And before the major civil rights advances in the South, a white called any black male "boy" regardless of age in order to hold the black in a kind of perpetual childhood of dependence and obedience. Each phrase symbolizes a cultural setting and is loaded with cultural baggage.

Part of becoming a qualitative interviewer is learning to recognize and then explore words that have rich connotative or symbolic meanings for the people being studied. Hearing the meaning of words that convey cultural information may be a different way of paying attention to a conversation, but not one that broadly challenges the researcher's values or point of view.

More challenging is to recognize that the way the researcher thinks and speaks reflects his or her own cultural assumptions and is not the only way to view the world. Learning to recognize that other people's view of the world is as legitimate to them as yours is to you is called *relativism.* Unless you can recognize the legitimacy of someone else's views, you will have a hard time communicating across cultural boundaries.

Suppose you grew up in a subculture where family members never hit each other and all conflicts were either suppressed or worked out nonviolently. You are now interviewing women who have been beaten by their partners, and because of your background you struggle with a nagging question, "Why are they staying in the relationship?" This question makes perfect sense in your world, but it is likely to be interpreted by the interviewee as "Why are you stupid enough to stick around?" If you ask the question "Why stay?" at the beginning of an interview, you demonstrate such a gap in cultural comprehension that you may lose the interviewee, who may conclude that you could never understand.

But by listening further to what she is saying you will discover her understanding. A long history of emotional dependence has left her without much confidence to strike out on her own. To her, your questions sounds like you are blaming her for the emotional and economic dependence that traps her in the abusive relationship.

Qualitative interviewing does not require you to drop your own cultural values and assume those of your interviewees, but it does require you to be self-aware. When interviewing, keep in mind that your cultural assumptions might affect what you ask. So as a kind of general prophylactic to cultural misunderstandings, try to word questions early in an interview in an open way, expressing little of your own sentiments until you figure out what not to ask.

Cultural and Topical Arenas

A second step in setting up a qualitative study is to figure out its scope and boundaries, the *research arena* that defines whom you will be interviewing and about what. A topical arena includes those who are affected by a problem or who interact intensely on a narrow issue. Thus if our topic were public housing, those within the topical arena might include tenants in public housing, managers of the physical plant, housing boards, and funders, including the federal Department of Housing and Urban Development. People in topical arenas can come from distinct cultural arenas and may have to deal with one another across cultural divides.

A cultural arena includes those who have similar understandings, expectations, and values; such people usually have had common experiences or a shared history. A cultural arena is not defined by a single belief or rule, or by a handful of phrases unique to the group, but by a whole set of understandings that is widely shared within a group or subgroup. It won't always be obvious how widely shared some understandings are, or who is in a group and who is not. An interviewer cannot presuppose that people who are in close proximity share common beliefs.

To find the boundaries of cultural arenas, we begin by assuming for the moment that those people who interact frequently share cultural premises, then check out this assumption in the interviewing. People in small American towns share many values and cultural premises, but to what extent were African American sharecroppers members of the same culture as the white landowners in their small rural communities? We can also guess that people who wear a particular kind of clothes or share a visible lifestyle, such as the Amish, are likely to share cultural premises, even if they live in scattered communities. We might start out thinking that people who wear jewelry in their noses share cultural premises, but we might find out during the interviewing that we were wrong.

Especially when we first begin the study, we are likely to make judgments about cultural arenas that reflect our own assumptions. A scholar from Mars studying Earth might see all humans as a cultural whole because we do so many things in the same ways. A Mormon might divide the world into Mormon and Gentiles, two large cultural categories. We have a tendency to map our own concerns onto the groups we are studying. As we go along, however, we hear what our conversational partners are saying. We change the boundaries of the study as we learn which persons share what beliefs.

To find the boundaries of a topical arena you may want first to find those who might have been involved in a process or decision on that topic, even in a marginal way. But as you do the study, you may find the topic changes a little, and the people you need to talk to change accordingly. You may start out studying curriculum changes in universities, focusing on faculty most involved in university governance. As you interview, however, you may find out that other topics intersect, such as how funds get allocated between research, teaching, and the construction of buildings. As the questions evolve, the relevant arena for inquiry and those with whom you speak also changes.

In the early stages of the research, the interviewer figures out how broad the culture is, or how narrowly to focus the topic of concern. Then, as the research progresses, the arenas can change to fit the evolving subject matter.

Forms of Information

In learning about both topical and cultural arenas, interviewers ask questions, and interviewees answer, explaining their ideas, presenting concepts of how they understand their worlds, and describing what they think occurred and why things are the way they are. Much of what we hear are the examples that people provide to explain what happened or describe events in their lives, trying to make us see the world the way they do.

Much of what we hear are simple and straightforward answers. Sometimes, though, people respond to our questions using narratives, accounts, fronts, stories, and myths. These different forms of information require alternate responses on the part of the interviewer. Depending on the form of the information, it may be appropriate to push for details and clarifications, or it may be more appropriate to just listen and later try to figure out what it is the interviewee is saying.

A narrative describes what happened, defines outcomes, or presents the stages of a social process. It is based on remembered history, with little elaboration, distortion, or intentional cover-up. It might begin, "So far as I can remember, this is what happened . . . " A narrative may be analytical, but is usually not particularly emotional. The narrative is what the person believes happened. Researchers interview a number of those involved to obtain narratives on the same subject, because people experience or remember different parts of an event. The researcher combines several narratives to portray what occurred (R. H. Brown, 1985; Maines, 1993; Mumby, 1993; Richardson, 1990; Riessman, 1993; Sarbin, 1986).

Narratives usually relate events or describe processes step by step. First this happened, then that happened. What events preceded the vote to change the zoning? Why were the criminal charges dismissed? Narratives are data that collectively speak to when, how, and why an event or process occurred. When researchers hear a narrative, they can listen for gaps or missing steps to ask about, or look for differences between the versions of the same event and try to figure out what they might mean. Researchers can also ask conversational partners to explain the importance of the process, whether it differed from what happened in the past or had a horrendous outcome.

Sometimes the answers that conversational partners provide have more emotional content, are less linear and more aimed at making a particular point, and are more interpretative, or even evasive. We call these responses fronts, accounts, stories, and myths. They require more interpretation on the part of the interviewer than do the narratives.

A *front* (Goffman, 1959) is an image given off to communicate an acceptable impression to an audience outside the cultural arena. For example, a police officer creates, through a variety of cultural symbols, the appearance of authority and control, to show that he or she is in charge. The waitpersons in a fancy restaurant create a front of elegance—that is what the patrons are paying for. A front is a kind of act, involving costume and symbol as well as language, but also revealing values and expectations. Professors at a conference try to convey confidence and competence, whether they feel confident and competent or not, because confidence and competence are expected. A front is not necessarily something to be taken apart; it can be considered information about how your interviewees feel that others think they should behave.

An *account* is a culturally acceptable justification for what is considered to be unacceptable behavior (Lyman & Scott, 1968). An account is meant to sound plausible and may or may not be true, as when a police officer pulls over a motorist and asks, "Why were you speeding?" and the driver answers, "I have a sick child at home."

You might expect to hear accounts when interviewing convicts, or from people engaged in criminal or often-criticized behavior. Thus if you were talking to men who failed to pay child support, or alcoholics, or women who had abortions, you might hear accounts. You would also expect accounts in evaluation research, when you are trying to find out how well a project or program worked or what went wrong with it.

An account communicates what the interviewee sees as an acceptable excuse; it also indicates that the interviewee feels challenged or threatened and in need of defending him- or herself. An account that pops up in the middle of an interview warns the interviewer that he or she has inadvertently made an accusation. The interviewer tries to both calm the discussion and figure out what he or she said to threaten the interviewee.

A *story* communicates a moral, a broad message, or a set of core beliefs. A story may be linear, like a narrative, but it may not be—it may have a more dreamlike quality to it, with a dream's disjunctive connections and symbolic events. Some stories start out as narratives and then become refined or altered to more poignantly communicate the underlying point. In a story, it is the messages, morals, or beliefs that are important; whether the specific events occurred or how they occurred is of minor concern.

Stories are valuable to interviewers, because they almost always contain some point that the interviewee feels an urgent need to make but does not feel comfortable enough to say directly. The content may be too emotional or it may contradict the drift of the discussion. Stories become subtle ways of communicating or deepening the level of discussion or redirecting the subject (Antaki, 1988). After hearing a story, the interviewer tries to learn the underlying lesson or clarify the theme, but pays little attention to the narrative-like details. Let's suppose an interviewer from Mars is interviewing about the core cultural values of Christianity. His/her/its conversational partners tell him/her/it that Christ died on the cross. If this Martian interviewer is any good, he/she/it won't ask what cross Christ died on, or at what time, but will try to explore what the symbols convey in the story, and particularly what Jesus' suffering means.

Sometimes histories that could be told as narratives gradually become stories and may be repeated so often they become shared *myths*. Myths offer some explanation of otherwise mysterious phenomena. They order social behaviors and action (Levi-Strauss, 1963) and create justifications of the social world (e.g., Hubert & Maus, 1964). Myths provide a powerful means of communicating a homogeneous set of social expectations for behavior. Myths can be especially useful to researchers who are exploring a cultural arena because myths summarize core underlying values.

Sometimes myths reflect the history of past conflicts and explain or sustain current animosities. Thus militant labor unions keep alive myths (not falsehoods, but historical stories) that justify anger and mistrust of management (Fantasia, 1988). When interviewers present myths, researchers must understand they are not hearing what is happening now, but are being told how to interpret the present as shaped through the cultural lens of a reconstructed story.

TYPES OF INTERVIEWS

Qualitative interviews differ in style. Some interviewers are more aggressive than others. They also differ in the relative emphasis on understanding culture as the main object of the study. In some interviews, the goal is to elicit narratives; in others, you are delighted if the interviewee tells you a story. The scope of the research arena also varies from one type of interview to another.

In *topical oral histories,* the interviewer seeks out conversational partners who have experienced a particular historical event, such as the Great Depression or the Cuban missile crisis, and through the interview reconstructs what happened and how it was understood. The interviewer is looking for narratives that explain what happened. Oral history interviews are also done on culturally important concerns, such as documenting a way of life that is fading out or a skill that is becoming rare. The narratives in this case are likely to be focused on processes that have changed, such as how we washed clothes before washing machines or how we built furniture by hand (Frisch, 1990; Grele, 1985; Lummis, 1988; McMahan, 1989).

Life histories focus more on the experiences of an individual and what he or she felt as he or she passed through the different stages of life. Life histories can tell us about life's passages; they can also provide a window on social change. Not that long ago, interviewers could talk with African Americans who began life as slaves and lived until the transformations of the civil rights era. It is still possible to find elderly people who have lived through several major wars; who experienced economic depressions and political repression; who took part in unionization drives; and who now must deal with retirement homes, home health care, or nursing homes. Life histories involve a combination of narratives and stories that both interpret the past and make it acceptable, understandable, and important (Helling, 1988; Watson & Watson-Franke, 1985).

Evaluation interviews attempt to learn whether new programs, projects, or other types of intentional changes are living up to expectations. Many states now require able-bodied welfare recipients to work. How are these programs working? Are they getting people off welfare? If so, how are these former welfare recipients doing? How are the police coping with requirements that they arrest husbands accused of battering their wives? Why are some public schools working so poorly? Because evaluation research focuses, in part, on what goes wrong with a program or project, accounts or justifications are common in this type of interviewing. Myths may arise as people try to explain present problems in terms of unresolved tensions in the past (Patton, 1990; Sink, 1991).

Focus group interviews are a form of evaluation in which groups of people are assembled to discuss potential changes or shared impressions. Matters discussed range from the narrow and specific—how people react to a new shape for bottles for a soft drink—to broader concerns of community members as they share their hopes and fears in a changing neighborhood. Because the interview takes place in front of other people, many of whom are strangers, there may be considerable effort to preserve front in these situations. People may be unwilling to indicate, for example, that they don't wash their kitchen floor regularly, because they think that others will consider that bad housekeeping (Frey & Fontana, 1991; Goldman & McDonald, 1987; Morgan, 1988). Oral history, life history, evaluation, and focus group interviews refer to specific approaches to hearing data. They can be encompassed within two broader categories of qualitative interviews. *Cultural interviews* focus on the norms, values, understandings, and taken-for-granted rules of behavior of a group or society. *Topical interviews* are more narrowly focused on a particular event or process, and are concerned with what happened, when, and why.

Cultural interviews probe for the special and shared meanings that members of a group develop, the kinds of activities that group members typically do, and the reasons why they do them. An interviewer learns about the culture by eliciting examples and stories that reveal how people understand their world; the researcher also hears the values that underlie both fronts and accounts. He or she asks for examples that show how particular words and phrases are used and deduces the meaning from the examples. Does the phrase "respecting women" mean that women are treated the same as men or does it mean women are sequestered at home and sheltered from outside contacts? If you hear lots of examples about "respecting women" you should be able to figure out the answer.

The style of questioning in cultural interviews is relaxed. With no preset agenda of issues to cover, there is no reason to rush through material or to steer the interviewee in particular directions. With adequate time and many conversational partners who can provide similar information, you can hold back questions that seem sensitive or ask them only to interviewees who are most willing to respond. Cultural interviews usually involve reinterviewing the same people several times so ideas and themes that emerge in the early interviews can be pursued in greater detail in later ones.

A cultural interview involves more active listening than aggressive questioning. The researcher asks the interviewee to describe a typical day or ordinary occurrence, allowing the conversational partner to define what is important. The interviewer asks for examples of cultural premises, norms, and common behaviors. The factual truth of an example is less important than how well it illustrates the premises and norms. A statement that sounds unbelievable can be an important piece of information, not something to tear down or get a corrected version of. If followers of David Koresh, who later immolated themselves when attacked by government agents, described Koresh as a messenger of God, the interviewer should not try to find out whether Koresh was or was not a messenger of God. That his followers stated it and apparently believed it is what is important.

Culture is often communicated through stories, so the interviewer listens at length to extended tales through which cultural lessons are shared (Hummel, 1991; McCall, 1990). If you were interviewing about Christian culture, you would be told about the Sermon on the Mount and the cultural value of behaving with concern for other people; if you were interviewing about Buddhist culture, you would be told about the lives of the Buddha and about enlightenment that occurs by withdrawing from earthly concerns. Such stories convey nearly opposite cultural values.

Stories convey values and themes, even in narrower arenas. In one university, stories circulated about an arrogant administrator who lost his job in under 9 months. The moral of the story is that in the university culture, administrators should not be autocrats. In this same university, new faculty are told in tones of wonder and approval about a job candidate who had 18 books on his job resume. The clear implication is that writing lots of books is a cultural ideal. Whether there actually were 18 books or only 14 is irrelevant; the point of the story would be exactly the same.

In contrast to the cultural interviews, topical interviews seek out explanations of events and descriptions of processes. The researcher is generally looking for detailed factual information. In topical interviews, the interviewer typically plays a more active role in directing the questioning and in keeping the conversation on a specific topic.

Topical interviews deal with more precisely defined subjects, such as why ecoterrorists sink whaling boats or what happens to little girls when they get to be about 12 years old and suddenly lose confidence and ambition. Often topical interviews trace a process or how a particular decision was made, such as the dropping of the atomic bomb on Japan during World War II.

Although cultural interviews are frequently repeated with the same interviewees, in topical interviews, the researcher may only have one shot at getting the specific information that is needed. As a result, the interviewer may adopt a more aggressive style of interviewing, developing a list of specific questions and pursuing them until he or she gets some kind of satisfactory answer. The interviewer may reject accounts or fronts if they stand in the way of understanding what happened. Nothing in topical interviewing justifies bullying, but topical interviewing is often considerably more directive than cultural interviewing.

Cultural and topical interviews also differ in the "ownership" of the resulting report. In a cultural study, the researchers report the ideas, expressions, and understandings that they heard in the interviewing as belonging to the conversational partners. To the extent editors permit, the report is presented in the words of the conversational partners. In preparing a cultural report, the researcher is like a photographer, making choices about what to frame within the picture, but reproducing exactly what was there.

In contrast, a topical study often is based on the interpretations of the researcher. The researcher may sort out and balance what different people say, especially if there are contending interpretations of the same events. Then the researcher creates his or her own narrative based on this analysis. The narrative can be as simple as the summary phrases "the program works" or "the program fails" in an evaluation study, or as complicated as the minute details of how environmentalists brought together coalitions to prevail over land developers (H. J. Rubin, 1988b). The words and evidence are those of the dozens of people interviewed, but the interpretations are those of the researcher.

Rather than being a photographer, the topical researcher is more like a skilled painter. The events portrayed did occur and were learned about through the interviews; the information is still grounded in the interviewees' lives and stories. But the narrative is the truth as heard and interpreted by the researcher. It is an artist's rendition.

The cultural report is credible because the story is told by the experts, the members of the culture, in their own words. Because the topical researcher reports more of his or her interpretation of what he or she heard, the report must show that the interpretation did not go far from the evidence, and show the reasoning and evidence that lead from the interviews to the conclusion. To the extent that the topical researcher combines different points of view to form a single narrative, almost every piece of information has to be confirmed. Interviewers must solicit information that can be checked against other sources, such as personnel files or meeting minutes, and interviewees must be chosen who are knowledgeable about distinct parts of an event or have different perspectives on what occurred.

In practice, cultural and topical styles are often mixed in a single interview. In a topical study of budgeting, Irene had to stop and figure out what the concept *superchiefs* meant and work out what interviewees meant by *political accountability*. Oral histories present peoples' narratives of important events such as the Great Depression or legal immigration to the United States, but those topical interviews can only be understood by exploring the cultural values of adaptability, honorable work, mutual aid, and hope. In such situations, the researcher may alternate between listening for nuanced cultural meanings and asking about events. You can mix topical and cultural interviews because they share the underlying assumptions that guide all qualitative interviewing.

THE QUALITATIVE INTERVIEWING MODEL COMPARED WITH OTHERS

Our model of qualitative interviewing emphasizes the relativism of culture, the active participation of the interviewer, and the importance of giving the interviewee voice. Our approach reacts against the limits of the positivist research model and borrows generously from both the interpretive and feminist approaches.

Our work is most closely related to the interpretive approach toward social knowledge. The interpretive approach recognizes that meaning emerges through interaction and is not standardized from place to place or person to person. The interpretive approach emphasizes the importance of understanding the overall text of a conversation and, more broadly, the importance of seeing meaning in context. This approach accepts the importance of culture and the necessity of a relativistic approach to culture in the interview, but it does not speak fully to the respective roles of the interviewer and interviewee in an interviewing relationship.

A feminist model of critical social research suggests how to go about interviewing in ways that respect both parties in the conversation. As part of a broader critical approach to social research, feminists reject many of the tacit political assumptions underlying positivism. Arguing that the way positivists do research distorts learning, feminists have set up their own guidelines for interviewing. We have incorporated parts of a feminist model into our own.

Our approach differs most dramatically from the positivist model. For many types of research, the positivist framework is appropriate, but it is not useful for hearing data and understanding meaning in context. Positivism, especially as seen in survey research, denies the significance of context and standardizes questions and responses, so that there is little room for individual voice. The positivist model usually plays down the importance of cultural distinctions in its search for rules or laws, like those of physics, that apply to all people all the time.

The Positivist Model

Positivist social researchers look for the uniform, precise rules that organize the world, much as physicists try to do. And just as positivists in the experimental sciences do, positivists in the social sciences examine simplified models of the social world to see how a small number of variables, for instance, gender and education, interact. The result is that they miss how the complexity in the real world affects human behaviors. A positivist model extracts simple relationships from a complex real world and frequently examines them as if time and context did not matter, and as if social life was stable rather than constantly changing (Denzin, 1989; Lincoln & Guba, 1985).

Positivists assume that knowledge is politically and socially neutral and that such knowledge is achieved by following a precise, predetermined approach to gathering information. They argue that a commitment to quantitative precision and an accumulation of facts is the way to build an ever-closer approximation to a reality that exists independent of human perception. They express what they learn through mathematical manipulation of predefined variables, usually deduced from an existing academic theory (Lincoln & Guba, 1985). Because they assume that Truth can be measured with statistical precision, positivists routinely reduce complex information to summary measures, often ignoring what is difficult to quantify and eliminating subtleties. Because positivists argue that objects and events that researchers study exist independent of people's perceptions of them, they believe that there can be only one version of events that is "true." The idea that there may be several different "realities," that is, different constructions of events by the participants, an idea that underlies much of qualitative interviewing, is unacceptable in quantitative positivism.

In learning how people feel about an event, survey researchers, as one type of positivist, make up precise and standard questions to ask all their interviewees. With certain constructs—age, income-on-which-taxes-were-paid, whom people (claimed) they voted for—imposing such standard definitions makes sense. But the further the researcher goes from ideas that are easily defined with widespread agreement, the more problematic these procedures become. People may be able to agree on how old they are, or understand that they could have voted for one of two people, but they may have different conceptions of justice or fairness, family values, or public accountability. These more complicated, culturally defined concepts have distinct meanings in different arenas; trying to impose one definition across cultural arenas may be misleading or confusing.

Although positivists do sometimes talk to people before they decide how to word a measure, their goal is to define a concept before they begin to interview, and these definitions are intended to apply to everyone being studied. In survey interviewing, a standard positivist methodology, a uniform questionnaire is constructed asking each respondent identical questions using the researcher's definition of the key terms. The researcher assumes that each question means the same thing to each respondent, an assumption that is often incorrect.

In surveys, interviewers are trained to act in a uniform way with every research subject and not to get involved in relationships with the interviewees, so that the answers cannot be attributed to the personality of the interviewer. Interviewers ask everyone the same questions and the respondents' answers are placed in categories that are predesigned by the researcher. The respondents are treated as interchangeable parts, with no particular individuality, except on background characteristics as defined by the researcher, such as age, gender, or education. Because the researcher prewords the questionnaire, the interview is intellectually dominated by the perceptions of the researcher, rather than the understandings of the interviewees.

Positivist researchers come up with overall sums and averages of their measures, ignoring the detail and richness of individual behavior. The result is often bloodless, but it is valuable for some types of research. For example, if one wants to know whether women are paid less than men for identical work, or if some geographic areas receive fewer mortgages, statistical data is appropriate. The economic background of those imprisoned, the number of air traffic controllers fired by President Reagan, or the number of homes built by community groups are all important objects to count and measure. You don't lose much, if anything, in translating these concepts to numbers, and sometimes you can see trends and relationships through statistical analysis that you cannot see with the naked eye.

However, if you stop the research at the counting stage, you miss a great deal. Does the economy in the prison mirror the economy outside? Where does the prison economy get its resources? What happened to the fired controllers? Did they maintain relationships among themselves, form a mutual aid network? If so, what happened to the network when some of the fired controllers were rehired? How did the community groups manage to get the resources to build housing? Were they able to maintain it better than other housing for the poor? Is there a model for building housing for the poor that can be extended more broadly? In short, the counting aspects of the research, although useful, tell only a small part of the story, and not always the most interesting or useful part.

An Interpretive Approach

The interpretive approach stands in sharp contrast to positivism (Berger & Luckman, 1967). What is important to interpretive social scientists is how people understand their worlds and how they create and share meanings about their lives. Social research is not about categorizing and classifying, but figuring out what events mean, how people adapt, and how they view what has happened to them and around them. Interpretive social researchers emphasize the complexity of human life. Time and context are important and social life is seen as constantly changing.

The interpretive approach argues that not everything that is important can be measured with precision and that trying to do so is a distracting and inappropriate task. Similarly, searching for universally applicable social laws can distract from learning what people know and how they understand their lives. The interpretive social researcher examines meanings that have been socially constructed and consequently accepts that values and views differ from place to place and group to group. There is not one reality out there to be measured; objects and events are understood by different people differently, and those perceptions are the reality—or realities— that social science should focus on. It matters less whether a chair is 36 inches high and 47 years old than that one person perceives it as an antique and another views it as junk.

Interpretive researchers try to elicit interviewees' views of their worlds, their work, and the events they have experienced or observed. To reconstruct and understand the interviewees' experiences and interpretations, interpretive researchers seek thick and rich descriptions of the cultural and topical arenas they are studying and try to develop an empathetic understanding of the world of others.

Feminist Critical Social Researchers

Positivists assume that social researchers can be *value neutral*, that they can study the world without imposing social or political values. Interpretive social researchers understand the importance of values: they study values. Their goals are to understand and accept the values of others, but not necessarily to bring about social or political change.

Critical social researchers argue that the purpose of research is to discover flaws and faults in society and in so doing promote actions that eliminate problems (Thomas, 1993). Critical researchers tend to study underdog groups, those facing oppression, suppression, and powerlessness. Qualitative critical research gives voice to the victims of crimes; to migrant workers; to the hospitalized ill; to AIDS patients, their lovers, and their advocates; to political and social minorities; and to the handicapped. The critical researcher looks for situations in which individual or group accomplishments were ignored, defeats were prematurely accepted, or careers were waylaid or ruined, and explores and reveals how and why these things occurred.

One variety of the critical approach, feminist research, pays particular attention to the problems of dominance and submission as they affect women. Feminist researchers have extended the implications of what they study to the methods of doing research. They have developed a model of how to ask questions that counters the positivist approach.[1]

Feminists criticize positivist research methodology as being anything but neutral, claiming that positivist researchers often ignored women and assumed an intellectual dominance of the researcher over the interviewee. For instance, the survey interviewing model does not let the interviewee talk or explain anything, precisely the complaint that feminists have about men more generally in their dealings with women. In their critique of positivism, feminists argue that the researcher frames the question and leaves the interviewee only a yes-or-no choice; an approach that has a kind of bullying quality to it. And to feminist researchers, the stripping away of context, the reduction of information to summary numbers, and the interchangeability of interviewees seems dehumanizing.

In response, feminist researchers worked out a methodology that was gentler, that listened and heard more and talked less, that humanized both the researcher and the interviewee, and that focused more on those who had little or no societal voice. Allowing people to "talk back" (hooks, 1989) gives a voice through interviews to those who have been silenced; talking back becomes a political act. If positivists disempowered interviewees, feminists intentionally empowered them.

Feminist researchers argued that because of the pretense of neutrality, the positivist researcher never examined his or her cultural assumptions, but transmitted them within the questions. If the dominant culture belittled women's roles, then the wording of the questions did too; there was no way for women to talk about their lives, no vocabulary that did not put them on the defensive or make them feel worthless. Some feminists argued that women should interview women, and that interviewer and interviewee should try to build a relationship in which they share responsibility for finding the words and concepts in which ideas could be expressed and lives described.

More broadly, feminists question whether people can share experiences across cultural chasms. Many feminists claim that successful interviewing requires that there be a considerable shared culture between the interviewer and interviewee. Not only should women interview women, but women in the same position—say, returning students with children—should interview returning students, and Chicanas should interview Chicanas. Otherwise, important information will not be reported or nuances will be ignored.

Feminist researchers emphasize the need for interviewers to avoid dominating the interview. They argue that a more open, loosely structured research methodology is necessary to learn about women, to capture their words, their concepts, and the importance they place on the events in their world. An interview, the feminists said, should not involve a scientific instrument sterilely applied to a passive object, but should resemble normal conversation in which the interviewee influences the exchanges.

The interviewer should not be neutral but should be, if not a friend to the interviewee, at least a partner or collaborator. Such collaborations should produce better interviews that help those being interviewed rather than merely using them for the purposes of the researcher.

In this relationship, the interviewer participates and shares. An interviewer is not justified in keeping all uncomfortable things to herself while asking others to reveal what is personal and private. Feminist researchers argue that being open about themselves to their research collaborators, the interviewees, is both fair and practical. You are not asking someone to tell you what you won't share with them, and by examining your own feelings on the subject at hand you become more aware of what you are asking others to reveal.

Feminist researchers argue that because there is a real relationship between the researcher and the interviewee in their work, it is important for the interviewer to be aware of his or her emotions and reactions. How does the interviewer respond to the neighborhood, the housing, the noise and the smell, the interruptions, the visiting, or the food sharing? Being scared affects how you hear, as does anger at the content of the stories. Too little identification with the subjects of the research distances and distorts, but too much identification can obscure the faults of the interviewees.

Sometimes, watching your own reactions to the interview can help you unravel the puzzle of the research topic. A feminist studying a prosecutor's office reacted with dismay to some of the patronizing behavior toward her and some of the sexism she felt. Stopping to analyze what she was feeling, she discovered that the attorneys' behavior to her was a clue to how they dealt with certain kinds of cases. They made light of cases where men defrauded women (gigolo cases) and paid more attention to cases of political corruption where their reputations could be enhanced (Gurney, 1985).

With the feminist approach, both the questions asked and the way in which they are asked contribute to learning about others. Understanding is obtained from what the conversational partners say and from the relationships developed between the researcher and the interviewee.

OUR MODEL FOR QUALITATIVE INTERVIEWING[2]

Our model for understanding the content of qualitative interviews follows much of the philosophy of the interpretive approach, but our techniques of interviewing have been strongly influenced by the feminist model. Like the interpretive social researchers, we prefer to let ideas emerge from the interviews, from the lives and examples of the interviewees, rather than to categorize answers initially according to preexisting categories from an academic literature. Like the feminists, we argue that interviewers should not dominate the interview relationship, and also like the feminists, we argue that interviewers cannot be completely neutral, and need to consider their own beliefs, needs, and interests as they work out questions and try to understand answers.

Our approach to qualitative interviewing assumes a continually changing world and recognizes that what we hear depends on when we ask the question and to whom. An interview right after someone's mother died is likely to be quite different from an interview conducted a year later with the same person. Qualitative research is not looking for principles that are true all the time and in all conditions, like laws of physics; rather, the goal is understanding of specific circumstances, how and why things actually happen in a complex world. Knowledge in qualitative interviewing is situational and conditional. The underlying assumption is that if you cannot understand something in the specific first, you cannot understand in the general later.

You can do qualitative interviews of couples that are divorcing, to try to figure out what went wrong in each case you studied. You can then look for common themes across cases, although you know that each person and each marriage is different. Qualitative interviews should sort out what is unique and what may be common while staying close to real examples. This is a better approach than creating a mental construct called an average or typical person or event that may exist nowhere and that blurs distinctiveness (Riessman, 1990).

We accept much of the feminist methodology's emphasis on gentleness and reciprocity in the interviewing relationship, but there are parts of that philosophy we do not accept. Unlike some schools of feminist research, our approach to qualitative interviewing emphasizes the ability to go across social boundaries. You don't have to be a woman to interview women, or a sumo wrestler to interview sumo wrestlers. But if you are going to cross social gaps and go where you are ignorant, you have to recognize and deal with cultural barriers to communication. And you have to accept that how you are seen by the person being interviewed will affect what is said.

Some feminists emphasize the need to be collaborators and perhaps friends with the interviewee, the need for the interviewer to be willing to share his or her thoughts and feelings in the interview in order to make the interviewing relationship more balanced. They argue that the result of a friendly collaboration is a natural sense of protection of the interviewee by the interviewer. Our model of qualitative interviewing is not limited to people we naturally socialize with; becoming friends with interviewees may not be a realistic goal and it may create draining obligations with which the interviewer cannot deal. A middle path involves understanding that you do have a personal relationship with the interviewee, but that relationship may not be a deep or lasting friendship.

Even though you may not become personal friends with the interviewee, the interviewing relationship still entails personal obligations. For the researcher, one obligation is to protect his or her interviewees from harm that might result from the study. You may not protect the interviewees out of love or friendship, but you still protect them out of obligation, because it is right, and because, by implication, you agreed to do so as a condition of the interview. We agree with feminists that interviews should not become power games in which you try to make the interviewee reveal all. The interview should not only not hurt the interviewees but, if possible, actually leave them somewhat better off for having talked with you. The concern for the interviewee that is core to feminist research is the basis for maintaining an ethical relationship with those being studied, a topic that we discuss at length in Chapter 5.

Our model builds on the feminist approach in that we recognize that the personality of the interviewer counts in social research. In qualitative interviewing, researchers develop different styles depending on who they are and the type of questioning they do. Some interviewing styles allow more active interviewer participation, more light chatter, or more self-revelation than others. If your personality does not allow you to reveal much of yourself, you may need to be extra cautious that you do not depend too much on deep revelation from your interviewees. You tailor the type of qualitative interviewing you do to the types of questioning with which you are personally comfortable.

IMPLICATIONS OF THE PHILOSOPHY FOR DESIGN

Research design, the subject of the next two chapters, helps us in choosing what we are going to ask, from whom, and why. How we design the research builds on our model for qualitative interviewing. Three themes from our model guide the design for qualitative interviewing research.

First, we are trying to find in detail how the conversational partners understand what they have seen, heard, or experienced. We want to elicit from the conversational partners examples, narratives, histories, stories, and explanations. These will help us understand what the person thinks and ground the answers in his or her experience to give us nuance, precision, context, and evidence all at the same time.

The second theme is that what we hear is affected by the ongoing interpersonal relationship with a conversational partner. We need to pay attention to how interviewees perceive us and how those perceptions influence what they are willing to say and how openly they are willing to talk. We also need to pay attention to our perceptions of the interviewee as these can distort what we hear. The third theme is that qualitative research is personal, not detached. Who you are counts. Your interest, curiosity, and concern encourage the conversational partner to discuss the topic at length. Your ability to recognize, accept, and share emotion legitimates its expression in the interview.

The interviewer is an important actor in another sense as well. Your self-confidence, adaptability, and willingness to hear what is said and change direction to catch a wisp of insight or track down a new theme is what makes the qualitative interview work. Without that confidence and flexibility, the qualitative interviewing model will fail. Research becomes more like the positivist model, where the design is fixed and depth of understanding is gone.

The qualitative researcher has to have a high tolerance for uncertainty, especially at the beginning of the project, because the design will continue to change as the researcher hears what is being said and learns from his or her interviewees. At no point in the research can the interviewer say, okay, from here on out, I can operate by rote and know in advance each step of the way. You always have to be prepared for multiple possibilities. Perhaps most important, the researcher has to be confident enough and curious enough to welcome challenges to his or her preconceptions. You can't do this kind of research well if you are afraid of making a mistake or finding out that you were wrong about something.

On the other hand, the qualitative interviewing model is tolerant. It allows for mistakes and recoveries, and it generates tremendous excitement because you have to do so much thinking on the spot and because there is genuine delight when you discover something new. And you almost always do discover something new.

NOTES

1. Synthesized from Anderson & Jack, 1991; Devault, 1990; Gluck & Patai, 1991; Harding, 1991; hooks, 1989; Oakley, 1981; Reinharz, 1992; Riesmann, 1987.
2. Also compare Bowman et al., 1984; Douglas, 1985; Mishler, 1986; Silverstone, Hirsch, & Morley, 1991. Many of our assumptions parallel those for field work in general; cf. Emerson, 1988.

3

Keeping on Target
While Hanging Loose

Designing Qualitative Interviews

*R*esearch design is about planning what you are going to ask, whom you are going to ask, and why (cf. Marshall & Rossman, 1989). You begin a project with a design in mind to keep you on target about what you intend to learn. But you don't have to follow the original design in every detail. The questions change during the research as new avenues of inquiry open up.

Metaphorically, designing a qualitative interview study is like planning a vacation. You have an overall idea of what you want to see and do, but you are not locked into a fixed itinerary. You allow sufficient flexibility to explore what you see along the way. You know which guidebooks and maps to take but are not sure what parts of each will prove useful. You change plans as new adventures entice you, but you keep the final destination in mind.

The design of the study helps you remember the original motivations for the research while encouraging you to explore the topic in different ways. Design helps you collect credible data and convince readers of your research that the material was collected in a systematic and thoughtful way. A careful design links research to the wider world of theory and practice to ensure that the results are significant, and by keeping the research on topic, prevents the nightmare of conducting a variety of interviews that you are not able to put together.

You cannot plan the entire design for a qualitative project in advance, because the design changes as you learn from the interviewing. But you can begin the work with a rough and tentative design, talk with potential interviewees, sort out initial ideas, refocus the research, and decide with whom else to talk and about what. At this point, you can write a research proposal describing the object of the research, explaining its importance, and presenting what you have already heard. In the proposal, you can indicate how you plan to proceed (Locke, Spirduso, & Silverman, 1987). In qualitative work, a meaningful research proposal for funders or a dissertation committee can be prepared only after the work is under way. But even after you have written a proposal, the design continues to change as you learn more about the subject and discover new perspectives.

Qualitative interviewing design is *flexible*, *iterative*, and *continuous*, rather than prepared in advance and locked in stone. In this chapter, we explain what we mean by flexible, iterative, and continuous design. We describe how researchers find and winnow their research topics while adapting the topics to their interests and personalities and to the interests and knowledge of the interviewees. Then we describe our goal of building meaningful theory out of the interviews and outline how to design the research to achieve this goal.

FLEXIBLE, ITERATIVE, AND CONTINUOUS DESIGN

In a qualitative interviewing study, design takes shape gradually, as the researcher listens and hears the meaning with the data. Concerns that appear important at the beginning of the research may seem less vital later, and points that seemed unimportant when the study began may turn out to be valuable. To adapt to what you are learning, your design has to be flexible. In preparing the design, you have to suspend your own assumptions about the way things work and actively solicit ideas and themes from your interviewees. You analyze these themes and gradually winnow them down to those that you want to examine in detail.

Doing so involves an iterative process during which the final design slowly emerges. At each stage of the interviewing, you gather information, analyze, winnow, and test; then, based on the analysis and testing, you refine or change your questions, and perhaps choose a different set of interviewees, and repeat the process. Each iteration focuses more on the core points the interviewees are trying to convey. After several iterations, you will have built an explanatory theory or narrative description that closely fits the interview data and is based on the experiences and understanding of your interviewees.

Doing design is continuous in the sense that you have to redesign the work at different points in the research. In the early stages, you spend more time defining and refining the subject of the research and exploring how the interviewees understand the matter. As the work continues, you listen to hear the specific ideas of the interviewees and determine how their ideas go together or clash and what they might mean. The design then focuses on ways to sort out these ideas, to see which ones are important, which are linked to others, and which ones are common or rare. In this midstream design you think of ways of testing these ideas, and reformulate whom to ask, how to ask, what sites or conditions to look for, and what inferences to draw. In the final stages of the research, you build and test a theory that is grounded in the data that you have heard.

Flexible Design

Adjusting the design as you go along is a normal, expected part of the qualitative research process. As you learn how the interviewees understand their world, you may want to modify what it is you are studying or rethink the pattern of questioning. Such flexibility is much better than persisting in a design that is not working well or that doesn't allow you to pursue unexpected insights.

Because so much of qualitative research focuses on relatively unexplored areas, it is easy to start off research with assumptions that later turn out to be incorrect. Our colleague Jim designed his dissertation research to explore the question of how government funding subverted critical scholarship in criminology. After his first morning of interviews with two federal officials at a funding agency, Jim realized that his thinking was wrong: federal funders did not operate in the way that he had read in the literature and his assumption that funding subverted critical research was naive. He revamped the focus of his study to find out how the funding agencies decided between proposals. You don't have to be wrong at the outset to warrant a redesign. You can also redesign if a better way to study the original question becomes apparent. When Jim was trying to study deviant computer culture, he singled out software piracy as a first approach to the subject. The software pirate he was interviewing, however, was reluctant to answer questions on how he acquired thousands of dollars of free computer programs. While avoiding answering the questions, the interviewee was fiddling with a computer and modem and Jim asked him what he was doing. The informant was engaged in "hacking" (getting into someone else's computer without permission) and was more willing to talk about hacking than about software piracy. Since hacking is another avenue into the deviant computer culture, Jim adapted his questioning and began asking about hacking.

Design remains flexible throughout the study because you have to work out questions to examine new ideas and themes that emerge during the interviews. Irene was studying how cities make budgets and discovered that professional staff and political appointees interacted in the budget process in ways she never imagined. She redesigned her questioning to explore the unexpected relationship between bureaucratic staff and political appointees (I. S. Rubin, 1992).

Flexibility of design is helpful in yet another sense. Rather than being locked into one set of questions for all the interviewees, you adjust the questioning so that individuals are asked about the particular parts of a subject that they know best. For instance, in his research on community development, Herb found some of his interviewees were better able to talk about their philosophy of community development, whereas others preferred to discuss project funding. Rather than try to force people to respond to questions that did not interest them, Herb accommodated himself to the topic the interviewees preferred to discuss and obtained a richer picture of the overall research arena (H. J. Rubin, 1994).

In qualitative interviews, flexibility to accommodate questioning to what you are learning and to what the interviewees know keeps the results fresh and interesting. The ease of redesign encourages you to truly hear the meaning of what the interviewees say without discarding pieces that don't fit your initial conception of the research problem.

This flexibility also lets you explore research arenas that were unanticipated.

Iterative Design

Design in qualitative interviewing is iterative. That means that each time you repeat the basic process of gathering information, analyzing it, winnowing it, and testing it, you come closer to a clear and convincing model of the phenomenon you are studying. In the early stages of the interviewing, design emphasizes more the gathering of many themes and ideas; toward the middle of the research, you concentrate more on winnowing to limit the number of themes that you explore. In the final stages, you emphasize more the analysis and testing of your understanding as you put themes together, begin to form theories, and run them by your interviewees and critical readers in your field.

In the early interviews, you actively solicit a wide variety of ideas, themes, and explanations and try not to limit how interviewees respond to your concerns. Suppose your research is on the topic of "vacations" among working Americans. Rather than impose your idea of what a vacation is, you start with a broad question, such as, "When we talk about vacations, what do you think about?" Some people may emphasize where they went or what they saw, others might talk about how they felt or what the vacations meant to them. Some of the interviewees will talk about how expensive trips are or their inability to get away from work. They may describe vacation activities that you never thought of as recreational. You ask the same broad question to a wide variety of people from different occupations and lifestyles.

Phrasing initial questions in an open way allows you to hear what your conversational partners think before you inadvertently narrow down the options for questioning. You want to cast your net initially as broadly as you can, both to get a range of responses and to make sure that what you later ask has meaning to the conversational partners.

The next step in iterative design is to narrow the topic. How you do so depends on your interests, the concerns in your professional field, and of course, what the conversational partners have said. A sociologist might pay particular attention to interviewees when they describe how vacations bring family members closer together. The sociologist might focus on how vacations tighten family bonds while trying to discover if this is better done through visits to relatives or trips to national parks. If you are a political scientist or policy analyst, you may be more interested in answers that discuss how perceptions of crime influenced the choice of vacation destination. You then adjust the size of the research to the time available. If you only have a limited amount of time, you would have to focus either on family values in vacations or the influence of the fear of crime. With more time to spend, you might decide to try to understand how vacation choices are made, including discussions of family values, crime, and the attractions of the destination.

You have decided on what you feel might be important, but do your conversational partners agree? Before you start interviewing in depth, go back to your original interviewees and informally talk with them a while to make sure their understanding of the subject meshes with what you are interested in learning. Make sure they have good examples, narratives, or stories to tell that elaborate on the topic you want to pursue. Make sure what you want to know is something that the conversational partners feel is significant to them.

The sequence of gathering broadly; analyzing, winnowing, and testing; and then focusing particular questions on those best able to provide the answers is done over and over throughout the research. You follow the pattern first when you are exploring the subject, then again when you are looking for concepts, again when you are examining themes, and again when you come up with either your theory or a tentative set of explanations that integrates several themes. How do you know when to stop? The iterative design stops when the information you are putting together supports a small number of integrated themes and each additional interview adds no more ideas or issues to the themes on which you are now questioning. Glaser and Strauss (1967) call this point *theoretical saturation.*

Continuous Design

The continuous nature of qualitative interviewing means that the questioning is redesigned throughout the project. A particular answer may suggest a new line of inquiry or it may suggest different people to talk to than you had originally planned. Or as you develop a picture of what is going on you may decide to change research locations to test out what you think you are hearing.

Herb was curious about how community groups built homes to house the poor. In the early part of his research he concentrated on community organizations working in the economically deprived areas of larger cities. During these interviews, he learned that community organizations within each of the larger cities competed for limited funds. To understand how the competition between community developers affected how they did their work, he redesigned the research to talk with community developers in small cities that had fewer community organizations and less competition among them.

Continuous design allows exploration of new topics while keeping the research organized and focused. It points you in a direction to ensure that you pursue core topics in sufficient depth to end up with adequate evidence for your conclusions and conclusions that fit your data. You cannot just touch on a new theme and move on. Rather you judge the relevance of the new theme, and if it is important, you explore the new theme by choosing appropriate interviewees and planning a new set of questions. You iterate in this way until theoretical saturation occurs. Continuous design allows you to be flexible yet organized at the same time.

In the rest of this chapter we discuss how to generate and winnow down the topics for research. Research design helps you maintain focus on a set of themes that both closely fits what the interviewees have told you and also reaches for theoretical significance.

CHOOSING A TOPIC

The researcher chooses the initial subject of the research, which is then modified by what the interviewees say. In choosing the original subject, you consider your interests, the feasibility of the work, and the appropriateness of the topic for qualitative research. As you narrow the topic you also make sure the subject is important enough to warrant the time and effort it will take to study.

For a topic to be appropriate for qualitative research it must be grounded in the lives of the conversational partners. It is their reality that you will eventually convey. But you also have to be interested in the topic. Make sure the subject grabs you, so you are willing to spend the time that qualitative research requires. Conversational partners can sense if the interviewer is bored and are likely to show less interest themselves when the researcher is not involved. Also, examine what biases you might bring to the project, what anger, fear, or repulsion. Strong emotional feelings are one reason why you might want to do the research, but they can bias both what you ask and how you understand the responses.

The Emergence of Research Topics

Where do ideas for qualitative research topics come from? They come from employers; from life experiences (J. D. Brown, 1991); from the researcher's personality; from ethnic, racial, or sexual identity. Some subjects attract researchers' curiosity; others appeal to researchers' political or social values.

Sometimes topics that are suitable for qualitative interviewing are assigned to us by employers. In a recent consulting assignment, Irene was asked to interview business people to find out if the financial incentives the government offered encouraged them to locate in a special area called an enterprise zone. On another consulting assignment, Irene was asked to explore why communication in a probation and parole office had broken down and how it could be restored. Herb has done evaluation research on economic development projects in the Philippines to find out if recipients spent foreign aid wisely.

Sometimes an assigned topic just grabs you; at other times to maintain enthusiasm in your interviewing you have to look for an angle that is interesting to you. Suppose the mayor asked you to evaluate a city's recycling program. Your first reaction might be, "Ugh, how boring." But then you begin to do some interviewing and find out that especially among the young, the prevalent attitude is, "What I do does not matter, so why should I bother to recycle?" You learn that many of the older people keep recycling, "Because it seems like the right thing to do." Suddenly, there are interesting ideas and themes to explore. Why do some people feel part of a larger group, a community, and others do not and feel no responsibility for what happens to it? You can get the information your boss or client wants while studying issues that are of interest to you.

Often topics grow out of life experience. After serving for years on a school board, one researcher wanted to know why voters accept or reject tax measures to support the schools. Another researcher who spent his life in the military was fed up with congressional micromanagement and therefore wanted to study congressional oversight of executive branch agencies. Interest in studying age discrimination can come from one's own experiences looking for a job; returning to college to complete a degree after raising a family may lead to research on how universities adapt, or fail to adapt, to new clientele groups.

Topics reflect one's personality. Herb, who in departmental votes is often a minority of one, is deeply interested in how people dominate others. A colleague who works most of the night, sleeps late, and owns only one sports coat is deeply interested in what behavior gets labeled deviant. Irene is interested in how organizations, political candidates, and individuals deal with defeat and decline in a society that emphasizes success and growth. These interests can be turned into specific topics for research, such as why people are afraid to complain, how law enforcement agencies treat those whose actions they don't understand, and how bureaucratic agencies respond to budgetary cutbacks.

Sometimes research topics develop out of the researcher's ethnic identity. African American researchers may be especially interested in how the civil rights movement of the 1960s shaped current politics. Jewish researchers might feel drawn to studying the political movement that denies that the murder of 6 million Jews took place in Europe during World War II. Those of Mexican or Caribbean ancestry might be especially interested in the impact of current immigration policies.

Sometimes research topics may evoke curiosity because they are puzzling or unusual. For example, a recent newspaper story described a killing at a Little League baseball game. Why should a killing occur at a Little League game? Was there a relationship between sport, a kind of stylized competition, and violence, an unstylized competition? Were the Little League teams divided on race or class, and if so, were these antagonisms being played out on the playing field? In uncovering the meanings in an isolated case, one can reflect on a series of larger issues.

Research topics can stem from social concerns and a desire to influence public policy. One might want to study the sources of pain and frustration, or of security and pleasure, in the lives of people with disabilities to find ways of helping them live independent lives. To help reshape programs to aid the poor, a qualitative interviewer might study programs in which the tenants are given managerial responsibility for public housing. Or one might want to study the system of medical care in the United States, to get a handle on why its costs continue to rise so quickly.

Is the Topic Appropriate for Qualitative Research?

As you think about a topic, ask yourself whether it is suitable for qualitative interviewing. Learning the number of people in prison is important and useful information, but the topic is not amenable to qualitative research. A topic that is suitable for qualitative work requires in-depth understanding that is best communicated through detailed examples and rich narratives. How does a prisoner learn to survive in a brutal situation? What does a community group do to refurbish an apartment house that had been a crack distribution center? How do local governmental deficits occur despite their illegality and visibility? If what you want to know is how something happened, or the details of the events, the subject is appropriate for qualitative interviewing.

Qualitative interviews are especially useful when you need to bring some new light on puzzling questions. Outsiders were unclear about why African Americans participated in civil rights marches despite the risk of arrest. One qualitative researcher asked Ivory Perry, a black activist in St. Louis, to explain why he got involved in civil rights protests when jail was often the reward. Perry answered, "I'm in jail anyway as long as there are places I cannot go and things I cannot do" (Lipsitz, 1988, p. 80). Such answers provide insight to help explain why things happened as they did.

Qualitative interviewing is appropriate when the purpose of the research is to unravel complicated relationships and slowly evolving events. It is also suitable when you want to learn how present situations resulted from past decisions or incidents. If you find the intensity of current labor disputes puzzling when workers seem to be well paid and reasonably well treated, you may want to use qualitative interviews to discover what set of past events has left such a legacy of bitterness. You could discover that in the past factory owners ordered private police to rough up the strikers. Although times have changed, the fear and anger linger.

Qualitative interviewing is warranted whenever depth of understanding is required. It is also the way to explore the broader implications of a problem and place it in its historical, political, or social context.

Is the Topic Important?

You don't want to get done with your research and then find out that no one is interested in what you found but yourself. As part of doing a design, you should ask yourself, why is this topic important? To whom would it be important? How could the results be used? What are the broader concerns of which this research is a part?

Sometimes a topic is important because it makes an invisible problem clear or gives a voice to a voiceless people. A study of wife beating in Japan may bring the practice to public attention. Interviews with cardiac patients and their doctors may help clarify why women, who experience roughly the same rate of heart attacks after age 50 as men, die more frequently of heart attacks than men. Interviews with imprisoned adults and their spouses about how they deal with their children may help give voice to the unintended victims of the current mania for incarceration—the children.

A topic may be important if it makes a visible problem more understandable (Broadhead & Fox, 1990). Studying reactions to plant closings and job loss speaks to how people respond to the decrease in the number of relatively secure, high-paying industrial jobs (Lord & Price, 1992). It also suggests the relationship between downward mobility and new political movements that are violently antiforeigner, antiethnic, and antiwomen.

A topic may be important if it addresses some riddle or unresolved problem of considerable scope. For example, in light of the collapse of the Soviet Union, why did the cold war last so long? The United States spent hundreds of billions of dollars every year preparing to defend itself against the Soviet Union because intelligence agencies continued to report that the Soviet Union represented a major danger. What does that mean about wasted resources and mistaken priorities? What does it say about democracy when policies are determined by secret information agencies that are either inept or twist information for their own policy preferences?

If you are evaluating a government program, the results will be important if your report is read and its vividness influences decision makers. If a study on the Department of Children and Family Services, whose role is to prevent child abuse, makes the agency more effective, you may save lives. If you are studying changes in the federal budget process, because there are so many dollars involved, almost anything you discover can have an impact.

A topic may be important if it suggests a way of interrupting negative cycles of causation, such as occurs with neighborhood deterioration. A major retailer has a fire, the business goes under, and the charred building remains unoccupied. Insurance rates in the neighborhood go up as a result. Locating in the area becomes more expensive and less attractive. Empty buildings attract derelicts who lie in the doorways and drink and harass passersby. Unless something happens to stop the cycle—say, a community group purchases and repairs the building—a negative cycle continues until the area looks like it has been bombed. Figuring out where and how to intervene in such negative cycles requires in-depth interviewing.

Qualitative interviewing focuses on the small, a single setting, one agency, one city or neighborhood, but the implications of the study should extend beyond the immediate arena. If you study the meaning of tattoos in prisons, you can learn about broader issues of defiance, group affiliation, self-expression, toughness, or responses to limitations of freedom. What you learn on these issues is not necessarily limited to a particular prison in which you did interviewing. If you study the closing of one industrial plant, cast the questions to help you learn about broader concerns, such as economic loss and adaptation.

One way to ensure that what you studied in the small has broader implications is to build into your design ways of extending what you have learned to other settings. Suppose you decided to do your study in a prison. You think that what you found may be a reflection of how people respond to loss of freedom. To check out this broader theme, do some interviewing in other types of organizations, such as nursing homes, mental institutions, and army barracks. It would be pretty exciting to find out that results you found in a prison also apply to a nursing home. Such a finding would suggest broader understandings about how people react to loss of freedom.

Reasons to Avoid Topics

Even when you have decided that a topic is important and appropriate for qualitative research, you might want to avoid the subject for personal reasons. The advice to know yourself before doing research is particularly important here. Skilled interviewing often evokes emotion and exposes crushing problems that the researcher might find too stressful. Talking with people who work in day care centers caring for AIDS babies might be a terrific project, but the stories volunteers tell might be too heartbreaking to pursue.

The researcher's feelings about some subjects might be so intense that hearing certain examples or narratives would be difficult. Someone who has been raped may not be able to pay proper attention to the narratives of rapists. If you feel that bankers and lawyers are parasites, you may conduct superficial interviews with them or goad them into angry responses.

Sometimes it is important to get both sides of an issue and to interview people of whom you strongly disapprove. Whether you can do so is a matter you have to work out for yourself. Our colleague Jim had trouble interviewing prison staff, because he found them hostile and racist. But he had to learn to curb his antagonism during the interviews because to understand prison life he also needed to hear their side.

Strong positive bias can also create interviewing problems. Community developers want to help the poor, but they know that the poor sometimes engage in self-defeating behaviors. Herb, whose writings advocate for the poor, had trouble listening to his interviewees express anger at the self-defeating behaviors of the poor.

The Feasibility of the Research

Another criterion for choosing between topics is whether you have time and money to do a particular study. How long will the project take? Can the scope be reduced to fit the time available? Can the project be broken up so separate pieces can be done at different times? A student who works full time during the day cannot interview most people at their places of work. Without financial support, you cannot travel to distant cities and stay overnight to do interviewing.

Sometimes feasibility revolves around gaining access. You might have a wonderful topic to study, for instance, how judges make their decisions, but simply cannot get the access to do the study. Irene tried to do a comparative study between private and public universities, but was not allowed access at the private universities and had to change the subject of her research.

If you begin with an overall question in mind, you can usually find a feasible arena in which to do the study. When Irene was picking dissertation topics, she decided to study problems of failure, decline, and losing. Her first pass was to find individuals who had failed at something, such as political candidates who lost elections or students who did not pass comprehensive examinations. Finding students after they failed comprehensive exams would be difficult, if not impossible. A politician who fails to win election may disappear from sight, unless he or she wins a later election. Even if she could find enough failed students or losing politicians, they might not want to talk about what they would probably consider personal failures. Instead she decided to study organizations that were suffering economic decline. Organizations cannot hide easily and individuals inside the organization might not blame themselves for losses and hence be more willing to talk about what was happening to them (I. S. Rubin, 1977).

Sometimes researchers, especially those doing projects while students, have other constraints on whether or not a project is feasible. Such researchers might have easy access to a place at which they work, such as a hospital, prison, school, or store, but lack the time to gain access elsewhere. They may want to carry out the interviews in the setting in which they already have access. In this case, rather than choosing a topic first, they look for a topic appropriate for the setting.

If you have access to prisons, you might think about topics that deal with freedom, privacy, sex, or violence. A hospital setting suggests research on the management of pain, family support of patients, the occupational hierarchy, the sick role, the informal organization, and the nature and role of humor. Among less obvious topics would be the invisibility of support staff, responses to unionization efforts, the practice of working two shifts back to back, hospitals' adaptation to restrictions on governmental payments, and romances between nursing staff and patients. The goal is to pick a topic that has some broader significance even though the study is limited to one site.

DESIGNING FOR THEORY BUILDING

From qualitative interviews, researchers obtain thick descriptions of a cultural or topical arena. Critical researchers use the data they hear to motivate people to bring about social change; many interpretive researchers consider it an appropriate goal of research to provide thick description of a situation or setting.

Other qualitative researchers, including ourselves, consider that the purpose of qualitative interviewing is to obtain rich data to build theories that describe a setting or explain a phenomenon. Qualitative researchers build theories quite differently from positivists. In a positivist's approach to research, an existing academic theory guides the design for the data collection; once the data are collected, they are used to test and perhaps modify the original theory. By contrast, qualitative researchers build theory step by step from the examples and experiences collected during the interviews.

In the early interviews, the researcher begins to test ideas of why things happen and chooses the concepts and themes to be explored. Then he or she designs subsequent interviews to examine these explanations and preliminary themes. The preliminary themes suggest what questions to ask; what is then heard indicates how to modify the themes and which themes to explore in more depth. The iterative process continues as the newly modified themes are tested and combined into a minitheory that is then retested through further interviews.

Early in his study of community developers, Herb heard the interviewees complain how business people and bankers did not treat them with respect. These comments suggested to Herb that he should work toward an explanation that would account for how community developers responded to the lack of respect and why it mattered. He designed questions to pursue this concern, for instance, by asking interviewees for examples of when they rebelled against disrespectful treatment and what such rebellion accomplished.

Through continuous and flexible design, the researcher then conceives of other situations, or different arenas, in which to test the emerging theory. Interviews are held with conversational partners in these different settings to see how far the theory extends or in what ways the theory should be changed. Is status deprivation primarily felt by the community developers in the smaller, less well-known organizations, or is it common even in larger, financially successful organizations? Do the feelings about status deprivation differ among blacks and whites? Do developers in organizations that are members of advocacy coalitions respond differently to the status deprivation from developers who are not? Based on what you find in different settings, you either support or modify the theory.

In building these theories, researchers listen carefully to hear the underlying *building block ideas,* or *concepts,* and the *themes* that both describe the culture and explain why events happen. Themes are statements that explain why something happened or what something means and are built up from the concepts. Concepts reflect the underlying ideas with which people label their descriptions and understandings of their world (H. J. Rubin, 1983, pp. 58-60). Concepts may represent relatively simple ideas, such as physical rest, or more complicated ideas, such as growing old or sexual attractiveness. Growing old may have different components to it, including fear of illness, loss of physical strength, loss of good looks, or financial insecurity. Sexual attractiveness may include ideas of biological drives, good looks, sparkling or vivacious personality, humor, warmth, and skill in relating to people.

Both in speech and writing, concepts are usually expressed in simple words or phrases, usually as nouns, noun phrases, or gerunds. These words, though, are simply the labels or symbols that represent the underlying ideas. One purpose of qualitative interviewing is to understand these building block ideas and then attach a word or phase as the label that summarizes the concept.

You become sensitive to concepts by listening to taped interviews or reading over transcripts of an interview and noting the words or phrases that interviewees use for examples or key explanations. These words might sound unusual, as in the technical jargon within a field. They might take on a special meaning within the arena. *Debt service* means something different in the federal government than it means in any other unit of government, because the federal government does not pay off any of the debt's principle, only its interest. Thus debt service implies an ongoing, permanent burden for the federal government, where it means a temporary burden everywhere else.

A concept may just be an ordinary term that interviewees repeat a lot because it is important to them or represents important parts of their work or daily life. Community developers describe their work using terms like *empowerment, social equity,* and *housing affordability;* budgeters use terms like *cash balance, earmarked revenues,* and *off-budget expenditures.* Among the police, terms like *perp* (perpetrator) and *mark* (victim of a fraud) are labels for underlying concepts.

Frequently used symbols and stories are often indicative of important underlying concepts or ideas that the conversational partner is illustrating. When you are listening to stories about the boss, you may hear about her kindness, her consideration for employees. You deduce that "benevolence" is an important concept, reflecting the interviewee's theory of how those heading a firm should behave. The famous Uncle Remus stories enabled people to share a sense of rebellion defined through the idea of "wiliness" whereby Br'er Rabbit kept outwitting his opponents without open defiance.

Most concepts are part of the specific language of those being studied. The interviewees use a particular word or phrase that you label as a indicating a concept. Sometimes you hear a set of ideas that you recognize as indications of how people understand, but the conversational partners don't express these ideas as a single word or phrase. For instance, in discussions on budgets, Irene heard frequent mention of *earmarked money,* money in a budget that has to be spent on a particular item and cannot be spent on anything else. She also heard talk about money that could be spent on any of a range of items. This second kind of money was highly valued, because it was more flexible and could solve a wider range of problems. Although the interviewees did not place a label on this second type of money, Irene called it nonearmarked money. She then explored this second concept, asking where the nonearmarked money came from, who controlled it, and how it was spent.

Part of what is done in continuous design is to think of questions to explore the meaning of new concepts as you discover them. As we explain later in this book, you ask for examples and refinements of the term and listen to how the word or phrase for the concept is used in different contexts.

In the following excerpt from Herb's notes, Herb had homed in on the concept *empowerment* and was trying to understand what it meant to those who were building homes in poor communities. Herb's question built on his knowledge that in the past community activists used empowerment to describe any victory over government, for instance, by getting the city to install a needed stop sign. Today community groups are building their own homes. Rather than ask, "What do you mean by empowerment?" which might elicit an abstract, textbook type answer, Herb asked the interviewee to compare empowerment in the old and in the newer sense:

Herb: How does a house really differ from a stop sign, in the empowerment sense?

Conversational Partner: It is bigger, for one thing. And, it impacts people, I think, in a different way. I think quite honestly, [if] people have a decent place to live, to go home [to] everyday, their ability to deal with every other issue that's out there is greatly increased. I don't have to worry about where I am going to live, what I am going to pay for rent, I can move onto that next step and worry about a whole lot of other things. If they got the stop sign and they are still worried about where to live, that stop sign doesn't take them to the next step. You know, it is a self-actualization thing. You take care of your most basic needs and then you can move on to the secondary level, up the ladder.

Without asking directly for a definition, Herb got one: empowerment was an increasing ability to solve personal problems.

You can listen for concepts, then ask questions that will help you understand what they mean and how they are used, and gradually weave the concepts together into themes, longer explanatory phrases, or statements. Sometimes the interviewees state the themes themselves to explain why things occur. Herb's interviewees might say, for example, "The bankers don't respect community groups, so we have to compromise sometimes to get funds." The two concepts are *respect* and *a compromise,* and they are linked to form a theme: lack of respect results in forced compromises. The researcher builds toward theories of how and why things happen by putting themes together that appear to explain related issues. The implications of the emerging theory are examined with further questions asked both to the original interviewees and to others.

To illustrate how the researcher moves from identifying and modifying concepts to hearing themes and to possible theories, suppose you were interviewing professors about problems they have had with students. The professors complained about students who missed deadlines and students who submit the same paper to several different professors. From what you have heard, you summarize the material initially as illustrating two concepts, *lateness* and *cheating.*

In interviews you ask about further examples of these concepts, but from what you hear you begin to worry that more is involved. Other professors complain about excuses students make, such as forgetting their assignments or being unable to come to class because of a family emergency. You think now that the professors are talking about "ways of getting out of work," a different underlying idea. Handing in the same paper to several instructors may be less "cheating" than just another form of "getting out of work."

In the interviews, you have also heard professors explain that they feel "put upon," that the students do not treat the faculty with the respect that their intellectual achievements deserve. These same professors condemned the students for spending so much time "drinking and partying."

In thinking how to continue, the researcher tries out integrative themes that might explain how the professors interpret their world. One theme might be, "Students try to get out of work because they lack respect for professors as intellectuals" whereas another theme might be, "Students try to find ways of getting out of work because they are caught up in a culture that emphasizes partying." These tentative themes then suggest future questioning to see if and when they hold.

In subsequent interviews, the researcher tests the emerging themes. This time, though, the researcher questions both professors and students because examining the themes requires understanding how both sides understand the issues. The interviewer asks students how much homework they do and why they sometimes fail to get assignments done. These interviews also include a set of new questions that encourage students to talk about whether they respect their professors and what that respect means.

In these follow-up interviews, you listen to hear how the concepts of respect, getting out of work, and partying relate. When, for instance, students describe a professor whom they do respect, you ask how hard they work in his or her course. If you find a connection, you have the start of a theory, but you need to do more work to explore what respect means, what partying is all about, and the details of how such understandings came about. Theory building and redesign can take you in a number of different directions. You choose which path to pursue depending on both what topics interest you and what audience you have in mind for your findings. Do you want to know what happens to the quality of teaching when professors perceive that many students are trying to get out of work? Do some professors become demoralized and reduce the effort they put into teaching, or do they become angry at administrators for admitting students who are not interested in learning? Do the professors try to sort out the students who are interested in learning and give them special attention and invest their egos in the success of these students?

A different avenue might be to inquire if the culture of excuses that grows up in the university affects other aspects of students' lives. Do students think such excuses are okay? Did they make such excuses when they were in high school? Do they offer similar excuses in their jobs? Each possible avenue of inquiry suggests further concepts to look for, questions to design, and a choice of whom to interview.

In this example from a university, we illustrated how to build a theory by picking the avenue that seems most promising and redesigning the research to pursue the new line of inquiry. Another way to build theory is to choose different sites and then compare what you find on the same topic. As you try to explain the differences, you formulate new themes.

From her interviews in Rochester, New York, on budget reform, Irene developed two themes on why budgeting reforms failed (I. S. Rubin, 1992). First, she heard that the budget reforms failed because department heads (of police, fire, public works, parks) never understood how the reforms were supposed to work. Second, she learned that politicians feared budget reforms because the reforms provide citizens with information on whether electoral promises are being kept.

With these two themes in mind, Irene continued the research in a second city, Phoenix, Arizona. Phoenix has a more professional staff and politicians who are more comfortable with citizens knowing what elected officials do. The major differences in interview responses between Rochester and Phoenix suggested that to understand budget change, the larger question of political reform had to be explored. How are citizens involved in the budget process? Are bureaucrats who deal with the budget professionals or political appointees? What do the concepts *citizen involvement* or *political reform* mean with respect to budgeting? To build her theory, she redesigned the remaining research to pursue the question of how reform and professionalism influenced budget changes.

You build and test the theory step by step. The testing helps winnow ideas, so the weaker ones and the ones not supported by the interviews drop out. The testing also helps modify the theory so it fits new cases or additional situations, making the theory more tightly linked to the evidence and more generalizable. You continue the study by examining other settings to see how the implications of the emerging theory work out. If the implications work out as you expect, you gain confidence in the theory. If not, you modify the theory to accommodate what you have learned in the new setting.

Suppose you studied a prison that had a riot, and the guards, the prisoners, and the warden all argued that bad food precipitated the riot. The theme linking "having a riot" to "quality of food" is what you want to explore and test. You choose additional sites, one a prison noted for having bad food, but relative social calm, and another reputedly with decent food, but that did have a riot.

Both of these situations potentially contradict your original theme. If the theme held in general, then bad food should lead to riots; by implication, good food should lead to the absence of riots. As part of the ongoing design, you have picked two situations in which the theme does not hold, and you need to know why, and what that means for your theory. Are there conditions that lead to social calm even when the food is bad? Are there conditions that lead to riots even when the food is good? In either case, you can modify and expand your theory by adding conditions to it. In each of the new settings, you interview guards, prisoners, and the warden about both food and social order. You also ask about prison life in general. You want to test the importance of "quality of food," yet not exclude other reasons why riots happen.

You now have three settings to compare. Suppose that in both prisons that had riots, you learn that guards and prisoners referred to each other in ways that showed mutual racial disdain. In one, the riot was triggered as the guards yelled out, "You [racial epithet] deserve to eat this slop"; in the other, the guards locked up the prisoners and yelled out, "You [racial epithet] should be kept in cages like the animals you are." The prisoners retorted, "Fucking [racial epithets]." You start to suspect that the riot stemmed from racial tension rather than food; the food was simply an excuse. This conclusion is strengthened as you learn that in the second prison, before the riot the food had improved because of an advocacy effort of the Good Prison Association, but that little effort had been made to improve the racial problems. Your conclusion is given further credence as you learn that in the prison that avoided a riot, the food was miserable, but the guards spent time commiserating with the prisoners over the terrible food and racial antagonism seemed relatively low.

As the prison example indicates, designing qualitative interviewing to build a theory involves not only thinking about what it is you test, but where or with whom you do so. From his early interviewing in a few locations, Herb learned that community development organizations feared that if they directly pressured government for additional support, government would retaliate and cut off all their funds. Instead of directly pressuring funders, community developers formed advocacy coalitions that were not dependent on government funds and that worked aggressively to get cities to fund community projects.

To test the emerging theme that community developers buffered their financially dependent organizations from retribution by forming coalitions, Herb chose to interview in different cities that varied in the strength of these coalitions. In each site, Herb asked how government and community development organizations worked with one another. In the cities with weaker coalitions, interviewees told Herb that government ignored the development organizations. By contrast, in cities with strong coalitions, interviewees gleefully described campaigns of the coalitions that changed governmental agendas. The emerging theory of the importance of coalitions was strengthened by the interviews from the comparative sites. The process of building theory out of your interviews, testing it, modifying the theory, and retesting it, continues until fewer and fewer changes are made with each cycle.

In qualitative interviewing, theories emerge from the interviews, not as mere extensions of the academic literature. The theories reach for broader significance but remain firmly grounded in the experiences and understanding of the interviewees. After you have a theory that you have built and tested, you can compare it to the literature and locate your study with respect to other people's writing, but if you start off with other people's theories and only test them, you will not be able to see anything new; you may not even be able to see what is out there. The theory you start with can operate as blinkers, limiting your vision. In qualitative interviewing, blinkers are not allowed. You have to be free to follow your data where they lead.

4

Choosing Interviewees
and Judging What They Say

More Issues in Design for Qualitative Research

*T*he design of a study guides you in what and whom to ask. It organizes the research in ways to provide you and your eventual readers reason to believe what you have heard. In this chapter we describe how to choose the people to interview who can provide credible information and how to plan questions to get deep, detailed, vivid, and nuanced answers. We discuss briefly how to plan a series of interviews so the answers hang together without too much overlap. We conclude the chapter by describing how you judge the quality of the research you have done.

SELECTING THE INTERVIEWEES

Whom you choose to interview should match how you have defined the subject of your research. If you are doing an oral history of a recent presidential administration, you include ranking officials in that administration, and if possible, the former President. But suppose you are examining the transformation of the economy away from the industrial and toward the service sector, and want to find out how blue-collar and middle-income individuals have adapted to the changes. With whom do you talk and why? The newly unemployed? People working in positions

65

below their level of skill? Those who have succeeded or those barely hanging on? Whom you talk to is crucial in qualitative design, so choose thoughtfully. All the people that you interview should satisfy three requirements. They should be knowledgeable about the cultural arena or the situation or experience being studied; they should be willing to talk; and when people in the arena have different perspectives, the interviewees should represent the range of points of view.

The kind of person you select to interview will change as the research progresses. In the beginning of the research, almost anyone in the arena knows enough to help orient you; as the research progresses, you have to talk to people who have particular knowledge to help you test specific themes; toward the end of the research, you may change research sites and pick entirely new interviewees to help figure out how far you can extend your results beyond the original arena of the study.

Finding Knowledgeable Partners Initially

When you first enter a research arena, you may not know all that much, so to get acquainted with the field, you want to talk to a variety of people. When Herb started his community development study, almost any director of a community-based development organization could tell him something of import. He traveled to several cities and talked with activists who had done different kinds of projects to learn about community development work in general.

As you learn more, you need to interview those who have particular knowledge or can discuss specific experiences that you want to know about. Herb learned from the first set of interviews that he should compare groups engaged in two different kinds of activities. He needed to find some community developers who had experience in building homes for the poor and some who had been creating jobs within poor communities.

How do you locate people to orient you to the research arena? When studying a culture, you look first for the "encultured informants" (Spradley, 1979, p. 47)—individuals who know the culture well and take it as their responsibility to explain what it all means. Sometimes a group designates an individual to answer questions from outsiders; in other cases, an older, more experienced member of an organization informally plays the role of encultured informant without any formal designation. The server at the restaurant with several years experience, the sergeant in the police district, or the full professor at the university are often knowledgeable about their respective settings. Many of these encultured informants will take it upon themselves to walk you through the cultural premises of their groups.

People who are in position to have the knowledge you want may not always want to share that information openly. They may feel that it is their responsibility to give the "company line," or tell you how people are supposed to act rather than how they really act. A spokesperson at a university might talk about the value of research for pure knowledge, when in fact the university encourages applied research because it earns the university money. To learn to distinguish an idealized answer from a real one, you talk to a variety of people early in the study. At this point, you might not fully understand the cultural conflict over research in universities, but you should hear enough to know that the topic is controversial and potentially interesting, so you can design later interviews to explore the matter.

In topical studies, to find those early informants who will sketch the overall situation, you can start with people whose job it is to monitor what goes on in that arena. For example, reporters for some newspapers follow specific beats, such as the art world, city hall, or the gay community; those in charge of computer bulletin boards normally follow developments in cyberspace; editors of newsletters for religious groups, or environmental groups, or model airplane clubs can guide you about current activities in their groups. People who run professional organizations or trade associations or who act as consultants to a field keep tabs on what is going on and may make good general informants.

When you are studying a historic or political event you may be able to find the names of initial interviewees by looking in court records, libraries, archives, or newspapers. You look for stories about the issue or group involved, or you can locate organization membership lists or other written documents that report the names of those who were involved.

Once you begin interviewing, you will find that your interviewees mention other people as they describe events. For example, in describing disputes, interviewees often praise their allies and point out those whom they oppose. If the interviewees don't mention other people, you can ask them to suggest names of persons with whom you should talk. By interviewing people mentioned by previous interviewees, you make a start on interviewing along a social network. Qualitative interviewers frequently choose interviewees along social networks. In cultural studies, it is common to start with a personal acquaintance who is a member of the group being studied. Felix Padilla began his interviewing of Puerto Rican gang members after being introduced by his student who was a member of the gang (Padilla, 1992). Both William Whyte (1955) and Elliot Liebow (1967), whose studies are widely read for their vivid descriptions of inner-city life, gained access only after they befriended local leaders who introduced them to other people in the community.

In topical studies, sometimes strangers are willing to help you because they recognize the importance of what you want to learn. Before interviewing officials at city hall, Irene attends meetings of professional administrators from that part of the country and introduces herself and explains what her research is about. Usually, these people tell her who is knowledgeable about her subject and often volunteer to make introductions for her.

Networked introductions allow a study to begin, but the choice of the first person to interview may color the responses of later interviewees. For example, in organizational studies, it may be courteous or required to begin by talking with those in charge. But by interviewing bosses or supervisors first, the researcher might be labeled a tool of management and others in the organization may be less open. In situations of conflict or settings with status cliques and factions, if your initial contact is seen as being on one side of the issue, getting help from the other side may be well-nigh impossible.

Sometimes you can avoid this difficulty by watching or reading to learn about factions before you start to interview. You then choose your early interviewees to represent different sides. For example, when Irene does organizational studies, she tries to meet with both upper-level management and union officials at the very beginning of the study.

When the project allows time enough for periods of observation, you can meet those active on contending sides in ways that avoid your being identified with either faction. From watching people interact, whether at city hall, in the computer lab, in the church, or on the street corner, you learn who is knowledgeable and what antagonisms exist. For a land use study, Herb attended dozens of public hearings at which environmentalists, developers, and government officials quarreled with each other. Herb introduced himself to these people at the meetings and explained what he was doing. He then chose as his initial interviewees leaders of each contending faction who had met him as a neutral observer at the public meetings.

Getting Different Points of View

Getting only one side of an argument is not sufficient. You have to go for balance in your choice of interviewees to represent all the divisions within the arena of study.

In cultural studies, you should note from your early interviews or observations distinguishing characteristics of people in the cultural arena. Key distinctions may be between the old-timers and the new recruits, or professional staff and elected officials; between those who primarily teach and those who also do research; or between PC users and Macintosh advocates. Differences may be based on age, gender, or ethnicity or on those who want to fight back and those who prefer to accept the status quo. You then interview representatives of each category to learn about their perspective on key issues or themes.

In topical studies, you can think of the research arena as a theater in the round and try to locate interviewees with different vantage points on what is going on in center stage. Then talk to at least one person from each of those vantage points. Such an approach helps ensure balance. For instance, when Pushkala Prasad (1991) studied the founding of the clerical union at Yale, she figured out who had different perspectives on the matter and talked to the key actors in each of those groups. She conducted semistructured interviews with union organizers, clerical and technical workers, faculty, students, representatives of the Yale administration, and members of the New Haven community.

When there is contention in the arena, you clearly need to talk to each side. In a business or governmental organization, you might want to speak to union members first, and then, armed with the union perspective, ask to talk to upper-level management to get their version. Upper-level managers may be irritated enough at the things the union is saying—or that they think the union is saying—to want to "set the record straight." You can then go back and discuss some of these points with the union. Be cautious, though, when cycling between contending sides that you do not reveal information that violates promises of confidentiality. Our experience is that when we alternate interviews between contending parties, each side becomes especially motivated to fill us in. One of our students was told by a mayor he was studying, "After you talk to Mr. Silk, come back and talk to me and I will set you straight." Herb's experience is that people from one side of a fight will suggest what to ask the other side and even provide needed documents. Such a procedure ensures not only balance but also considerable depth, as people want to make sure you really understand their views.

Testing Emerging Themes

In your early interviews, you are likely to talk to several people who know the overall arena and then to a number of people who represent specific factions or points of view. As you continue the research, you want to find other interviewees who can provide insights on more specific themes that emerge from the interviews.

In studies of organizational culture, you might learn that people are afraid of criticizing those in the data management department. You wonder if the wariness is based on fear of computers and ignorance of technology, or if the director of the data management department knows everyone is dependent on her and has abused that power. You are referred to an old-timer in the accounting department, who tells you that years ago in a fight, the data management people fouled up his division in revenge for an imagined slight.

You have to choose with whom you talk depending on which theme you are trying to test. Suppose you are studying a bureaucratic squabble over an item in a municipal budget and want to compare three possible explanations of what the squabble means. Is this a narrow fight about whether the city should reduce funding for day care and increase funding for highway repair? Or does it represent a bureaucratic quarrel between the public works department and the city manager? Or is it symbolic of deeper schisms in the community and resulting disagreements over how political decisions should be made? Defining each idea suggests with whom you should talk to and what you should ask in order to test its validity.

If the argument is about trade-offs between types of expenditures—day care versus highways—then there ought to have been similar quarrels about trade-offs between other projects. To explore this possibility, you would ask department heads about past conflicts concerning the allocation of funds between projects.

If the quarrel is really about whether the city manager's office has authority over the public works department, then there should be evidence of conflicts over nonbudgetary issues. You might want to interview both present and past city managers and directors of public works and ask what issues provoked controversies in the past, and whether the relationship is currently problematic.

To explore the third possibility, that you observed only the edge of a mighty social cleavage, you might want to interview council members, the mayor, interest group representatives, and maybe homeowner's association activists and organized groups representing the poor. You could ask them about the kinds of issues they get excited about and the frequency of clashes, and then have them compare the current conflict over whether to fund day care or highway repair to the other issues they have battled about.

Choosing Interviews to Extend the Results

If you have picked interviewees who represent separate points of view or had different experiences and obtained rich interviews from each perspective, you gain confidence that what you heard describes the arena in which you did the interviewing. But how far can you extend what you learned?

Does a narrative describing 20 homeless people or the travails of a battered woman speak to broader questions of social injustice? Do interviews with police officers in one large city portray a broader image of police culture in the urban United States? Has Irene only learned about budgeting in three cities or about budgeting in cities more generally? Does Herb's knowledge of community development pertain only to selected places in the Midwest, or does it provide insight into what is happening all over the country?

Sometimes, you don't have to worry about generalizing. For instance, if you are working on a biographical oral history, you can treat what a particular interviewee says as descriptive only of that individual. Or if you are interviewing on the health policy debate, you may not care whether the lobbying and negotiating that you heard about extend to other issues. More often, though, you want to build upon what you learn from a few conversational partners to describe broader arenas or different settings.

How can you choose conversational partners so that you feel comfortable about extending the themes? Choosing interviewees in qualitative interviews in order to generalize is radically different from choosing interviewees in survey research, but unfortunately, people sometimes confuse the two.

Survey interviewers make several assumptions to allow the generalization of their results. They first assume that a research concern can be boiled down to a series of simple questions that can easily be asked of and understood by hundreds of people in a uniform way. Next, they assume that respondents can be treated as interchangeable, so long as they are randomly picked from a broader population defined in advance. Survey researchers randomly choose several hundred to a few thousand respondents to interview from a predefined population. Using complicated mathematical procedures, survey researchers can project, based on this limited sample, who will win an election, how many people watch a TV program, or what percentage of the population know where Rwanda is.

Surveys are appropriate when what you want to generalize are numbers or categorical responses—yes or no—and people can be treated as if they were alike. But in qualitative interview studies, researchers want to make broader statements about more complex responses than yes or no, approve or disapprove. Rather than asking simple facts or opinions, researchers ask about complicated cultural behavior and multistep processes. Interviewees are not treated as the same as each other or picked at random, but rather they are chosen for their different perspectives or particular expertise.

To extend what we hear from qualitative interviewing to other arenas, researchers use two principles. The first principle involves *completeness*, that is, you keep adding interviewees until you are satisfied that you understand the complex cultural arena or multistep process. When each additional interviewee adds little to what you have already learned, you stop adding new interviewees. This is called the *saturation point* (Glaser & Strauss, 1967). The second principle allows you to extend this complicated information to other sites by testing for similarity and dissimilarity. Here you interview in different sites and under different conditions to see how far what you have learned still holds.

With the first principle of qualitative sampling—what we label *completeness*—you choose people who are knowledgeable about the subject and talk with them until what you hear provides an overall sense of the meaning of a concept, theme, or process. Sometimes interviewing one very well informed person is all that is necessary. For instance, if you were asking about how to build an automobile, you would want to find someone who had experience building cars and could describe it to you. In practice, the first person you talked to might not know all the steps, so you keep asking among those who are informed and put together their answers. The test of completeness is if you can follow the directions and build a car.

What is important is not how many people you talked to, but whether the answer works. Can you put a budget together or finance low-income housing or explain to others the norms of courtesy on the computer network?

You interview until you gain confidence that you are learning little that is new from subsequent interviews. The point at which you are not learning any more new material is called *saturation* (Glaser & Strauss, 1967). In studies of social or political processes, you continue until narratives repeat the same events and the same variety of interpretations. You talk to leaders of a grape boycott and the opposition growers, and interview back and forth until you don't hear anything else that is new.

In the first round of his interviews with community developers, Herb heard descriptions of "economic empowerment," "building community," and "the dangers [for the organization] of being small." In his next round of interviewing, he asked other community developers to expand on these core ideas and heard further illustrations of each, but he also learned about the concept of "lack of prestige" for nonprofit organizations. He returned to his original informants and questioned them about "lack of prestige." They recognized and discussed this idea but said little that was different from what Herb had already heard. Herb had reached a saturation point, though he asked a few more community activists just to be sure.

Through completeness and saturation you gain confidence that what you learn holds for the particular arena being studied. The second principle, sampling for *similarity* and *dissimilarity*, suggests how far beyond one arena you can extend what you have learned.

First you test to see if *similar* themes and concepts hold elsewhere by interviewing people in arenas very much like those you have just examined. How did the experiences of Ernesto Cortes, an organizer in Texas, compare to those of Cesar Chavez, an organizer in California? Sometimes, rather than doing the extended interviewing yourself, you can read studies done by other researchers and compare your work to theirs. For instance, Herb's students interview other students at Northern Illinois University (NIU) to learn about the school's culture and then they wonder if their findings apply to other universities. To answer this question, Herb has his students read Michael Moffatt's (1989) book on student culture at Rutgers University, another large state university quite similar to NIU. When the students find the same themes and ideas in Moffatt's book that they heard in their own interviews, they begin to believe that their themes hold beyond NIU.

With a tougher test for generalization, *dissimilarity* sampling, you interview people with background characteristics different from those of your original interviewees, or you interview people in varying settings or who work in places other than the one you researched. You want to see whether the themes you discovered hold in these different situations. When people with diverse backgrounds or in different situations behave the same way or express the same values as your original interviewees, you gain confidence that what you have learned holds more broadly.

Suppose you have interviewed white male fraternity brothers on academic probation (a background characteristic) from Playboy Private U (a site characteristic) and heard the theme that "going to school is just buying a degree." You then interview African American females (background characteristic) who are graduating summa cum laude (background characteristic) from Prestige Tech U (site characteristic) and hear the identical theme. You start to reason that "buying a degree" might be a broader theme within student culture, though of course you would check it out in more than these two cases.

Sometimes dissimilarity sampling is done by choosing additional sites that have contrasting circumstances and interviewing people in each site who are in similar roles. Your reasoning is that if you change the context or setting but the same themes emerge from your interviews, you believe that what you have learned can be generalized to people in similar roles.

When we were researching the rural bureaucracy in Thailand, our interviewees described rules of how ranking officials ought to behave toward subordinates (H. J. Rubin, 1973). We wondered if these rules reflected an underlying belief in the organizational culture or were simply an artifact of the particular social, political, and economic circumstances in the first site. To check the generalizability of what we had found, we chose a second site, markedly different from the first in economic and social characteristics. In spite of these changes of environment, the interviewees in the second place presented the same descriptions of the obligations of a bureaucratic superior that we had heard before, strengthening our belief that what we heard was a widely shared premise in the organizational culture.

Core to this logic of extending what you have learned is figuring out how best to vary background features. Assume you are trying to learn how married faculty women combine career and family. Interviewees tell you that they are pressured to spend more time with their children and feel guilty for every minute they are not at home with the children. You then vary the background characteristics of the women interviewed—the subjects they teach, the professions of their husbands, the type of university at which they work. If you find that your newly sampled interviewees—some teaching physics, others nursing; some married to academics, others to business professionals; some working at community colleges and others in the Ivy Leagues—each feel the pressure to be with their kids and express guilt in a similar way, you gain confidence that the themes are descriptive of academic women in general.

The same logic holds for generalizing about processes. If you were doing a study on health care and the interviewees told you about how lobbyists and elected officials negotiated over the content of the health care bill, you might wonder whether the stages of bargaining you learned about pertained to other areas of legislation. The health care bill was of concern to many lobby groups, such as those representing hospitals, the insurance industry, and organized labor. You could pick a policy area with completely different characteristics, such as foreign policy, an issue that has had little interest group participation. If you hear about similar types of bargaining processes in this very different type of legislation, then what you have found may be generalizable. You would probably try several other areas of legislation before concluding that your results were in fact generalizable.

To summarize, to extend results from qualitative interviews, choose interviewees who can provide grounded and accurate information, and talk to enough of them to get a complete picture of the research arena and feel confident that you understand it. Keep adding interviewees until what you are hearing from the interviewees begins to repeat. Then you can extend what you have learned beyond the original setting and the original interviewees by a logic of comparison.

DESIGNING INTERVIEWS FOR
DEPTH, DETAIL, VIVIDNESS, AND NUANCE

One of the key differences between qualitative interviewing and survey interviewing is that the surveyors are trying to generalize relatively simple information, such as who are you going to vote for, whereas the qualitative interviewers are trying to learn about complex phenomena. Qualitative interviewers don't try to simplify, but instead try to capture some of the richness and complexity of their subject matter and explain it in a comprehensible way. But the richness from qualitative interviewing doesn't happen by itself; it needs to be designed into the pattern of questioning. One of the goals of interview design is to ensure that the results are deep, detailed, vivid, and nuanced.

Depth means getting a thoughtful answer based on considerable evidence as well as getting full consideration of a topic from diverse points of view. In early interviews you may have to encourage conversational partners to provide depth. In the introduction to the interview, you explain what you are interested in and why you are interested in it, so the interviewee will feel comfortable talking in depth on that topic. And you word questions to suggest the desired level of thoughtfulness or depth of the answer. "How do you like being a college senior?" conveys little information about the expected depth of answer, but, "Tell me how being a college senior differs from being a junior" invites the interviewee to think about the differences and explain with examples.

People are more willing to talk in depth if they conclude that you are familiar with and sympathetic to their world. When possible, before the interview begins, immerse yourself in the setting to learn what you can about the issues and start to understand the vocabulary that the interviewees use. When you use this vocabulary, you are telling the interviewees you are familiar with their world. To indicate sympathy, you might mention past experiences you have had in a similar agency, or an experience that you had that woke you up to the problems the group is facing. Or you can show your sympathy by describing the goal of your research in terms of getting more attention for their group.

Follow-up questions are a major way to get more depth. Suppose the initial question to a school administrator was, "What are some of the key problems you confront?" You may get a quick answer such as, "Oh, political problems are troublesome." To get more depth, you have to ask follow-up questions, such as, "What do you mean, 'political problems'?" or "Could you give me an example?" Then you could ask something like, "Are the problems getting worse or better?" and ask for a new set of examples. You can follow up again with a request for further elaboration by asking, "Why is it getting worse; what is changing?" or "How are you dealing with these pressures?" or "What are the impacts of these pressures?" You have series of questions, each asking for more depth.

Another way to obtain more depth on a subject is to come back to it later and ask for clarification. You can schedule a second interview with the same person and say, "I read over the interview that we did last time, and there were some places where I did not fully understand what you told me. Could I ask you a few more questions about that?" Or you can pick an event that occurred between the first and second interview that illustrated what you had discussed in the first interview and ask for elaboration. In the first discussion, you may have talked about controversies on the school board. Then, after the first interview and before the second one, there may have been a brouhaha at a school board meeting when one board member demanded that the students be taught creationism instead of evolution in biology class. You can ask the interviewee's reaction to that event as a way of obtaining more depth on a matter you have already discussed.

You can also go for depth by asking questions that unravel issues backward in time. When Irene was studying the effect of President Reagan's budget cuts on federal agencies, she understood why people were upset—they could lose their jobs—but did not understand what seemed like paranoia about the way the cuts would be administered. Maybe some past event had taught professional staff to fear the politicians. So she began to ask interviewees about their prior experiences with cutbacks. She found that President Reagan's attacks on the bureaucracy reminded many of the agency staffers of the partisan, personal, and anti-Semitic attacks on the bureaucracy of President Nixon's administration a decade earlier. Asking about the past elicited the depth that made the present understandable (I. S. Rubin, 1985).

You ask for detail by requesting particulars. Life is lived in details; the evidence for the generalizations you draw is in the specifics. You ask how hoboes find a place to sleep (Spradley, 1979), how hospital employees recognize and deal with patients' pain, or how elected officials maintain contact with their constituents (Fenno, 1978). You learn about each step of how a budget is balanced or how funds are put together from many sources to help finance housing for the poor.

Having technical knowledge of the field makes it easier to ask questions that will elicit detailed answers. For example, Irene once began an interview with a high official in the Department of Housing and Urban Development by asking what had happened to the "O" regs. Her question indicated her awareness of the ongoing debate over this technical matter and suggested to the official that she was interested in detail.

To solicit detail, you design interviews in ways that ask for specifics early on. If the interviewee mentions several cases, and you follow up on each one, you are signaling interest in detail. Each time you ask for an illustration or a step-by-step description of what happened, you are asking for detail. Once the interviewees understand that you want this detail, they will usually continue to provide specifics without being prodded.

Another way to suggest that you want to hear about things in detail is to ask people how they carry out specific tasks for which they are responsible. The following excerpt from interview notes taken in Tampa, Florida, illustrates how well this can work:

Irene: How do you put the management system, the SLA [service level analysis], and the budget together?

Delilah: We start at the lowest part of the chain, the micro level, working with the management reports. . . . For example, hole patch-ing, you put the number and location, estimating by recent history, or how many lane miles you will pave. It's accomplishment oriented. It specifies the level of service we want to be at, for example, mow everything twice a year. Or will we only have a certain amount of money, and will only be able to afford 1 1/2 times a year? We do the ideal one first, based on standards. At the average productivity rate, how many could we do if everything is normal? Translate that into crew days. We may not have that number of employees, so we have to revise it. Then, with a staffing estimate, we produce costs at standard rates. We find the total dollar value of labor, equipment, and materials. It's like the budget, but the budget is more detailed. But we can see how close we are to the budget target we have been given.

Each activity has different levels of priority, a, b, and c. If we don't get 1.2 [million?] we will start with [cutting] the c's, and go up to the a's. We know how to play with it. If we reduce mowing from 2 times to 1 1/2, will that create idle crews? Where would they go? What will it cost? Can they go to another c activity? If so, that might be okay.

This answer is wonderfully detailed and it stimulated the conversational partner to go into depth on related subjects in later answers. Although the detail seemed overwhelming at first, it opened up the theme of how bureaucrats respond to political demands, how they comply with demands to cut the budget, and how those demands translate into reduced services. Asking for a mess of details no one could love turned out to be the means of obtaining answers to a much larger question about how technical systems and political systems interact.

By asking detailed questions on technical points that are of interest to the interviewee, you convey interest in learning about the details. For example, toward the beginning of Herb's interviews, when his interviewees talked about "tax credits," Herb asked what "internal interest rates" they received, a rather specific concern, but of great importance to the developers, who know the amount of funds they receive depends on this rate. By asking this question, Herb signaled his concern in hearing about details.

Depth and detail differ but complement each other. To illustrate the difference between going after depth and going after detail, suppose you are doing a life history with a middle-aged woman and she tells you that she recently invited her mother to move to her town. Going for depth, you ask questions that require a thoughtful response, such as, "Was encouraging your mother's move a difficult decision for you?" To suggest your concern with details, you can ask, "What was happening in your mother's life when she decided to move?" "Is she more dependent on you now?" "Can you give me some examples of her increased dependence?" Clearly, depth and detail are related, and much of the time you want both. Detail adds solidity, clarity, evidence, and example; depth adds layers of meaning, different angles on the subject, and understanding.

You get details by asking for examples, and then you explore the examples, step by step. In the interview with the woman whose mother came to town, she might say, "Yes, my mother depends on me much more than she did. For instance she expects me to take her to the dentist and to her doctor's appointments." You can then ask for details, "What happens when you take her to an appointment?" She answers, "You know, I pick her up and bring her to the clinic and sit with her while she waits for the doctor, then I take her home." You are getting detail, but still lacking depth. You continue looking for depth, asking, "Why don't you drop her off and come back for her?" She answers, "I can't go anywhere else and come back for her, she gets too nervous." You would begin to understand what this dependence meant and how it was felt. You have the depth of the interviewee's reasoning and the details to back it up.

In addition to depth and detail, the interviewer should also design the questions to evoke vivid responses that will convey the range of feeling of the interviewee to those who read your report later on. To be vivid, an anecdote or example need not be dramatic or extreme, but it should create a strong vicarious experience for the audience.

One way to encourage vivid answers is to ask for firsthand descriptions of events and not interrupt them when they occur, even if, for the moment, they seem off the topic. Consider this example that Jim Thomas shared with us from his prison research:

[This guard would] mess with guys, and then he'd say, "Go ahead and beat me." And one day, somebody came up to him and hit him with a pipe, he's got a plate in his head now, [laughs] and he was lying on the floor, and blood was gushing, [laughs] and he was crying like a baby: "Please don't kill me, please don't kill me." He thought he was going to die right there.

The story is vivid. It could be used in conjunction with others similar to it to provide a convincing description of prison violence. Talking about violence in the abstract just doesn't reach the reader the same way that episodes like this do.

Qualitative interviewing seeks a realistic description of a situation or cultural pattern. Realistic description includes shades of gray, not just black and white. *Nuance* means precision in description, not blue, but cornflower blue, not just love, but love with energy and joy. It explores subtlety of meaning. What exactly does it mean to say you love someone? Is there a little fear mixed in with the love? Or a little dominance? How is the idea shaded or toned? You design questioning to elicit nuance and to reject unshaded answers.

Some people's speech is naturally nuanced, but many people talk with bold distinctions, requiring you to ask for shades of meaning. First, you indicate you want nuance by presenting questions that show you expect something other than black-and-white or yes-or-no type responses. "Did you want to go to Thailand" asks for a yes-or-no answer. "How did you feel about the offer of a trip to Thailand" encourages a more nuanced answer.

You elicit nuanced responses by asking follow-up questions, such as, "Does it always happen like that?" or implying that there must be another side or that something in the answer was too simple to be complete. The following excerpt from Irene's interview notes illustrates how to imply that an answer is too simple:

Irene: I am curious about the effect of changing from at-large to partly at-large, partly district elections.

Budget Director: [We] mix three at-large [councilmanic seats] and 4 district. If they were all district, we would have ward politics. We would have to locate 7 things in 7 wards. You want segments to be represented—it is more like a house and senate.

Irene: There must be some pressure from the districts. How do you accommodate to that?

Budget Director: This question reminds me of my PA days, worrying about ethics, how will you distribute resources. Equity may not be enough, you may have to combine equity with other distributional criteria. You can't just do the downtown either, the neighborhoods need some too. . . . Part is equity, part is a vision of what the community needs. It is also influenced by other sources of money; partnerships direct money where it wouldn't be if there weren't matching funds.

The answer to the follow-up question was much more nuanced in its implications that there are multiple competing interests that affect financial allocations and that the interests all get juggled so that everyone ends up getting something.

You can also follow up on the nuances that conversational partners provide in their answers, to show that you are interested and want to hear more. In this interview, the budget director was explaining the advantages of a new budget system called *target-based budgeting*, and Irene asked for nuance by offering a simple summary of the interviewee's answer, a summary so simple the interviewee reacted against it and gave a more complete and subtle answer:

Budget Director: It makes the departments and coordinators understand, and makes them prioritize and do the reasonable [thing]. It's not me or the mayor that says, "I don't want to hear that." They [the department heads] have to define what is important. Early, people are being creative, [asking] what should we be doing. As they go from thought process, [and] put pencil to paper, [and then] put detail behind it, some of them [the ideas] drop out. As the department looks at their [staff's] request and talks to the coordinators, things start to sift out, departments adjust the request list to those that are more appropriate. It's not top down, it's not "I only want to see 4 projects instead of the 10 you have."

Irene: . . . it forces the departments to winnow? . . .

Budget Director: We force the departments to manage, they are new and innovative, there is incentive to do things. There is self-investigation, self-inspection, [they say] "can we do this better," they talk of things. It's not done by the internal auditor, that creates hostility. The departments get involved and question how they do things. They do preliminary staffing [analysis], they meet with accountants and permit people to find out if things are possible, they don't just say, "mayor, let's go with it."

Another way of getting nuances is to listen for signs of ambivalence or apparent contradictions and then inquire into them. In Herb's early interviews, community developers seem to vacillate on how much they still believed in protest actions, at times saying they were terrific, and later on indicating that they were highly problematic. Herb designed follow-up questions to explore these mixed feelings and obtained thoughtful and nuanced responses on when protest is appropriate and when it causes more harm than good.

PUTTING THE INTERVIEWS TOGETHER

One major goal of design is to ensure that you get the depth, detail, and nuance that are the strength of qualitative research. Another purpose is to help you put together the separate pieces of information that you gather. An interview project is more than a single interview; you may interview the same person several times, you may interview many people in one site, and you may do interviewing in several sites. All this information has to come together at the end, and unless you build into the design some means of putting the pieces together, you may be very frustrated when it comes time to write your report.

Combining examples, descriptions, and illustrations from different interviews to form a narrative is much easier if the individual interviews are designed originally in ways that help them fit together. We describe in later chapters how to draw an outline for yourself that serves as a guide across the interviews, ensuring that the pieces you collect fit together. The outline allows you to ask different people different questions and still have a place for each piece of information you get.

You also have to weigh the versions of a variety of people. The interviewees know different things, the strength of their memories may differ, and their openness may vary. You don't necessarily want to weigh what each interviewee says exactly the same.

Sometimes you want to judge how well people remember events, how accurate their social memory is, or how well they remember specific dates and places. One way of checking is to guide the interview to a discussion of events for which you have a record and compare the record with the interviewees' oral versions. You are not checking whether people are being truthful, but what types of things they recall. Some people remember better who was there, others what was said. Some remember budget sizes and others draw a blank when a number is mentioned. You want to rely more on the numbers of the person who remembers in that way, and more on the social details of the person who is good at recalling them.

Another way to figure out how much weight to put on a specific part of an interview is to *norm* the answers, that is, measure them against a standard that you form. If you and the interviewee have watched a meeting, you can compare the interviewee's version with your own, in terms of the level of emotion, the degree of antagonism, or the under-standing of the outcome. If you saw the meeting as emotional, and other interviewees agreed, except for one who described the meeting as if nothing emotional happened, you suspect that this interviewee has a tendency to flatten out emotional narratives. Then you know how to interpret other things he or she describes that you did not see and you know how to compare this interviewee's reports with those of other interviewees that report more excitement or more controversy.

If you cannot compare the interviewee's descriptions to something you have both seen, then you may have to build some *norming* questions into the interviews. A norming question is a way to learn a person's overall opinions on a subject so as to be better able to interpret his or her answer on a specific matter. People norm each others opinions all the time in ordinary conversations. Herb, for instance, is well known to be highly critical about the motivations of university administrators, so when Herb praises what a dean has done, his colleagues assume this administrator must be really spectacular.

If researchers know their conversational partners well, they can norm the way they ordinarily do, by comparing the current answer to what they know the person has said before on the general topic. Without such background information, the researcher designs questions to test people's opinions on a subject. Having learned from such questions that a person is a political conservative, you would weigh his or her description of a welfare program differently from that of a social activist.

If you keep an overall outline of the information you are looking for, so that each major piece of information you collect belongs somewhere on this outline, and you pay attention to how people remember and how they know things, and also think about whatever slant people may bring to the interviews, you should be able to put the pieces together at the end of the interviews.

MAKING THE STUDY CREDIBLE

At the end of the research, you will present a report, or write an article or book to share what you have learned. But why should anyone believe what you say or write? And for that matter, why should you accept what your conversational partners have told you? If your research is well designed, it should convince both you and the readers that what you have concluded is accurate.

Research design suggests standards for good and convincing research. In quantitative research, the standards most frequently used are those of *validity* and *reliability*. If research is valid, it closely reflects the world being described. If work is reliable, two researchers studying the same arena will come up with compatible observations.

Most indicators of validity and reliability do not fit qualitative research. Trying to apply these indicators to qualitative work distracts more than it clarifies. Instead, researchers judge the credibility of qualitative work by its *transparency, consistency-coherence,* and *communicability;* they design the interviewing to achieve these standards.

Transparency

Transparency means that a reader of a qualitative research report is able to see the basic processes of data collection. A transparent report allows the reader to assess the intellectual strengths and weaknesses, the biases, and the conscientiousness of the interviewer. Interviewers maintain careful records of what they did, saw, and felt to make their research transparent to others and to themselves.

The original records of notes or recordings of the interviews should be kept in ways that others can read or play back. It's best to prepare a written version of each interview, called a *transcript*. In a log, describe how the transcript was made, whether directly from tape, from notes, or from memory, and indicate when and how the transcripts were verified, and whether the transcript includes pauses and other nonverbal indications of what occurred. If the transcripts are edited versions of the tape recordings, you should also note the kind of material that was left out.

Also keep a record of how you organized and analyzed the transcripts. Such a record will include the original coding categories, that is, how you sorted out what people said. Maintain the marked-up transcripts and include in the transcripts the in-text comments that you jotted down to indicate what was happening in the interview. These comments might include observations like, "He seemed to think this was very funny" or "She was very nervous at this point, standing up and sitting down again."

On notes that you reconstructed from memory, you can add comments such as, "This was my term, not his" or "I am not sure of the order here, the point about her mother may have preceded this." If you have paraphrased a question or response, mark that too, so you know later that you cannot use it as a direct quotation. You can also add your feelings about the whole interview, such as, "This interview was filled with tension" or "The group was friendly and teasing, and it was hard to get past the small talk." Be sure to keep one copy of the original transcription untouched and keep the raw notes or tapes as backup. Make editing changes or notes only on copies that you make for the purpose.

In a notebook separate from the rest of the interview notes, you should also keep a record of how you went about doing the research. If you did participant observation, describe what occurred, when it took place, how long it lasted, where you are keeping the notes. Also provide a summary of what you learned. You can keep a running file of ideas as they emerge. You can also note what was happening in the research—how you felt, with whom you were speaking—when you made major decisions, such as determining to follow a particular theme or explore a specific concept.

This notebook should also record discussions you had with the interviewees about how the material would be written up, whether they asked to be kept anonymous, or whether any particular information was received "off the record." You may want to refer to this log when you write up the report, and it should be made available to others in the unlikely event that they want to examine it.

The requirement that the research process be transparent encourages the researcher to stay close to his or her data in writing up a report. Flights of imaginative fancy are controlled when the original interviews are publicly available and quotes from the interviews are used in the report to support each major conclusion. The logs can help you reconstruct the process of decision making, so that you can tell readers with some precision exactly what you did. These logs should be kept and made available to readers on request. Hardly anyone ever does ask for them, unless you are charged with research misconduct (which can happen to anyone). In that unlikely event, your research logs should provide evidence of your careful methods.

Consistency

A credible final report should show that the researcher checked out ideas and responses that appeared to be inconsistent. You show that you examined themes in one interview for coherence with the themes presented in others. You indicate that you checked it out when a single interview seemed to present contradictory responses, and you explain how you examined for consistency across settings or cases.

In qualitative research the goal is not to eliminate inconsistencies, but to make sure you understand why they occur. When people present different versions of the same event you either have to offer evidence why you accept one version or the other, or show why in these circumstances people can hold contradictory understandings. If you find inconsistencies of themes across cases, you either modify the emerging theory, or limit how far your findings extend.

Coherence of the Themes. Coherence means that you can offer explanations for why apparent contradictions in the themes occurred and what the contradictions mean. Suppose you were doing a study of street people and discovered they held widespread norms of food sharing, but felt that it was okay to steal from each other. By itself, such a finding appears somewhat inconsistent. To increase the credibility of your report, you show that you explored this difference in norms. Perhaps you asked why it is okay to steal, or what is okay to steal and what is not okay to steal. Or perhaps you asked from whom is it permissible to steal. You might find a resolution of sorts if you discover that it is okay to steal from those who have something, but that your interviewees felt they had to look after those who have nothing, because they might die. What you thought was an inconsistency becomes coherent.

To check for this level of coherence you have to ask for responses that are deeper and more detailed than the original answers. In studying community development organizations, Herb learned that some developers felt their goal was to build homes and stores that would improve the community, whereas others chose to emphasize social programs that helped individuals. A reader would probably want to know why the split was there and what it meant. Herb explored the issue further, and found that the community developers had already worked out an answer: The social programs taught the poor how to maintain and pay for the new homes built for them or provided them with training to work in the newly opened stores. What appeared to be two separate approaches ended up being logically consistent and coherent.

Sometimes, though, what appears to be inconsistent across interviews is irresolvably inconsistent. Two interviewees may give contradictory versions of what happened. The researcher may have to pick between versions, weighing the quality of evidence, the nature of the interviewees' memory, and evidence of slant to sort out which version is more credible. Alternatively, you may decide to present the two different versions because they help explain the nature of the conflict and are strongly held and believed by the interviewees. If you present both views, you can make your research more credible by showing that you checked out why your interviewees offered different versions of what happened.

The Consistency of Individuals. Readers might doubt the credibility of what was learned if the report shows that an interviewee was saying things that did not mesh and the researcher failed to examine why. When an interviewee responds in an inconsistent fashion you have to check it out, carefully and courteously.

The most common way of handling contradictions is to ask, gently, about the contradiction, with the assumption that there is an explanation. "I noticed that you mentioned earlier that you did not like the planning aspect of the budget process, but now you are talking about the importance of planning in revenue projection. That sounds contradictory . . . " Then let the conversational partner explain the apparent contradiction.

Sometimes the interviewees hold contradictory views simultaneously, and both are true, in the sense that the interviewees believe them. To gain credibility with readers, the interviewer has to show that he or she explored the apparent contradiction. Suppose an interviewee has expressed racist sentiments, yet is friends with a person from the disliked group. Pointing out the contradiction directly would probably create discomfort, but you could ask about the matter indirectly. For example, you could ask about the perceived negative characteristics of the disliked group at one point, and then at a later time, ask if the friend has these characteristics.

Sometimes checking out an inconsistency increases the report's credibility by adding depth to the understanding of the culture. As an example, in a study of young male prostitutes, another of our colleagues, David Luckenbill, suspected, by observing their clothes, that these teenagers were inflating their reports of nightly earnings, probably to elevate their status to him and to their peers.

Later in the interview, Luckenbill asked "Uh, how much money do you have on you right now?" or "Do you have change for a $10?" Using this ploy, he discovered that his suspicions were correct: Not only did his informants have little money in their possession, but they in fact made little. Discovering the inconsistency was not important in itself, but because in doing so, Luckenbill learned about a crucial aspect of the culture—that the young prostitutes wanted so badly to be rich that they pretended they had money.

In demonstrating consistency, the researcher need not show that peoples' beliefs are fully coherent or that interviewees told some idealized version of the truth. But the researcher does have to show that he or she bothered to check out inconsistencies. The benefit of doing so is twofold. The reader is more likely to believe that the interviewees are responding openly, and the researcher is more likely to get more thoughtful and nuanced answers.

Consistency Across Cases. Credibility is increased when the researcher can show that core concepts and themes consistently occur in a variety of cases and in different settings.

For instance, early in his community development research, Herb learned that community developers resented it when property in their neighborhoods was owned by outsiders. Herb was alerted to this concern by an activist in a poor Hispanic neighborhood:

> This area is coming back. But a lot of stuff is all owned by people from outside. . . . There are eight bars. . . . They don't hire anybody from the community to tend bar. They are all owned by people from outside. . . . I mean all the cash those eight bars generate, none of it changes hands in the community even once. It leaves at 2 [a.m.] and it is gone.

Herb explored this concern further and learned that the strategy followed by this community developer was to help people in the community buy and own property and to concentrate on physical development projects rather than providing job training to individuals who might then move away from the community.

But how common was this rather elaborate strategy? Does this theme appear elsewhere? Is it mainly found in the inner city? Does it also apply in African American or Caucasian neighborhoods? To find out, Herb asked questions about this topic in other types of communities, in bigger and smaller cities, in rural areas, in areas populated by Caucasians, and in those in which African Americans lived. Herb found that indeed this community-ownership approach to development was widespread.

Another way of showing credibility across cases is to think through the implications of a proposed theme and then check to see if the implications occur as you expected. For instance, if Irene was right that the degree of political reform in a city affected the budget process, as she had heard in earlier interviews, then more reformed cities ought to have more open budget processes in which citizens find it easier to affect budget priorities. Irene checked out that implication by continuing her interviewing in more reformed cities and asking about citizen involvement. She found out that the pattern continued to hold. To show credibility, it is not necessary that a proposed theme holds generally. But your research report should show that you explored it carefully and that when the theme failed to hold, you continued the work by either revising the theme or figuring out under what conditions the theme holds and what conditions it does not hold.

Communicability

The portrait of the research arena that you present should feel real to the participants and to readers of your research report. It should communicate what it means to be within the research arena. Your conversational partners should see themselves in your descriptions, although they may not agree with every detail or interpretation. Other researchers should understand your text and accept your descriptions because they complement what they and others have seen.

Readers who have never been in your research setting should feel confident that they now can find their way around the arena that you describe. The richness of detail, abundance of evidence, and vividness of the text help convince those who have never been in the field that this material is real. You add to their confidence by describing how each major theme was tested and retested under different conditions before you accepted it.

Another way of increasing how well the research communicates is to make sure that those being interviewed talk about their firsthand experiences, rather than acting as informants on the experiences of others. Readers are usually much more willing to pay attention to someone who has "been there" or "had their feet to the fire." Accounts by people infected with AIDS are more convincing than summaries by uninfected physicians. In qualitative research, the author does not impress the reader with his or her credentials; it is the experiences of the interviewees that give legitimacy to the argument. Insider accounts give the reader a glimpse backstage.

Research that is designed to garner lots of evidence; that is vivid, detailed, and transparent; that is careful and well documented; that is coherent and consistent is going to be convincing. These are the standards through which qualitative interviewing studies gain credibility.

A SUMMARY OF ITERATIVE DESIGN

In the last two chapters we have shown how to design qualitative research cycles to bring together what you want to learn with what the conversational partners know and experience. The design guides the questioning and suggests how the questioning changes over the course of a study. In the next five chapters we discuss techniques of interviewing that carry out the iterative design.

An iterative and self-corrective design ensures the accuracy and credibility of the research. To gain that credibility, you have to choose interviewees carefully and be sure that they are knowledgeable, will speak openly, and have firsthand experience. You have to custom-design each interview to build in depth, detail, and nuance. Specific questions are added to interviews as the project proceeds to test out ideas along the way. Whom you talk to later on depends in part on what you have learned in earlier interviews and what you failed to learn.

The iterative testing of concepts, themes, and theories improves the credibility of the research report. If you feel uncomfortable with what you are hearing, if the narratives do not ring true or ideas described are not consistent, or if you learn new and unanticipated things, you redesign questions and shift the setting and/or the interviewees until you can figure out what is happening. You gradually build a consistent portrait that is close to the evidence and will persuade your readers that what you have found is credible.

Readers must be able to see the evidence and the logic that led the researcher to his or her main conclusions. To convince the readers, quote generously from your interview transcripts to back up key points. Make your research process visible, but not intrusive. The reader should not only be able to see and follow the logic of the analysis, but be swept along by vividness and clarity of the examples. The voices of your interviewees should be clear and compelling.

5

Building Conversational Partnerships

*R*esearch design tells you what types of information you want to collect and from whom. You obtain this information in long interviews with individuals who feel comfortable talking to you openly and in depth. Much of this chapter describes how to build a conversational partnership that encourages such discussions.

But a conversational partnership is much more than a gambit to encourage conversation. It involves personal and ethical obligations to the people you are studying. You want to obtain and report accurate information in ways that cause no harm to those you study. Further, to ensure that you are fair to those you are studying and accurate in what you report, you should note your own reactions to the interviewees and your responses to what you learn during the course of the study.

ETHICAL OBLIGATIONS IN
CONVERSATIONAL PARTNERSHIPS

Research ethics are about how to acquire and disseminate trustworthy information in ways that cause no harm to those being studied (Neuman, 1994; H. J. Rubin, 1983). To obtain high quality information in interviews, you are dependent on the cooperation of your conversational partners. When you encourage people to talk to you openly and frankly, you incur serious ethical obligations to them.

These ethical obligations require avoiding deception, asking permission to record, and being honest about the intended use of the research. Your obligations also include ensuring that interviewees are not hurt emotionally, physically, or financially because they agreed to talk with you. You have an obligation to warn interviewees if something they are saying may get them in trouble and to give them an opportunity to retract what they said or tell you not to use the material or not to identify them as the source. You should not take material from the interviewee for your own purposes, leaving the interviewee feeling diminished or "ripped off" (Mishler, 1986, p. 118).

Protecting interviewees from harm might mean leaving out exciting material from the final report or slightly distorting the results so as to keep people out of trouble. If interviewees do not want you to use something they said, even though they told it to you in their interviews, you should leave it out. You may have to make some trade-offs between the accuracy and punch of your report and protecting your interviewees, but with some thought you can usually protect individuals and still get your points across.

You can find advice on how to handle ethical concerns in the codes of ethics published by professional associations whose members do social research (cf. Neuman, 1994, pp. 461-467). At the core of these ethical codes are admonishments to be open and honest with those you are studying and cause them no harm.

To encourage such ethical behavior, a number of federal agencies have imposed a legal requirement that before research is eligible for funding, researchers must demonstrate that they will not harm their interviewees. Whether or not a researcher is seeking federal funding, many universities and other social research organizations insist that researchers (including students) show in advance how interviewees will be protected before the research is allowed to begin. *Institutional review boards* (IRBs) composed of professionals from the researcher's organization and informed community members review research proposals and can request changes to protect the subjects of the research before approving the proposal. Be aware of these requirements and use them to force yourself to think beforehand about the possible consequences of your research.

Most professional codes of ethics and IRBs encourage researchers to obtained signed *informed consent statements* from people they are studying. An informed consent statement describes the purposes of the research, provides background on the researcher, and points out both the benefits and possible risk to those involved. It usually promises to share results with those being studied, indicates the degree of confidentiality of the findings, and most important, emphasizes that participation is fully voluntary. Participants in a study sign these forms to show they understand the risks described in the statement and agree to be in the study.

Codes of ethics, institutional review boards, and informed consent statements all force the researcher to think out the possible harm his or her work might cause. These measures encourage researchers to determine if information can be obtained in ways that are less disruptive to those being studied. Most important, they emphasize to the researcher that those who are providing the data in the research are people who deserve respect and concern, not objects or impersonal cases.

But this formal approach to research ethics creates difficulties for those following the iterative design model. Before approving research, institutional review boards want to see formal questionnaires and precise descriptions of those to be studied. But in qualitative research the questions to be asked evolve during the course of the study and can differ from person to person. Further, with iterative design, who you are studying and the core topic of the research may emerge only after the work is well under way.

Letting people know what you are studying, that you want them to participate, that their participation is voluntary, and that, if they wish, you will keep their answers confidential are important routine steps in qualitative research. But whipping out an informed consent statement and asking for a signature can be awkward at best. To the extent that interviews are an extension of a conversation and part of a relationship, the legality and formality of a consent form may be puzzling to your conversational partner or disruptive to the research. On the one hand, you may be offering conversational partners anonymity and confidentiality, and on the other asking them to sign a legal form saying they are participating in the study. How can they later deny they spoke to you—which they may need to do to protect themselves—if you possess a signed form saying they were willing to participate in the study?

You may have known people in your research arena as cooperative and helpful partners orienting you to the field before you decide to interview them. The transition from general informant to interviewee should be as natural as possible; pulling out legal consent forms for them to sign is an abrupt departure that says this is something different and possibly risky. Moreover, with its flavor of medical experiments and hospital informed consent rules, the form suggests manipulative research in which the interviewee is a passive recipient of treatment rather than an active partner.

Institutional review boards are not geared for qualitative research. Often the qualitative researcher cannot come up with the detailed proposal the board demands. You cannot achieve ethical research by following a set of preestablished procedures that will always be correct. *Yet, the requirement to behave ethically is just as strong in qualitative interviewing research as in other types of research on humans—maybe even stronger.* You must build ethical routines into your work. You should carefully study codes of ethics and cases of unethical behavior to sensitize yourself to situations in which ethical commitments become particularly salient. Throughout your research, keep thinking and judging what are your ethical obligations.

In extreme cases, qualitative researchers have gone to jail to protect their interviewees and keep their promises of confidentiality. When Mario Brajuha interviewed restaurant workers for his dissertation in the early 1980s, he had no reason to suspect that his data would ultimately land him in jail—he was only studying the social construction of the workplace (Brajuha & Hallowell, 1986; Hallowell, 1985). Brajuha promised his interviewees confidentiality to ensure that nothing that was said would be used against the workers by their co-workers or supervisors. However, when a fire occurred in the restaurant, the police suspected arson and subpoenaed Brajuha's interview notes as part of their investigation. Brajuha was in a difficult ethical position: He could surrender his data to police and break his vow of confidentiality to informants, or he could keep his promise and go to jail. He chose to honor his promise and went to jail.

Most of the time you won't have situations that are this difficult, but you should always anticipate ways of preventing such harm. For example, people's real names are often not important in your research, and by leaving them out or giving people pseudonyms, you protect conversational partners in case your notes end up in the wrong hands. You should be prepared to destroy your notes rather than allow access to them by people who would hurt your conversational partners. If you carry a tape recorder into a prison to do interviews, be prepared to quickly destroy the tapes. If you think you might be stopped and searched and your notes confiscated, don't take notes, memorize the conversation as best you can. At worst, you lose that one interview, which is a lot better than losing the whole research project and harming a conversational partner.

In general, if you promise anonymity or other measures, such as giving the interviewees a final veto on the written report, in order to encourage their participation, then you should come through on these promises. Failure to keep such promises is more than discourteous; it is also unethical, because it means the interview material was obtained under false pretenses. In addition, breaking such promises makes it more difficult for anyone else to do research, because it jaundices interviewees about the whole research enterprise.

If you think you may not be able to keep a particular promise, don't make it, and don't even imply it. If you cannot imagine yourself going to jail for contempt of court for refusing to turn over interview notes, then you should not promise confidentiality to an interviewee who might be engaged in some unlawful activity.

You might, however, find yourself in a situation where the ethics of keeping your promise are less clear. You may have promised confidentiality, because you could not imagine getting information that you would have difficulty keeping confidential, and then learn about an upcoming crime and feel that you have to report it. Avoid this situation if at all possible. For example, if there are limits to your promise of confidentiality, make them clear up front. "Unless you tell me that you are going to kill someone, I will keep this material confidential." That is a warning not to tell you some kinds of information (cf. Jankowski, 1991).

Another potentially ambiguous ethical area is the decision on how hard to press someone for information. Your overall guideline might be to push for information, but to stop if it seems the interviewee feels upset or threatened. But what if you get people to give you answers that they then feel uncomfortable about having revealed? What if thinking about the topic in depth recalls some pain or frustration and leaves the interviewee depressed? In Herb and Irene's research in Thailand, one of the most open and helpful conversational partners was a junior-level administrator. About 2 months after we left the field, he committed suicide, leaving us wondering if our encouraging him to talk about his problems may have made them more salient to him.

Our obligation as researchers is to get past superficial answers, but how much knowledge is worth what degree of tension on the part of the conversational partner? Clearly, you should not push someone hard for a minor piece of information, but beyond that, the researcher has to make judgments. Often it depends on the type of research being done. AIDS patients find it painful to talk about their suffering, yet some want to talk about their illness if it will help others avoid AIDS or learn to handle their illness better (Weitz, 1987). Because these AIDS patients understand that what they are doing will be painful for them, but still want to do it, an interviewer could ethically press them for information.

Irene feels pretty comfortable pressing for information when she is interviewing public officials in their roles as guardians of the public weal. If a city budget is out of whack, she wants to know why and thinks it is the ethical obligation of the public officials to tell her. If she were interviewing single mothers about the difficulties in their lives, she would draw some different lines, because she would be interviewing about those things that are most stressful and most personal, and her interviewees would be under no moral obligation whatever to talk to her.

If you are in a situation where you feel wary of pressing for information, you can use a nondirective questioning style to encourage your conversational partners to determine the boundaries of what they discuss. If you are concerned that a question might be too stressful, you can give the interviewee a choice of whether or not to answer. "If this question is still too stressful, don't answer, we can talk about it another time, but you mentioned coming home to an empty house. Do you feel like talking about that?"

Fortunately, not pushing usually results in better rather than worse interviews. If you press hard for a piece of information before someone is ready to share it, he or she may shut down and tell you nothing of consequence or lie or distort the answer. You need to listen hard to figure out if your questions are evoking stress and back off when stress levels threaten to get too high. You can usually cycle back to stressful questions later, when the relationship is firmer.

You have to try to anticipate ways that your research can hurt someone and be constantly alert during the interviews to the possibility of bringing up excessively painful or stressful material. You also want to avoid harm to the interviewee in other, more personal ways, through how you ask questions and respond to answers.

For example, don't take interviewees for granted. Make it clear how much you appreciate your conversational partners' help. Avoid mockery or sarcasm. Don't assume you know the rest of an argument they are presenting and prevent them from finishing what they are saying. Don't interrupt a story that is obviously important to the interviewee even if it doesn't appear to be on the topic. Asking for permission to use specific quotes indicates that you think the answers are worthy of quoting and shows that you respect the interviewees' ownership of their words.

You can also show respect to your interviewees by being reasonably honest if you are asked about what you feel and where you stand on issues, but this is an area that requires balanced judgment. It can be very tempting to try give an answer that agrees with the interviewee whether you mean it or not, but in the give and take of interviewing, honesty is easier and usually works better. You can usually express your opinion briefly in a nonthreatening manner. "I started out thinking maybe the agency wasn't doing a good job, you know, all that stuff in the newspapers. But that is why I wanted to hear what you had to say. I was getting only one side of the story." Or "I grew up in a household where guns were considered evil, so I just accepted some negative ideas about hunting. This is the first time I am really hearing the other side." You will usually get better information if you are honest about your opinions because your spontaneity and openness communicate to the interviewee.

Honesty does not require complete revelation. You should not respond to a request for your opinion by blurting out everything you think or feel. Nor do you need to tell your interviewees every time you disagree with what they say. You just listen and record. You are not lying if you fail to respond to blatant racism, anti-Semitism, or sexism that is often revealed in interviews. The problem does not get sticky unless the interviewees ask for agreement. You can take evasive action, with some innocuous sounding statement like, "Yes, well, you know, but what about . . . " and return to the question. Or you could say, "I am not sure I agree with you on that, but that is neither here nor there. I would like to hear what you think about . . . "

If it is important for you to disagree, then do so, but try not to do it in a way that will terminate the interview. If you feel that you cannot refrain from expressing sharp disapproval at the mention of abortion, or alcoholism, or child abuse, you probably should not be doing interviewing on these topics. You should not feel that you have to make convincing statements of your own morality in the middle of an interview where the focus should be on the other person. But short of that bit of advice, where you draw the line on appearing to agree or disagree with obnoxious opinions is a judgment call.

As you write up your report, you should clearly keep in mind your ethical obligation of not hurting those you study. In preparing a report, respect what your conversational partners have told you. Don't put words in your interviewees' mouths, and make sure you render quotations accurately. When possible you should share your findings with your interviewees and obtain their responses to your interpretations before publishing a report.

Reporting honestly on what you learned may hurt your interviewees. Even if what you write is accurate, if portions of it are unflattering, you may do damage and invite others to misuse the information. Interviewees went out of their way to help the researchers, spending their time and exposing their hopes and pains; it is poor repayment to hurt them in the report. Writers need to be aware of this tension and perhaps not automatically come down on the side of harmful truth. Some truths are not worth the pain that they cause. Others might be necessary for the pain they can prevent.

Treating interviewees seriously, going out of your way to prevent them from being hurt by the research or the write-up, being honest and keeping your promises are all ethical obligations that the researcher knowingly takes on. But some obligations that may arise from the interview relationship have more ambiguous status. Some interviewees may feel that the granting of an interview entitles them to a range of favors or intimacies that the interviewer is not prepared to grant. Some may ask for money loans that the interviewer fears may never be repaid; others may ask for rides or make desperate phone calls for help with a child in jail or ask the interviewer to testify for them in court.

It may be helpful to decide in advance what favors are appropriate, offer them freely and comfortably, and refuse just as clearly inappropriate requests. Better still, signal well in advance what might be considered an inappropriate request. Researchers on teenage gangs are often requested to purchase alcohol for minors, for instance (MacLeod, 1987). If you think that is wrong, tell your interviewees that you won't do that. If the atmosphere and joking suggest that a sexual proposition may be forthcoming, it is better to head it off than to allow the proposition to be made and then reject it. Such rejection may well embarrass the interviewee and ruin the research situation. Irene finds that occasional references to her husband in the conversation generally work to keep the tone appropriate.

ENCOURAGING PARTICIPATION

Being ethical and gaining a reputation for being ethical encourages people to be more open with you. People in a research arena talk with one another about the interview they had with you. If you failed to treat them with respect and dignity or if you broke your promises, word will get around your research arena. So being ethical is not only right, but useful.

But how do you start such conversational relationships in the first place? How do you overcome the reluctance of some people to talk and share their world with others? To do so, you try to figure out why people may be reluctant to talk to you and address those concerns, both as you set up appointments and in the early stages of the interview. You think about what might motivate people to talk to you and describe the interview to them in ways that they can see its use to themselves and others.

Overcoming Initial Barriers

Sometimes, the interviewees fall smoothly into the conversational partnership role, work hard to make you comfortable, and seem eager to share their world. On other occasions, your interviewees may be fearful and insecure, and need some encouragement to feel comfortable. Or the conversational partners may be overly eager to make a good impression, to be liked or respected, and as a result exaggerate their experiences or accomplishments. They might avoid answering particular questions for fear that they will reveal their own ignorance or that you will strip away their rationalizations or question their achievements. Some conversational relationships begin with a defensiveness that the researcher must work to overcome. You can overcome these initial barriers to a conversational partnership. Through letters, calls, or meetings you reassure the interviewee that he or she knows enough to talk to you. You encourage future interviewees to talk with people you have already interviewed to find out that you care about their world and that the interview is fun. When possible, you can demonstrate your interest in their world by taking time to observe it.

When meeting nervous interviewees, you try to relax them by showing them respect, if not deference, but in a low-key manner that does not appear patronizing. In interviews one mark of respect is to dress appropriately. In our research, done in offices and in peoples' homes, that often means dressing somewhat formally for the interview (generally a jacket and tie for men and dress or skirt and blouse and nylons for women). Researchers talking with members of a street gang out of doors would choose other apparel to match the research roles chosen.

Another mark of respect is to arrange the appointment sufficiently far in advance to suggest that you know they may be busy. Courtesy dictates that you arrive on time for an appointment, but not too early. Arriving late says your time is more important than their time, but arriving too early inconveniences others who might feel they have to begin to talk, but resent the intrusion.

Early in the interview, you should reassure interviewees about how you will use their material. It is courteous to ask interviewees for permission to tape-record an interview or to take notes; you can at the same time make it clear that they can go off the record if they wish. You can offer to let the interviewees review their interviews and make corrections or modifications and additions later on. If you are using informed consent statements, this is the time to discuss them with your interviewees.

The researcher needs to play by ear the presentation of his or her own credentials. Some interviewees are flattered by being interviewed by a famous person—a well-known journalist or author—but other interviewees are intimidated by being questioned by someone with much more education or experience. Some want interviewers to be deferential, a novice who will learn at the feet of the master. But too much self-effacement also can be a problem if the interviewee treats the researcher as a hired hand or a credulous dimwit who can be easily manipulated. Some conversational partners may see the interviewer as someone who will convey a touched-up picture of their life and accomplishments; these people may only cooperate so long as the interviewer appears to be a fan.

You normally need a balance between too much deference and too little. You indicate that you can learn from the interviewees and respect what they say, but that you have sufficient background to understand and benefit from what it is they want to share.

Why People Like to Talk

Although for a variety of reasons, some people may be afraid of being interviewed, most people want to share what they know. Being aware of the reasons for reticence gives you confidence to approach strangers and suggests what to say early in the discussion to encourage people to talk to you.

At a basic level, most people like to talk about themselves; they enjoy the sociability of a long discussion and are pleased that somebody is interested in them. The interviewer provides the conversational partner with both attention and recognition. To build on this motivation, the researcher learns what the interviewee has achieved and makes a request for an interview by mentioning the person's successes, for instance, by saying, "I came to you because people thought you were the most skillful weaver" or "I wanted to talk to you because I thought the budgeting system you worked out was very impressive." This kind of introduction increases the interviewees' sense of competence to answer your questions. The researcher is also offering a kind of memorial or testimonial to a particular craft, a way of life, a religious practice, or a bureaucratic innovation.

Being interviewed allows people the opportunity to teach others and combats the feeling many people have that although they do some things well, almost no one cares. Now you come along and say, yes, what you know is valuable, it should not be lost, teach me, and through me, teach others.

People can teach a variety of things, including sharing some terrible experiences they have had or know about. Teaching others about such travails becomes a way of handling grief or terror, a way of making the suffering meaningful. One researcher explained that those suffering from AIDS often felt that it was their mission to share how they felt through an interview:

> Many of my respondents explicitly refer to their interviews as "legacies." They are participating in this project despite the pain it might cause them because they believe I will use their stories to help others. Thus they shoulder me with the responsibility of giving meaning to their lives and their deaths. (Weitz, 1987 p. 21)

The interview assures the participants that what they have done, or what they have experienced, will accomplish something useful.

Sometimes being interviewed becomes a confirmation of the interviewee's status, as the conversational partner learns he or she is important enough to be included in the group of those being interviewed. "Who else are you talking to?" the interviewee might ask. "Oh, I have an appointment with the city manager tomorrow, and I saw the mayor yesterday and will speak with the budget director this afternoon."

As the opening quotation in Chapter 1 showed, interviews give people a chance to reflect on their life or work, an opportunity that most people lack. For example, oral histories of the Holocaust let survivors remember their experiences although the people around them wanted them to forget (Lewin, 1990). Support groups of bereaved parents complain that other people tell them to get on with their lives, to forget the dead child, but they do not want to, they want an opportunity to talk about and remember the child, to grieve openly.

People sometimes participate in interviews in the hope of gaining favorable publicity for their political or social concerns, type of work, ethnic group, or whatever they identify with. Librarians may want to talk about their efforts to combat censorship; historical preservationists may want to make a case for restoring an old building; members of a religious group may be eager to explain how they celebrate particular holidays. In each case, interviewees want their activities to be viewed in a favorable light. Interviewees whom others look down upon, such as prostitutes, illegal aliens, or victims of discrimination, may hope that the researcher can gather their hurt and angry voices to call attention to their problems.

People sometimes talk to interviewees to get out their side of a story, to balance out what others have told. For instance, management may control how newspapers describe labor disputes, so spokespeople for the unions may be eager to talk to someone who might get their perspective across. Herb had failed to get an appointment with a funder of community groups, though he had made a variety of attempts. Finally, Herb wrote again, including a paper that explained why community groups were angry at the funder. The funder then agreed to talk to explain why the community groups were wrong.

Another approach to gaining people's cooperation is to get help from their friends and co-workers. When you call or write to the suggested conversational partner, you can say, "Bill Cash suggested that I call you." The person knows and works with Bill Cash, and talking to you is doing Bill Cash a favor.

People usually want the opportunity to do such minor favors. Once, Irene was trying to get an appointment at a distant city hall and was not getting anywhere when a gentleman walked up behind her and asked her where she was from. "DeKalb, Illinois," she said, thinking the person would never have heard of it. "Oh," he said, "your mayor is Greg Sparrow, do you know him?" "Yes," she said, "I know him well, he was a student of mine, and he appointed me to the budget review committee." "Okay," her new friend said, "I know Greg well, I will get the appointment for you." Irene not only got the appointment, she got a lesson in what she is supposed to do to get appointments at distant city halls, namely use her mayor as part of a network. When she returned home and told her mayor the story, he said, "Irene, you should have told me what you were doing, I could have arranged the interviews for you."

As you phrase a request for the first interview, you can choose from among these different motivations for interviewees to participate. If you want to present both sides of a controversial case, let future interviewees know; if you are going to write a book about the lives of illegal immigrants and make recommendations for reform of the Immigration and Naturalization Service, be sure to mention the proposed book when you introduce yourself. If you have gone along a network to find the interviewee, tell the interviewee who recommended that you speak to him or her.

SETTING UP APPOINTMENTS

When interviewing is part of a participant observation study, the shift to a conversational mode may be as casual as an invitation to join you for a cup of coffee. But with people who work in offices and must be approached from a distance, researchers first send a letter requesting an interview and then follow up with a phone call.

A letter requesting an interview should be reasonably brief, but include information describing the project, why the person has been chosen to be in the study, and why he or she should participate. The letter should radiate professionalism, indicate concern and interest in the life or work of those to be interviewed, and reassure interviewees that the information will be used in accordance with their wishes. An example of a request for an interview might read as follows:

Dear Ms. Lobbyist:

I am a student working on my dissertation at Northern Illinois University on the topic of what makes health care legislation politically feasible. As you have been a key actor in developing and pressing for health care proposals over the last few years, I wanted to talk to you about how you judge feasibility, and how you think others judge it. I will be talking to a number of other people active in trying to shape health care legislation, beginning on March 17, in Washington. Would you be willing to see me some time that week? Ideally, I would need about an hour. Any time at your convenience, morning, noon, or night would be fine. I will give your secretary a call next week.

If you have any questions about the project or about me, please give me a call at 815-753-xxxx.

Sincerely,

Marilyn Wantstoknow

In this simple example, the research role is that of student. The material will be part of a dissertation so presumably should not be widely circulated. The topic is delineated, as is the reason why the person was picked to be in the study. The letter could be improved by adding a sentence such as "Before I began my Ph.D. research, I was a health planner, so I am very sensitive to the technical aspects of these proposals, but never fully understood why some of the best technical proposals did not make it through Congress." Such an addition establishes the interviewer's sympathy with the group or individual about to be interviewed.

Herb makes three main points in his cover letters: Talk to me, I am legitimate, and the interview will be a chance to get your side across. In addition to the letter, Herb sends along several manuscripts based on prior interviews. These manuscripts help establish that Herb is a legitimate scholar, and that his work will be published, so he can be a useful voice to the outside. The manuscripts are also helpful in demonstrating that the final version of his work does not hurt the interviewees or even name individuals. Further, the published work illustrates that Herb is sympathetic with the group. His letters look like the following example:

Dear Mr. Executive Director:

I am an urban sociologist who for the last several years has been studying community-based development in the Midwest. As part of this project, I have visited Cleveland on several occasions. During one visit, Ms. R____ was quite helpful in sharing some background on housing projects accomplished by [organization name].

In my writing I try to provide a flavor of the ethos of community-based development. To illustrate the approach I have enclosed two manuscripts. The first, entitled *Community Empowerment Within an Alternative Economy,* is an advocacy piece portraying the upbeat flavor of the CBDO movement. The second, called *Renewing Hope in the Inner City: Conversations with Community Based Development Practitioners* examines dilemmas that community development practitioners face.

I am now in the second stage of the research and am gathering missing material that will be incorporated in a book entitled *Renewing Hope in the Inner City: The Community Based Development Model,* for which I have just received a contract. To complete the book, I am revisiting organizations. During these visits, I try to learn a little more about the structure of the organizations as well as how the changing political and funding environments influence community-based development. For example, I would like to learn about the changes for [organization name] that have occurred since the advent of NPI. In addition, I follow up on projects that were planned or under way during my last visit.

I am hoping to visit Cleveland the third week in November and will call to try to schedule an appointment. I'll telephone sometime in early October about a November appointment.

Thanking you in advance,

Herbert J. Rubin
Professor of Sociology

Depending on the circumstances, Irene sometimes encloses a resume with the letter requesting an interview. She has found that many public officials become interested after they see she does consulting, because the consulting to them is real world and indicates Irene might know something of interest to them. City officials want to know, "How do we stand, compared to Phoenix or Boston?" Finding out gives the interviewee a reason to participate.

Other variations of the introductory letter are sometimes appropriate. You can include a list of the specific topics to be covered. For example, in the health care proposal study, you could say, "I am particularly interested in the contribution your office made to changing House Bill 75." If you are representing yourself as someone who supports a movement and wants to publicize its successes, then your credentials that back up these claims should be offered. "I spent three years in ACT-UP [a militant gay rights group] from 1985-1988." To support the claim that you are working on a book, you might mention what you have published related to this topic, especially material that is supportive of the agency, program, or movement.

In short, whether or not you get the appointment can depend on how well the letter answers some basic questions, how well it handles fears, and how successfully it motivates people to participate. The letter also indicates your research role and the level of your expertise so interviewees can figure out how much detail to provide in the interviews. The letter should tell them whether you can give them publicity, help them think about their problems, or mediate for the group with a broader society.

As a practical matter, when scheduling appointments, try not to make the interviewing schedule too tight. If you space interviews comfortably, the quality will be better, even if you do fewer interviews. You can usually do two a day, but if you have to do three on a particular day, you will probably need a day to catch your breath and examine your notes.

In scheduling appointments keep in mind that after every interview, if you have been taping, you need to play back the tape to make sure that the tape recorder was working properly. You will probably want to make a few notes on the tape too, explaining to yourself who the voices were that came in the middle of the interview or what people were doing at some point that caused general laughter. If you took handwritten notes, you have to look them over immediately to make sure every word is legible and fill in what you remember that you did not get down.

If possible, schedule interviews in such a way that you have time to transcribe the interview the day you do it. This is desirable whether you taped it or took handwritten notes, because it forces you slow down, read your interview carefully, and revise your questions for the next interviews.

You also need to plan time to rest or exercise between the interviews. During an interview, your level of concentration is high, you are listening hard, trying to extract themes, deciding what to follow up on and how, and asking for explanations and examples. And you may be doing that for a couple of hours. Doing so is exhausting. Do it too long and you end up missing obvious places to follow up. You may also come close to falling asleep during an interview.

Interviewing can not only leave you exhausted, it can leave you wound up, because of what you heard or just from drinking coffee that the interviewee offered and you politely accepted. Especially if the interview is particularly emotional or exciting, you need time to calm down, lest you show up for the next person looking like you are on some mood-altering substance.

Even with careful planning, schedules sometimes run tight and you enter the second interview frazzled. Herb scheduled a 2 p.m. appointment in a city about 45 minutes from where he was doing a morning interview that started at 8 a.m. The person he interviewed was ebullient and on target and kept on providing one wonderful answer after another. At 1:15, when the person was finished, Herb sped to the second interview, dictating into a tape recorder on the car seat. He made it, but wasn't able to concentrate fully on the second interview.

If you have spaced the interviews appropriately, there should be plenty of time so that if an interviewee is elaborating in rich detail, you do not have to be the one to say, "Sorry, I have to get to another meeting." We try to build in buffer time between interviews, doubling our estimates of transportation time, and when possible, scheduling ourselves for a meal between the interviews. If someone runs late, you can always skip the meal. Herb keeps bagels in his car in case he needs an energy burst and hasn't got time for lunch. Irene keeps a high-energy (healthy) snack bar in her handbag.

You cannot keep up a pace of two to three interviews a day, looking them over, transcribing them, preparing for the next one, and still have time or energy to think about what you are doing. You need to take periodic time-outs to catch up, discuss your work with colleagues, consider the interviews you have already done, and work out a revised design and a more focused set of questions.

DEEPENING A RELATIONSHIP

Interview relationships grow and change, and may go through phases of openness, withdrawal, trust, secrecy, and even embarrassment. As a study proceeds, you are no longer treated as a stranger. You may not ever get to be friends with your conversational partners, but you get to know each other a little, learn to take each other seriously, and treat each other with respect. As relationships become more involving, both partners develop expectations about what is going to be said. Sometimes, the conversational partners end up creating a shared language of discourse. Creating a shared language is more important if the interviewer and interviewee come from different backgrounds and have different patterns of communication.

Hearing Across Social Cleavages

Many interviewers are afraid to interview across class, sex, race, or ethnic lines. In practice, bridging these gaps is often less difficult than anticipated, and there are advantages to sharing the life and experiences of someone with a background quite different from your own. In fact, interviewing people similar to yourself can pose difficulties, because the interviewees assume that you know what they know. They may not explain taken-for-granted meanings in the way they would to an outsider.

Some evidence suggests that interviewing across class, gender, or ethnic barriers can actually be more effective than matching the backgrounds of interviewer and interviewee (Cannon, Higginbotham, & Leung, 1988). For instance, researchers investigating how ethnicity affected conversations on sensitive topics compared the content of conversations between Chicana women and Anglo interviewers and Chicana women and Chicana interviewers. They found that

> in terms of both the quantity and quality of references to sex-related topics . . . the women did speak more, and more freely, to the Anglo about sex-related matters. It was also predicted that this pattern would reverse itself when the topic was switched to discrimination. It was assumed that the speakers would be more inclined to discuss their feelings about prejudice with another Chicana and would be apt to avoid or minimize such discussions with an Anglo. This did not prove to be the case. (Tixier y Vigil & Elsasser, 1978, p. 95)

Part of the reason that cross-ethnic interviewing was more successful may be that interviewees strive to explain their ethnic experiences to those who do not share them. Other studies of interviewing across race have come to similar conclusions. Jay MacLeod (1987), who is white, found in his study of career aspirations of street gang members that the black gang members were far more forthcoming than were the white gang members. Herb's experience in interviewing African Americans is that the conversations on race, so long as Herb introduces the topic first, seem brutally frank. His conversational partners switch into teacher mode and instruct him how they feel about the consequences of racism in American society.

We are not arguing that conversations are the same between men and women as they are between women and women, or that conversations between black and white are the same as those between black and black. The differences, however, do not preclude effective communications. To help get across the gap, the interviewer should pay attention to the differences in *how* people from distinct groups communicate stories and narratives.

For instance, Riessman (1987) described the marked differences in how Anglo and Puerto Rican women described stressful relationships they had with men. In their narratives, Puerto Rican women first mentioned the crucial events in their relationships, irrespective of when the events occurred, and then described why these events took place. In contrast, Anglo women narrated what happened in chronological order, making less distinction between important and unimportant events (p. 173).

In general, men and women also respond to questions and provide answers in different ways. The recent set of popular social-psychology books by Deborah Tannen (1990) indicates that for women, unlike men, the way in which the message is exchanged is as important as the message itself. Women understand messages as part of an established pattern of communications, not as isolated utterances. To understand what a woman is trying to communicate, an interviewer should probably ask a female conversational partner to elaborate on the context in which an answer should be understood. In addition, women may be more likely to give multiple messages at the same time, requiring the interviewer "to listen in stereo, receiving both the dominant and muted channels clearly" (Anderson & Jack, 1991, p. 11). The interviewer may need to listen to hear the implications of what is said as much as to pay attention to the actual words themselves (p. 17).

Women often develop conversational patterns that allow them to get around male dominance. Devault (1990) argues, "While much feminist research in linguistics is designed to show how language and the organization of talk contribute to the subordination of women, it also shows, often, how skillfully and creatively women speakers circumvent and subvert the processes of social control, whether they do so by 'talking back' (hooks, 1989) or 'telling it slant' (Spender, 1985)" (p. 112).

Women may be more likely than men to hesitate before answering. A woman's hesitation should not necessarily be interpreted as showing ignorance or fear; rather, women may be thinking of ways to express themselves that avoid [male] dominant vocabularies (Devault, 1990, p. 100). The researcher should be patient with such hesitations and not jump in with a suggested word or phrase.

In cross-gender interviews, other differences in conversational patterns occur. A blunt question from a male to a female may get a less detailed and thoughtful response than a more indirect question. When a woman is interviewing a man, the male conversational partner may be troubled if the interviewer seems too assertive. He may be used to women's more indirect language, and it may be difficult for him to express his views fully if the interviewer is too aggressive. Yet, a passive role on the part of the female interviewer reinforces the image of women as dependent. Female interviewers may need to work out a style that combines being nonthreatening and professional (Gurney, 1985, p. 43).

There is not much literature on qualitative interviewing across social class gaps, but what there is suggests that middle-class interviewers do better in working-class settings if they start with a period of participant observation (Macleod, 1987; Padilla, 1992; Whyte, 1955). As relationships develop during the observation period, those being studied take it on themselves to explain or interpret particular occurrences. Interviews then emerge out of an existing relationship. A period of participant observation before beginning interviewing may also be useful in interviewing middle- and upper-class people across class gaps, but there are not many examples in the literature.

Elite interviews present particular barriers for the interviewees. In an elite interview the researcher is questioning wealthy or upper-class people, or those in high positions regardless of their economic status. First, elites may assume interviewers are like journalists, who are to be manipulated or used but never fully trusted. Second, elites often limit the length of the interview, because their time is too valuable to spend in long discussions. Short interviews make it difficult to build trust slowly.

Getting past these barriers requires you to assume a role that the elite interviewee can accept and trust, a role that suggests you are knowledgeable, yet nonthreatening. You can show knowledgeability through the questions that you ask, questions that demonstrate that you have done background work. Such questions indicate you are unlikely to accept the sort of formal statements offered to reporters.

It is easier to build a relationship with an elite interviewee over time. If after one interview the interviewee discovers that nothing untoward happened—you did not tell the newspapers or any colleague—he or she may be more willing to tell you something more revealing in the second interview. Another approach is to define the interview as a chance for the conversational partner to step back and reflect on matters with someone who is knowledgeable but has no immediate stake. You, like a biographer, are both an interviewer and a sounding board for what the interviewee is thinking.

In short, crossing class, rank, ethnic, and racial lines takes some attention and an ability to recognize and tolerate different styles of conversation. But such interviewing can result in depth and detail that probably would not be communicated between people who share similar backgrounds. Not every interview will work, but neither will every interview between individuals with matching backgrounds.

Negotiating a Research Role

What research role you take and how that role is seen by the interviewee affects the quality of the conversation (cf. Adler et al., 1986; Briggs, 1983; Douglas, 1985; Gorden, 1987; Horowitz, 1986; Snow, Benford, & Anderson, 1986). People talk differently to hard-nosed investigative reporters and ivory-tower academics. As part of negotiating a relationship with the interviewee, the researcher works to define a mutually acceptable research role.

Calling yourself a researcher often doesn't work because researcher is not a meaningful category in many interviewees' eyes. This point was made dramatically clear to Irene once, when a director of a probation and parole office that Irene was researching asked, "What do you get out of this?" He was completely puzzled, as there was no role in his world for someone who was simply trying to understand what was happening in the organization. She responded, "I use the examples I pick up from you in class. The examples make the class vivid, and I know that what I am teaching is what people in the field actually do. Students like it when I use real examples." He nodded his head. Irene had conveyed something from her world that he could understand.

Although you have to take some understandable role, you can take different roles with different interviewees. In Herb's project with community development activists, some of his interviewees treated him almost as a therapist, a person who listens to their travails, whereas others cast him as an activist scholar promoting the social change movement. Most of his interviewees treated him as a historian of their collective efforts, a sympathetic recorder of their experiences. In this role, Herb was expected to translate the interviewees' experiences into a language that outsiders could understand. The roles into which Herb was cast affected what was said in the interviews. With a therapist, the interviewees could expose weaknesses and stresses. With a social activist they could discuss strategies. To a historian of their movement, they could describe their triumphs in a world of adversity.

Sometimes people won't talk to a researcher because they identify the researcher with a disliked role, perhaps a journalist, social worker, or university professor. Pauline Bart, who studied Jane, the abortion cooperative, reported that the women whose cooperation she sought initially refused to speak with her because, "They were antiacademic and antiprofessional" (Bart, 1987, p. 340). She had to negotiate a research role that would allow the interviews to take place. First, Bart explained that she had been a feminist activist in Chicago, that is, she was one of them. Next, she mentioned that she did not have a grant. That was interpreted by her interviewees to mean that she had not been co-opted or bought off. Finally, her low-key interviewing manner calmed her conversational partners, indicating she was not a journalist, and induced further cooperation.

Sometimes the interviewer is immediately cast in a role that fits into the culture of the group being studied. In poor neighborhoods, people who come around asking questions may be seen as social workers, landlords, undercover police, or repossession agents, roles not encouraging openness in conversations. When Herb and Irene were in rural Thailand, they were often viewed as missionaries or Peace Corps volunteers, because rural Thais knew Americans primarily in these roles. The role that you have been cast into influences what interviewees are willing to talk about and how openly they are likely to talk. In one extreme case, a woman in Thailand cast Irene as a Peace Corps volunteer, was sure she was a nurse, and only would talk about health issues.

Roles that are more or less generally acceptable to interviewees include student/novice, professor, or author. MacLeod (1987), for instance, had been tutoring and playing basketball with gang members. He moved into the role of student to begin more formal interviews with two of the gangs:

> I needed to explain to both groups the proposed study, my role as researcher, and their role as subjects. This I did in a casual way before initiating a conversation on their aspirations. I simply explained that to graduate from college, I must write a lengthy paper and that instead of doing a lot of research in a library, "I'm gonna write it on you guys down here and what kinds of jobs you want to go into after school and stuff like that." (MacLeod, 1987, p. 174)

The role of the professor allows more intensive questioning than the role of student, but at the same time, a professor can be seen as a threat, as a person who knows a lot and evaluates people. The related role of author has some of the same freedom to ask questions without some of the negative baggage of the judgmental professor. The author role also communicates that the interview will become part of a book. Interviewees may be flattered to think that academics and authors want to know about their lives.

Irene often presents herself as a writer of textbooks. Her interviewees like the idea of being used as a positive example in a textbook. To make the role of writer credible, she gives her conversational partners lists of books she has written and published. Although this could be seen as an intimidating thing to do, her interviewees tend to view her list of books as legitimating the time they spend with her, because it is likely that she will publish what they tell her.

Choosing between different research roles does not mean that you distort who you are, but rather that you select those aspects of who you are that make sense in the world of the interviewee and that facilitate conversation. Sometimes you have to feel your way a bit before you know how to translate what you do into terms that are meaningful to interviewees. You may be a medical sociologist, but also a daughter, and can use either role in exploring the pill-taking experiences of your elderly interviewees.

It is generally not advisable to pretend to be someone you're not in order to gain entrance to a group. Many people consider it ethically wrong, because it is manipulative, and hence disrespectful to interviewees. It is also extremely hard to carry off. If you don't know everything that you are supposed to know, you might give yourself away and destroy the interview and the relationship.

It is legitimate, however, to take on the role of a casual acquaintance, a person who has shared some experiences with the interviewee. Through casual conversation at the beginning of the interview, you may find that both researcher and interviewee went to the same schools or worked in the same place. Often your interviewees will search for such commonalities, maybe teasing you about an accent and asking you where you grew up, or commenting on your background. Sometimes these questions lead to connections, such as, "My son went to NIU in business." (The authors of this book teach at NIU, but not in the business school.)

Even if the connection seems tenuous, it may be important. People are often uncomfortable dealing with outsiders because a stranger can deceive you and disappear. Through casual chat, the interviewee links you to a place of employment. Sharing a mutual friend may make you seem more responsible. Mentioning that you have had some relevant job experience may make interviewees more confident that you will understand their answers. If you have family nearby, or have friends in common, or work somewhere they know, you can fit into their social structure in a way that they can understand. You are not a rootless stranger.

Whatever role you pick, it should be one that allows you to be warm and responsive. If you try to be a neutral recorder of the interview, you won't be able to make a relationship. If an interviewee is telling you about a painful experience of being fired, you can grimace with sympathy; if the interviewee expresses tremendous satisfaction at an accomplishment, you can grin with pleasure along with him or her. If the interviewee is interested in a particular topic, you can ask him or her to talk more about it and listen as you would when a friend or acquaintance tells you a story with emotional content.

Creating a Shared Language

As an interviewing relationship evolves, a language of shared experience develops. The conversational partners can construct a vocabulary, a set of events or symbols, that they both know and can use to communicate. Both partners can refer to past events as a shorthand to explain something in the present.

One approach to developing this shared language is to ask how the interviewee feels about some event that has just occurred that both of you have witnessed. This is easiest to do as part of a participant observation study. Herb and his conversational partners listen to the same speeches at conferences both attend and witness the same squabbles. They can talk about these events and use them to discuss and explain other incidents.

Another way shared language grows is that conversational partners describe and discuss a concept or idea during the interview. For example, Irene heard a conversational partner report on a meeting, claiming that he was "mushroomed." "Mushroomed?" she asked, "what does that mean?" "They kept me in the dark and dumped shit on me." After an appropriate grin or chuckle, she asked for the details of that event, and then asked about other occasions on which the interviewee felt "mushroomed." After a term has been explained and the context given, the interviewer can use it even though it was originally the interviewee's word. It is now a word that both partners share.

Sometimes the researcher and interviewee invent terms together or give new meanings to old terms that emerge during the interview. Devault (1990) describes this process in feminist interviewing: "We often need to go beyond standard vocabulary. . . . By speaking in ways that open the boundaries of standard topics, we can create space for respondents to provide accounts rooted in the realities of their lives" (p. 99).

HOW CONVERSATIONAL
PARTNERSHIPS AFFECT THE RESEARCHER

In conversational partnerships, the first goal for the interviewer is to develop a relationship in which an interview can comfortably take place. You do this by paying attention to the reasons that people agree to be interviewed. You handle their fears and concerns and respond to their answers with empathy, building a common language by finding or creating shared experiences. Each step encourages people to share what they know.

But conversational partnerships are two-way streets. The interviewee responds to you, and you respond to the interviewee. What you hear and understand is affected by your own reactions to the people you interview and what they tell you.

Sometimes you are enthusiastic and in full agreement with what the conversational partners say, at other times you quietly wonder how somebody could be so perfidious. You may feel bored when you are listening to an explanation of a core cultural concept for the umpteenth time. You may feel betrayed when somebody you like tries to deceive you. You may be frustrated if you can't patch up simple disagreements between your interviewees. You may get carried away when a conversational partner is ebullient and informative on a point of joint interest and perhaps join in the conversation, forgetting to ask the remainder of your questions.

You may well get into a situation in which you are interviewing two people who are on opposite sides of an issue. You recognize that each is sincere in what he or she is saying and that it is your job later on to sort out the differences. But at this point you agree with one person and have to make sure your feelings don't distort how closely you listen to the other one.

You may find that the borderline between showing empathy for another person, listening with concern and belief, and overrapport, identifying so much with those you study that you forget who you are, is easily crossed. If this happens to you, it may affect the work, because you lose sight of lines of questioning that would otherwise be clear to you and may have to withdraw from the field in confusion. Think for minute about how confusing it could be if you identified so closely with (male or female) prostitutes you were interviewing that you began to see yourself as one of the group, or how you might feel if you identified so closely with Wall Street stock manipulators that you began to think of yourself as one of them. People in your study may become so central to your life that their continuing approval becomes important to you. Finishing the study and leaving them behind may become emotionally difficult.

Personal reactions to a conversational partner affect what you hear and how well you hear it. In his community development study, Herb enjoyed talking with African American women activists whom he truly admired, but he felt uncomfortable with extremely religious white males. How well did he hear what each was saying? Does Irene listen as intently to people she suspects are violating the law? On the day Herb visited a community-based day care facility for children with AIDS was his subsequent interviewing overly gentle? After he learned about corruption in the field did he become more aggressive?

Because our reactions to those we interview and to what we find out affect what further questions we ask and what we hear and fail to hear, it is a good idea to maintain a record of how we reacted to our partners in each interview. This record makes our notes more interpretable and helps us figure out later how much to rely on our interpretations of each interview.

Many qualitative researchers maintain a running diary of their thoughts and responses to the people they are studying. During interviews and immediately thereafter we record on our tapes or jot down in our notes how we felt about the people with whom we were talking and what they said. We include in these records where we feel that we misspoke or failed to ask an appropriate question, or whether we were feeling up or down, sad or angry, or nervous. Herb noted that early in his community development study his interviews lacked depth on questions of race and ethnicity, because he was afraid to ask follow-up questions on this topic. Irene marks in these notes when her attention wandered and the notes became a little confused. The resulting portrait of ourselves doing the interviewing can be extremely helpful as a clue to what kind of material is likely to be missing, as a warning of where bias may enter the analysis, and as an indicator of what parts of an interview or which whole interviews may be less rich or even less accurate than others.

None of us is sufficiently self-aware to always know exactly how we are reacting to an interview or interviewee or interview situation. It can help to chat with a colleague or friend about how the fieldwork is going. You may be able to tell from the excitement you feel describing an interview to a colleague how you felt at the time. In trying to explain a sudden loss of motivation to stay in the field, you may discover that you have slid over into feeling part of the arena and are feeling frustrated by your inability to play a more active role in the world you are researching.

Keeping diaries, jotting notes on interview transcripts, or exploring your interviewing experiences with your colleagues also let you step back from the conversational relationships and obtain a necessary distance. The observing of yourself as researcher can help you remember that you are a scholar, a student, or an evaluator, not a planner, community developer, or city budgeter. The distance provided by taking notes on yourself also makes it easier to end a study and withdraw from the conversational partnerships. It reminds you that you have a role outside the research arena to return to.

Your relationship with the interviewees does not have to end when the interviewing stops and you withdraw from the field. Interviewees can become friends. But even if they don't, your life will be greatly enriched through the conversational partnerships in which people whom you otherwise might not know open their lives and share their experiences with you.

6

Interviews as Guided Conversations

*I*nterviews work best if you and your conversational partner are in a small room, maybe sipping coffee while quietly discussing an event or exploring some aspect of a culture. Both parties concentrate on the matter at hand, talk, respond, and reflect. Such interviews build on the skills of ordinary conversation.

In this chapter, we describe the similarities between interviews and ordinary conversations, and then we examine some important differences. Next, we discuss the stages through which interviews proceed and consider the types of questions that can be asked at each stage. We conclude the chapter with suggestions for handling some unusual interviewing situations, such as interviewing several people at once, interviewing by telephone, and conducting a focus group interview.

INTERVIEWS AS ORDINARY CONVERSATIONS

Although qualitative interviews are more focused, deeper, and more detailed than normal discussions, they follow many of the rules of ordinary conversation. As in ordinary conversations, only a few topics are covered in depth, and there are smooth transitions between the subjects. People take turns speaking and acknowledge what the other has said. People give off recognizable cues when they don't understand and clarify ambiguities on request.

Both interviews and ordinary conversations deal with only a limited number of subjects in detail. A conversation in which five or six topics were discussed would probably leave the participants with headaches. Similarly, raising more than a limited number of main topics in an interview would be overwhelming for an interviewee. The result would be a jumble, with inadequate depth on any one subject.

If you can limit the number of main topics, it is easier to maintain a conversational flow from one topic to another. Transitions should be smooth and logical. "We have been talking about mothers, now let's talk about fathers," sounds abrupt. A smoother transition might be, "You mentioned your mother did not care how you performed in school—was your father more involved?" The more abrupt the transitions, the more it sounds like the interviewer has an agenda that he or she wants to get through, rather than wanting to hear what the interviewee has to say.

People who are chatting usually indicate that they have heard and understood the other person's response. Interviewers do that too. They can indicate nonverbally, with a nod or an intent expression, that they are paying attention and have followed the answer. Alternatively, they may summarize what they understood from the answer they just heard or refer in the next question to what they learned from the last question. For example, "So, you are in favor of orphanages for children of poor families. How much money do you think the federal government should spend on such orphanages?"

Just as in an ordinary conversation, in an interview the parties take turns speaking and indicate when their turn is through. The interviewee might end his or her comments by asking the researcher if the answer is alright or if the researcher has understood. Wrap-up statements, such as, "So that is my opinion on that," also indicate a turn is complete. Sometimes people may get to the end of an answer and just pause. In interviews, unlike ordinary conversations, the researcher may want to wait a bit rather than immediately taking a turn. The interviewee may fill the gap by continuing, that is, taking a second turn, and modifying or adding to what was just said.

Both ordinary conversations and interviews follow similar ways of clearing up misunderstandings (Schegloff, 1992). Linguists call such exchanges *conversational repairs.* Whoever did not understand looks puzzled or asks for clarification. A conversational repair usually occurs right after the misunderstanding (Moerman, 1988, p. 52). Maybe the interviewee said "park" with a Boston accent, which sounds like "pahk," and you might have interpreted it as "pack." You might respond, "Why did you pack the car? I thought you were going to the office." If the interviewee picks up the accent difference, he or she should respond with a chuckle, "I didn't pack the car, I parked it."

In spoken language, people often make ambiguous or vague statements. They may use pronouns where the noun being referred to is unclear, such as, "She told me she wanted to run for office." Who is the first she, and who is the second she? In a conversational repair, you can ask for clarification by suggesting what you thought the person meant and asking for confirmation. You could ask, "You mean Bella said that Edna wanted to run for office?" Or you could follow up a confusing description of legislative process with a question like, "Is it the chair of the committee who does that or the subcommittee chair?" The answer might be, "Neither, it is done by the chair of the rules committee."

If the interviewee has misunderstood one of the your questions, you politely listen to the mistaken reply, and then, without reference to the mistake, rephrase the question so it is clearer and ask it again. That is far less awkward than saying, "No, what I meant was . . . ," which suggests that the answer you just got was worthless to you.

In normal conversations, you don't just walk off at the end of the discussion. You might say, "Well, it has been good to chat with you. I will see you again soon." You indicate that the conversation is over and yet leave the door open for further contact. Similarly with an interview, you wrap it up but try to leave a door open for further contact.

INTERVIEWS AS VARIANTS
OF NORMAL CONVERSATIONS

Although generally following the rules of normal conversations, interviews also have distinctive features. A normal conversation can drift along with little goal, but in interviews, the researcher gently guides the discussion, leading it through stages, asking specific questions, and encouraging the interviewee to answer in depth and at length. The interviewer might ask about the meaning of specific words, a rare circumstance in a normal conversation. In addition, in interviews the entire conversation is recorded one way or another.

Conversational Depth. In normal conversation, people customarily answer questions briefly. "How are you?" "I am fine, thanks," is a perfectly acceptable exchange. People usually don't expect long and detailed answers. In qualitative interviews, however, the interviewer may ask one question and expect the conversational partner to give a long answer, sometimes hours in length.

Part of your job as interviewer is to unobtrusively teach the interviewee the level of depth and detail you want and expect. If, for instance, you ask a limited number of questions, listen intently to the answers, and ask for detailed information about some responses, the interviewee will get the idea that you want him or her to respond in detail. By not interrupting a long rendition of events, you communicate that you want the interviewee to talk at length.

If the interviewee responds to a question superficially, as he or she normally would in a conversation, then you follow up the answer with a series of other questions that press for a more thoughtful answer and explore various aspects of the subject. In a casual conversation, one person may ask another, "How's business?" and the second person responds, "It's been great." That is not much of an answer, but it is acceptable and appropriate in casual conversation. In an interview, however, if you ask, "How is your project coming along?" and the conversational partner answers, "Fine," you would have to follow up with questions such as, "Did you get the financing you were expecting?" "Have you started construction yet?" "What problems have you run into?" and so on. The interviewee will get the idea that a superficial answer was not sufficient and that you expect more depth.

Keeping a Record of What Is Said. In ordinary conversations no records are maintained. In interviewing it is imperative to keep a record so the report you write will be based on accurate renditions of what was said.

To keep a record, you first choose the technology for recording, whether it is videotaping a session and preserving every detail, using a tape recorder, taking handwritten notes during the interview, or jotting down the important points after the interview. Which you do depends on the detail you need, the degree to which recording equipment disturbs the interviewee, and the comfort of the interviewer with the various techniques. The choice also depends on the circumstances of the interview. Herb once interviewed a person while he was on the back of a motorcycle traveling over the tops of the dikes between the rice paddies in Thailand. A tape recorder would not have worked in such a situation. On the other extreme, focus group interviews are frequently videotaped to preserve a complete visual and audio record.

Recording interviews on audiotape helps get the material down in an accurate and retrievable form. Tapes keep until you get a chance to transcribe them, that is, write down what they contain. Some interviewees appreciate being recorded because they see the tape as a symbol of your ability to get their message out accurately. Herb routinely records his interviews and feels that taping allows him to concentrate on what is being said, plan his follow-up questions, and be less concerned that he has gotten everything down.

Using a tape recorder does have some disadvantages, though. In any situation that is intentionally informal, the recorder looks out of out of place. You probably should not try to tape a "deep throat," that is, a secret informant. Irene doesn't use a tape recorder when interviewing public officials. By not tape-recording she gives her interviewees deniability—that is, they can always say, "I never said that" or "She took that out of context." Irene also feels that when public officials see a tape recorder they answer as if were talking to a reporter, with short sound bites or guarded answers rather than with depth and reflection. Other researchers, though, find that conversational partners share revealing information, even though they know they are being recorded. They trust the researcher not to misuse the information.

Another disadvantage of taping is that the mechanics of recording require attention. You need to ensure that the batteries are fresh and you may have to switch tapes in the middle of an interview, make sure the volume and the microphone are turned on, and that the tape does not break. The quality of sound can vary and background noises can wipe out interviewee comments. (Some noises are informative, such as the gunshots and police sirens on Herb's tapes when he is recording in areas dominated by gangs.)

Interviewers who routinely tape develop procedures to handle these possible problems. They carry spare batteries and change them long before the number of hours the manufacturer claims the batteries last. They check immediately after an interview to see if the tape recorder worked and keep handwritten notes during the interview in case they have to reconstruct the interview if the tape has failed. Many interviewers keep two tape recorders running, just in case.

Remember also that with taping, you are obligating someone (often yourself) to 4 to 6 hours of (tedious) transcription time for every hour on the tape. Some researchers try to save the time and expense by taking summary notes of key points while replaying the tapes. For some interviews this may be adequate, but it seems a shame to tape for accuracy and then not have a full transcript at the end.

Taping can contribute to some less-than-optimal habits. Taping encourages you to do several interviews back to back, with the idea that the tapes will keep. But it is better practice to space the interviews, both to allow time to refresh yourself and to study what was just said to adjust your future questioning. Another problem is that people who rely heavily on a tape recorder tend to lose their ability to recall conversations and events from memory. As a result, in those situations in which you cannot tape and taking notes is too obtrusive, you may be unable to remember a lot of valuable information.

Even if taping, you should still take some notes. Taking notes forces you to listen and hear the main points, and also provides backup in case of the inevitable technological foul-up. Notes allow the researcher to scribble down possible questions to use later in the interview and keep track of where you are in the discussion if the interviewee leaves or is interrupted and then asks you, "Where were we?" Further, note taking helps pace the answers of the conversational partner, as the interviewee is likely to slow down until you finish writing. Also, you can indicate that you think a point is important and should be elaborated by making a little ceremony of writing it down.

We strongly feel that you *must* receive permission before taping. Permission is legally required in most states when taping a telephone conversation, but you should request permission to tape whether consent is legally required or not. If you are not clear about the ethics of recording, err on the side of caution and kindness. If a third person walks into the room when you are taping an interview, you might point out that the tape is on and offer to turn it off. If interviewees seem to forget the tape recorder is on and says things you think they would not have said if they had remembered the recorder was running, you might say, "Some of that was pretty open. I will send you the transcript in case you want to edit some of it."

Taking notes requires practice and skill. To be effective at note taking, you have to write quickly. Irene uses alphabetic shorthand, supplemented with a trained memory. Immediately after each interview she rereads her notes and writes down in full any points that were only briefly sketched. Reading your notes immediately after the interview or making transcriptions promptly encourages you to review what you heard and improves subsequent questioning.

If you are trying to work without a tape or if an interview continues less formally after you have shut off the tape recorder, try to memorize the conversation and write it down as soon as possible. To reconstruct from memory, first jot down the main points, in the order they occurred. Then go down each point and try to remember as much as you can of the conversation, including your questions as well as the interviewee's answers. You may find that recalling one piece of the conversation triggers your memory about other pieces, and you can reconstruct a fair amount of the conversation. Herb jots down notes and then expands what he recalls by dictating it into a recorder to encourage him to associate one idea with another.

Some people become very good at reconstructing conversation from memory and can get close to a transcript of the conversation. However, no one's memory is perfect and the longer you wait before you write up your notes, the more you will forget. Especially if you have a second extensive conversation with someone else before you write up the notes, the later conversation will seriously interfere with your memory of the first one.

THE STAGES OF AN INTERVIEW

One of the main differences between normal conversations and interviews is that the interviewer guides the conversation in an interview, not only in terms of the questions asked and the flow of the topics, but also in terms of the emotional tone and intensity of the interaction. Interviews develop in several distinct stages. An interviewer guides the discussion through these stages, paying attention to how well the intensity and emotional and intellectual challenge of the questions matches the depth of the relationship between interviewer and interviewee. Our better interviews go through seven stages, although not every stage occurs with each individual, and stages may blend into each other or be scattered across several interviews. We pay attention to what stage we are in but recognize that the stages are not meant to be followed inflexibly. Rather they serve as a kind of an interpersonal scaffolding, giving the interviewer some guidance about how to deepen the interview relationship and how to ensure that the questioning is appropriate to the level of the relationship.

Creating Natural Involvement

You typically begin an interview with an informal chat that points in the direction of the topic. The tone should match the situation. When Herb reinterviewed an activist whose organization was in serious financial trouble, they first chatted for a while about how the activist was personally responding to the pressure.

If it seems appropriate, you might want to try to put the interviewee at ease by beginning with a mild joke or tease. When Irene interviewed in Phoenix, city staff were holding a fair outside city hall and had rented a snow-making machine. Her comment that she had come from the north to the sunny south in the deep of winter and they welcomed her with snow set a tone that said, "This should be fun, relax."

To suggest the main topic during the informal talk, you can comment on something you have seen or experienced that is on the topic, but that does not require an immediate answer. On more than one occasion when interviewing in the inner city, Herb turned an encounter with a mammoth pothole into a lead-in to an interview by suggesting that the neighborhood had been neglected by the city government.

The early chat should convey an interest in and a supportive attitude toward the interviewee's life or work. You can mention experiences that you have had that made you interested in the topic or that show some commonality with the interviewee. When interviewing in Boston, Irene mentioned that she had grown up there and still loved returning to the city. If you are interviewing in a prison or an intensive care facility, you can describe how you felt when the door shut behind you.

After a few minutes of chat, you can move into a more formal introduction. Interviewees want to know that you are on their side, they want credible information to that effect, or at the least, evidence that you are not a loose cannon, a person with an axe to grind and nothing to lose. You need to think of ways of getting that message into the introduction as you describe what it is you want to know. The following example from Irene's field notes will give you some idea what an introduction sounds like in a first interview:

Irene: Good morning Mr. Sette, it's good of you to agree to talk to me. As I mentioned in my letter, I am writing a book on municipal budgeting, that focuses on how it has changed over the last 20 years. I will be studying six case study cities, and Rochester was one of my cases.

Sette: Can I ask why you picked Rochester?

Irene: I looked at the budget and was struck by the level of openness in it. It's a good clear budget. Also, I was fascinated that Rochester gave up the city manager system a few years ago, and wondered what impact that had, if any, on budgeting.

Mr. Sette asked the key thing he needed to know, why Irene picked Rochester. By indicating that she found the budget a very open document, she was telling him that she was not out to vilify the city or make it look bad. By explaining that she was also interested in the shift away from the city manager government, she was saying, "I have done my homework, I know the specifics of your political environment, I picked you because you are a laboratory with an important experiment going on." This answer calmed Mr. Sette's anxiety and began the interview relationship.

Encouraging Conversational Competence

Some interviewees are nervous and may be unsure they can answer your questions. Early in the interview you spend a little time tactfully reassuring the conversational partners that they are competent and that you are interested in what they say. You can mention that other people identified them to you as knowledgeable people or you can refer to their experiences. "I've been told you've been making wooden chairs for over a decade." Or "I know you have been a senior manager for 20 years." By asking questions about the interviewees' personal experiences early in the interview you signal that their personal experiences will frame the discussion. People gain confidence to talk when they realize much of what will be asked is about their own life.

Early questions should be core to the subject, but not threatening, and should deal with matters that the interviewee almost certainly knows about and, ideally, feels good about. Herb finds out in advance about the successful projects community developers have completed and begins the questioning by asking about these projects. Further, he casts the question in ways that show he knows about the difficulties the person had to overcome to complete the project. "As the director of a new organization, how did you *ever* get so much funding for your first project?" The question allows the interviewee to show competence and triumph, a good way to begin.

Showing Understanding

Throughout the interview you should work to encourage your conversational partner to be frank and open, as well as to provide answers in depth. To do so, you show that you understand the factual content of what is being said and empathize with the emotional undertones. This is most important early in the interview as it sets the tone for the entire discussion.

To show that you have understood the factual content of what interviewees have told you, ask a follow-up question that demonstrates that you have followed the discussion and pulled out the main themes. For instance, when Herb's interviewees told him how lawyers fees dramatically increased the cost of building affordable housing, Herb followed up with the question, "With these expenses, how do you keep your organization alive?" showing he understood that lawyer's fees came out of the minuscule profits that the organization could make. His question showed that he understood how financially tenuous these small organizations were.

To show emotional understanding, you can begin by letting interviewees know that you share their background or have had similar experiences. Instead of directly asking a community group about its new project, you can say, "I was reading in *City Limits* about your new project. How did you get started on it?" By indicating that you read this neighborhood-oriented news magazine, you are suggesting that you are sympathetic to the community group and the movement of which it is a part.

You want your conversational partner to know that you are a willing and empathetic listener. You want interviewees to know you are paying attention to how they feel as much as to what they know. Sometimes you show such concern by the posturing of your body and expression on your face. Sometimes you offer a brief statement of sympathy, "Oh, that sounds so bad. That must have been horrible for you." Or just, "Oh, dear." Or "Oh, my."

You can show emotional understanding by using a tone of voice to indicate that you recognize the difficulties of the work or the magnitude of the accomplishments. For example, "You reorganized city hall from the budget office? How ever did you do that?" Your amazement should come through in your voice. However, if you are talking to someone who has really suffered, you might want to limit your verbal comments, and let your face and body register the shock and sympathy you feel. Anything you might say will sound inadequate.

When conversational partners seem to be trying to decide whether to describe their feelings and they pause in the conversation, don't jump right in and ask a question. Wait a while, keep still, and provide the silence that encourages people to continue.

Another way of showing emotional understanding is to briefly offer incidents in which you had similar experiences. "Yes, I remember when my mother was in the hospital. It was incredibly stressful." Or "That is nerve wracking, isn't it; the one time I had to take over the switchboard, I cut off the boss in the middle of a call." Or "I know about that call from the hospital at 5 a.m." Be cautious, though, in sharing your experiences during the interview. Make sure your example does not minimize the interviewee's suffering by presenting a false analogy. Keep your comments brief enough so that your experiences do not become the center of the discussion. Keep in mind that expressing emotional support is better done through suggestion or brief empathetic utterances.

It is not too difficult for most interviewers to convey a level of emotional understanding when they really feel it. But what about those situations in which you do not empathize with the interviewee? On one hand, you should not communicate disgust and reject out of hand what people are doing. On the other hand, you should not pretend to accept behaviors that are shocking to you, because your pretense may come across as hypocrisy. What you want to communicate is that you are interested in what they are saying and trying to learn from them.

You can suggest the importance of what interviewees do without expressing unqualified approval or sympathy. A researcher might not approve of sinking whaling boats as a political protest against killing whales, but can still honestly say that people who live their values and actively try to protect species are doing something important that should be recorded and broadly understood.

Opportunities for showing support without unqualified approval can arise when you precede the interviewing with a period of observation. During the observation period, you communicate respect for the culture overall, even if there are some practices that you find disturbing. In Thailand, Herb and Irene learned when and where to take off their shoes, not to hold hands with each other in public, and to hold hands with those of the same gender. We did these things because they were local customs and suggested that we accepted and respected those customs. We ate deep-fried insects (they taste crunchy like potato chips), drank moonshine, and chewed fermented tea leaves while interviewing people who were doing these things. Against the background of this general willingness to be involved in the culture, we could disagree with some things and get away with it. Some interviewees even felt comfortable enough to share with us things they knew we would disapprove of, such as an overcrowded prison or an instance of political corruption.

Showing understanding does not require becoming a member of the group you are studying. You can study trophy hunters without being one. You can be understanding and still be yourself in an interview relationship, agreeing with some things and disagreeing with other things. As an author who studied aggressively proselytizing groups observed, "Disagreement does not necessarily conflict with empathy and rapport in fieldwork" (Gorden, 1987, p. 269).

Getting Facts and Basic Descriptions

Once you have established that you can understand your conversational partner both cognitively and emotionally, in the next stage of the interview you concentrate on obtaining the basic information about the topical or cultural arena. You encourage the conversational partner to talk at length on the subject at hand, initially covering a broad territory and then focusing in on more specific matters. In a cultural interview, you might ask people to talk about a typical day as experienced by students, jazz pianists, textbook authors, or high-wire acrobats. In a topical interview you ask for broad descriptions of the events or processes you are studying. Irene might request a history of the new budget process at this point or ask what happened at a specific meeting.

You probe the answers and ask follow-up questions, exploring the field of inquiry. (We describe how to do this in the next three chapters.) You listen to a lot of descriptive material at this stage of the interview, but generally hold off asking emotionally or intellectually difficult questions until the next stage. You are encouraging the interviewees to sketch how they understand their worlds without posing complicated questions that follow up on what they say.

Asking Difficult Questions

So far in the interview, the researcher has indicated that he or she understands the subject and is sympathetic to the interviewees. The conversational partner has provided large amounts of basic information. By this point, it is usually possible to deal with more difficult, emotional, or sensitive matters. Sometimes getting to this stage takes several interviews.

A sensitive question might concern a cultural taboo, such as plagiarism among professors or corruption among accountants, or it might deal with failures, losses, or defeats. If the subject is marital breakup, you may be able to ask about infidelity at this stage in the interview. You can explore compromises interviewees have made between what they think is right and what they feel they had to do to survive.

One way of figuring out what people find difficult or sensitive is to pay attention to places earlier in the interview where the conversational partner seemed hesitant or avoided some part of a broader question. For example, the interviewee may have told you about an episode in which colleagues ignored her input, but then she did not say any more about it, and you went on to discuss something else. Now you can come back to this issue that the interviewee found troubling.

You should only ask about stressful material if it is important to understanding the subject of the research. Otherwise, let it go. For example, finding out about the compromises people make on the job can explain a great deal about how organizations work. But exploring why someone was fired from his or her last job may not be crucial to the research and may be highly stressful for the person to discuss. It is cruel to go after something like that unless you really need to know, even if the interviewee is willing to talk about it.

Sometimes you discover by accident what is sensitive. When Irene was interviewing in Rochester about the budget process, she learned that the technical issue of "fund account surpluses" was highly sensitive because the press had been using the surpluses as a cudgel to beat up on the city. Irene had never imagined that people would get upset about the size of positive fund balances. Herb recently stepped by accident into a sensitive area when he asked about the internal politics of an organization, only to discover an ongoing battle stemming from racial and gender tensions. Fortunately, it was his fourth discussion with a cooperative partner, who chided Herb, but then continued. If you are lucky, you will blunder onto sensitive issues at a time in the interview when that won't do much harm. If you accidentally raise an overly stressful issue too early, back off and raise it again later.

Sometimes it is not the emotional or political sensitivity of an issue that causes stress, but the conceptual difficulty of the question you pose. People are rarely asked to reflect in depth on a subject, and your asking them to do so can cause momentary dismay, especially once your conversational partner is aware that you will not accept a superficial response. You began the interview with comments and queries that made the interviewee feel competent and able to answer questions easily; now you may be challenging that feeling. But if you need to ask such questions to fully understand what is going on, now is the time to do so.

Sometimes you might ask questions that are just intellectually diffi-cult to answer, such as when Herb asked community activists, "What do you mean by 'community?'" or when Irene asked how technical requirements of budgeting conflicted with the political aspects of budgeting. Interviewees can answer these questions, but not without some thought and maybe some initial fumbling.

At this stage of the interview, you can ask provocative questions. In interviewing about sexual harassment, you might ask, "What efforts were taken, if any, to curb the inappropriate actions of the boss?" Or in interviewing about the culture of a police force, you might say, "You told me that police officers have a deep sense of good guys and bad guys, and get off on being society's protection from the bad guys, and yet we continue to see corruption in drug units. Is this a real contradiction? Is it factually correct? How would you explain it?"

You can get away with asking provocative questions at this stage because the interviewees already know which side you are on and have learned that you will pay attention to their answers and truly try to understand. When you have this support from the interviewee, you can question for depth in almost any way that makes sense, short of rudeness or excessive pressure. Interviewees, though, become exhausted answering difficult or draining questions, so you can usually only ask one or two in a single interview and must carefully decide which ones to explore.

A onetime interview might not be long enough to build enough trust to get good answers to tough or sensitive questions. If follow-up interviews are possible, you might want to wait until later interviews before asking stressful or difficult questions.

Sometimes a helpful conversational partner will teach you how to broach a sensitive topic with others. When Irene was doing a study of a city running deficits, a sensitive subject because running deficits is illegal, she explained to the city manager what her project was about. The city manager helped Irene frame the sensitive issue by telling others Irene needed to interview that she was studying the budget process. This change in emphasis from budget deficits to the overall budget process cast the matter in a less threatening way to the other officials and made Irene's questioning far easier.

Toning Down the Emotional Level

Once one or two sensitive topics have been discussed, the goal becomes bringing the interviewee down from the intellectual or emotional high without losing the openness of discussion. After eliciting depth and emotional honesty, you don't want to leave interviewees exposed, but help them calm down and feel protected again. Otherwise they are likely to feel violated. For example, you can shift from discussing the emotional stresses of living in prison to what the interviewee plans to do the first day he or she gets out.

After talking about stressful matters, such as racial tensions in the development field, Herb has found that then asking community developers to narrate their victories in getting money from a city or foundation relaxes them yet maintains a good level of openness. Irene asks people to explain the organization of the budget office as a way of continuing an open conversation yet pulling back from more provocative topics such as the role of politicians in financial administration.

Another approach to lowering the emotional tone is to direct the conversation back to earlier subjects that are of import, but little threat, and ask for additional information or documents on these matters. Herb requests annual reports, budget documents, financial estimates for projects, or grant proposals. Irene may ask for an organization chart. In cultural studies, you can ask where you should take pictures, talk about artifacts, or ask for details on how a ritual is carried out. Thus you return to the descriptive part of the interview while requesting help from the interviewee in ways that allow the interviewee to feel good about helping you.

This is the time in the interview to let the interviewee turn the discussion around and ask you questions that you can answer in depth. You can say, "Is there anything you would like to ask me at this point?" After the interviewee has been so open, he or she might feel it only fair that you expose yourself some too. Or you can ask, "Now that you know what the research is about, is there anything that I should have asked but didn't?"

It is often the case that by this time interviewees have truly become partners and will try to help guide your work by suggesting further topics or clarifying concerns that they think you have missed. In one interview, Herb had finished up his questions, stood up, and was ready to leave. The interviewee backed Herb down into a chair by stepping in his direction and loudly stated:

> One of the comments I was going to make to you about this work was
> . . . the most common experience that I have is absolute either disregard or

disrespect for CDCs [a type of community development organization].
. . . There is a very, there is palpable disrespect and animosity, you know,
toward CDCs.

The interviewee had added a major theme that she felt Herb had totally
missed. Herb picked up the thread and continued the interview along
the lines she suggested and later explored that theme in other interviews.

Closing While Maintaining Contact

You now need to indicate that the interview is ending, and that you
are grateful for the time and ideas that the interviewee has shared. "We
are just about out of time. This has been great, you have given me a lot
to think about." You might ask, if you have not done so before, if the
person wishes to be identified by name or wants the name of the group
used. This is a reminder that the material is theirs and that you will use
it with respect.

You should try to keep the door open to continuing the discussion or
asking additional questions. You can say, "Would it be okay if I give
you a call after I look over my notes if I have any questions?" Or "Would
you like me to send you a copy of my notes when I type them up, so you
can see if I got it straight or if there is anything you would like to add?"
Or "I wanted to ask you about how the house arrest program was
working, but we never got to that, could we continue this at another
time?" Once you get the idea, you can work out your own wording.

After you have finished with the formal closing, the interviewee may
resume the more casual chatting that marked the opening. This is
another way to wind down the intensity of the interview, but it can be
a very informal and indirect way of delivering additional information,
so you should pay close attention, make notes as soon as you leave, and
look them over in conjunction with the interview.

This stage model is not meant to become a rigid guide. The stage
model warns you not to jump right into the middle of a conversation—
unless the interviewee pushes you there. It cautions you that there are
emotional highs and lows in any conversational relationship, especially
one exploring in-depth topics that are core to who and what people are.

The model reminds you that people won't stay at emotional or intellectual highs for long periods of time. And the model makes you ask how well you have meshed the questioning with the steps of building a conversational relationship.

INTERVIEWS UNDER UNUSUAL CIRCUMSTANCES

Interviews sometimes occur under unusual circumstances. For instance, Herb has interviewed on the back of motorcycle, riding on top of foot-wide dikes between flooded rice paddies. He has also carried out interviews while walking across an uncompleted bridge 20 feet above a stream. He and Irene together interviewed a paranoid public official who was sitting in middle of his living room floor with a rifle in his lap. Less dramatically, but more noisily, Irene has carried out interviews in parking lots and restaurants to prevent the discussion from being overheard. One of her former students has been accompanying the mayor of Rochester, New York, and interviewing him in the back seat of his limousine between his public appearances.

In each of these cases, though, the interview was part of an established conversational partnership. The location might have been unusual, but both parties knew each other and had worked to establish shared rules for discussion. In some situations you may need to carry out an interview without the opportunity to build much of a relationship and you have to adapt the interviewing as best you can.

Interpersonal Relationships and Focus Groups

One situation lacking opportunity for building a natural-seeming relationship is a focus group interview (Morgan, 1988). In a focus group, the researcher calls together several people to talk about a concern held by the researcher or clients of the researcher. The members of the focus group might be consumers of a product or service, viewers of a movie, or persons who weathered some event together. An increasingly common use of focus groups is to bring together a group of people who have experienced the same problem, such as residents of a deteriorating neighborhood or women in a sexist organization. The interviewer becomes a group leader who facilitates the discussion, asking questions and listening to the answers of the whole group.

In most qualitative interviewing, the purpose is to obtain depth and detail from individuals. In focus groups, the goal is to let people spark off of one another, suggesting dimensions and nuances of the original problem that any one individual might not have thought of. Sometimes a totally different understanding of a problem emerges from the group discussion.

In focus groups, the researcher cannot build a deep relationship. The focus group meeting, involving 6 to 12 people, usually runs but an hour or two. There isn't time to get to know anyone or build trust slowly. Instead, the researcher tries to create a comfortable atmosphere so that people are willing to talk in front of strangers.

The interviewer can allow folk time to greet one another, serve coffee, seat people around a table, and create a social break in the middle. People in this group interview situation are most comfortable when they feel they are contributing to a professional project and that a professional is in charge. The researcher gives overall direction while communicating the expectation that the focus group members will do most of the talking.

Rather than trying to set up a personal relationship with 12 strangers, the moderator conveys through dress and manner of speaking that this is a professional environment and the panelists are the experts. The moderator explains the topic of discussion—a new design for a coffeepot or a child care leave policy—and indicates he or she will be saying very little. The researcher labels himself or herself as a *moderator*, a person who is going to guide the conversations of others.

During the conversation, the moderator pays close attention to the relationships between members of the panel to ensure that people don't step all over each other. Some people are frightened to speak before strangers and are willing to let others talk, so the moderator may have to take special measures to get their opinions. "Thanks, Bob that was interesting. Now Mary, you haven't spoken yet, have you had any experience with the drug pushers? Are they on your block?" The moderator thus gently moves the focus away from an overly talkative person and highlights the experiences, and hence competence, of the person whose opinion he or she is soliciting.

Telephone Interviews

Given the need to build a relationship and the importance of visible cues in conversations, you'd rightly expect that telephones are not a major way of conducting qualitative interviews. In phone interviews, all sorts of conversational cues are missing, making for difficult interviewing under the best of circumstances. Yet researchers have found that for following up specific topics with people with whom they have already established a conversational partnership, the phone may be useful. One of Herb's best informants in a distant city was a talkative and knowledgeable person. In face-to-face interviews, Herb leaned closer to indicate real interest in what she was saying and pulled back when he was less involved. She quickly picked up on these cues, and without Herb having to say a word, minimized discussion of what to Herb were extraneous topics. When Herb telephoned her, he had some very specific questions in mind, but without the body cues, the phone conversation drifted in and out of Herb's topics. Short of interrupting, Herb had no way of redirecting the irrelevant discussions. The interview was useful because the interviewee already knew what Herb's project was about, but less of it was on target than the previous face-to-face interviews.

It is much more difficult to interview someone on the phone when you do not have an established relationship, but sometimes it is necessary. Three people knew parts of a puzzle Herb was trying to solve; one was in Baltimore, another was vacationing on Cape Cod, and a third was in San Francisco. Herb would have loved to visit them but didn't have the time or money. He had never met any of these people, but he had to interview them by phone if he was going to talk to them at all.

Having absolutely no research literature to advise him on how to interview strangers on the phone, Herb improvised. He reasoned that he had to communicate a threefold message: that he was an appropriate person for them to talk to; that what they could contribute was important; and that depth and detail, even on the telephone, were important.

First, Herb prepared a professional-looking cover letter that explained who he was, what he had accomplished so far in the project, and most important, what it was that the individual telephone partner could contribute. The letter included information on the people who had referred Herb to the phone partner. Herb also included some of his manuscripts. The long quotes in the manuscripts showed that he was after detailed information, and the lack of names demonstrated that he protected the anonymity of his interviewees. It was safe to talk to him. Next, he called each person during business hours to arrange a time for the discussion. This call accomplished several things. It enabled the person to ask Herb a little about the project, and Herb could suggest that a large chunk of time would be needed for the interview. In each call, Herb and the telephone partner swapped tales about people in the field that they both knew. In part they were gossiping, but in part, Herb was being grilled to see if he really knew people in the arena. Herb and one of the people discovered they were going to be at the same convention and arranged for a face-to-face interview there. The other two readily agreed to a longer conversation on the telephone, and Herb actually had to dissuade one from talking then and there. Herb knew that few interviewees can spontaneously spend an hour on the phone in their office without blocking out their schedule in advance.

By the time the actual interview began, Herb was already involved in a relationship with the phone partner. The face-to-face interview was best of the three because it allowed a major refocusing when a new concern was raised. It was more difficult to refocus on the phone. Nevertheless, all three provided the specific information Herb needed.

Strangers in Our Midst

One of the oddest interpersonal relationships in interviewing occurs when the researcher plans to interview one person and ends up unexpectedly interviewing two or more at the same time. The researcher remains conscious of his or her relationship to the original interviewee, but now has to pay much more attention to the relationship between the new person and the original interviewee. The dynamics become less predictable and less controllable.

When the two interviewees are bureaucratic subordinate and superior, the subordinate is often reluctant to talk openly in front of the boss. Because they are paying attention to each other, rather than to the interviewer, the interviewees may not talk about what you want them to talk about. Still, their interaction over the questions, the places they defer to each other or disagree with each other, may provide information that is excellent and of a depth that could not have been intentionally arranged. Instead of leading with questions and pursuing with follow-ups, the interviewer encourages a dialogue between the two participants and watches what occurs. When such discussions occur between interviewees, the topic is usually important, and it is best to just listen.

On one occasion, Irene had intended to interview a city manager who was unexpectedly joined by the mayor's assistant, who just walked into the room. Irene quickly readjusted and rather than focus on her original topics, encouraged the two to give the mayor's views and manager's views on some common concerns. To her surprise, they began a conversation with each other about what the labels *Democratic* and *Republican* meant in city affairs, a question that was important to them and laden with implications for their careers. Irene had not thought about city managers in cities with nonpartisan elections having a political party, so the discussion was eye popping.

Keep in mind that the interviewees, unlike the interviewer, have consequence for each other's lives; how each hears the other is of far more concern to them than their answers to the researcher. What makes such situations interesting is that everyone knows you are there, but your presence is not very important, and the social structure in which the interviewees operate is unfolding in front of you. You can often follow up one of these accidental twosomes with individual interviews building on the insights you picked up earlier.

CONCLUSION

To summarize, the trust and interest needed for an in-depth interview grow as part of an ongoing relationship. The interviewer's enthusiasm for the topic and interest in what is being said encourage people to expand on what they say. By showing concern with who the interviewee is and what he or she feels, the researcher reduces the stress of talking openly to strangers. The strongest relationships evolve when interviewer and interviewee talk face-to-face over several separate encounters, but good working relationships can develop even in a single interview.

When circumstances preclude building such relationships, you may have to modify your expectations and interviewing patterns. In focus groups and other multiple-person interviews, you do less questioning and pay more attention to how the interviewees interact; in telephone interviews, you try to get more information across in your introductory letter and preliminary phone calls.

In the next several chapters, we discuss how to prepare main questions, probes, and follow-ups, and how to use these three types of questions to structure an interview. This structure helps make the pattern of questioning intelligible to the interviewee and helps you get the depth, detail, and accuracy that qualitative interviews aim for. But it is the stages of the interview described in this chapter that encourage open and thoughtful answers. If you match your questions to the stages of the relationship, your interviewees should enjoy the interview more, feel more satisfaction in what they have told you, and be more willing to talk to you again.

7

Assembling the Parts

Structuring a Qualitative Interview

*I*n qualitative interviewing, you change the questions you ask depending on what you learned or failed to learn. Overall through the interview, though, you have to maintain balance between separate lines of inquiry and ensure that there is time to go into depth on each major subject. To allow flexibility to change questions while maintaining an overall structure, researchers pattern interviews around three types of questions—main questions, probes, and follow-up questions. Further, by preparing conversational guides— written outlines, protocols, or checklists—researchers set up an overall framework for the interview to keep the interview on course yet allow sufficient flexibility for exploring uncharted paths.

THREE TYPES OF
QUALITATIVE QUESTIONS

An interview is built up from three kinds of questions. Prior to talking with the interviewee, the researcher prepares a handful of *main questions* with which to begin and guide the conversation. Main questions change during the course of the research, as the researcher learns what to ask and to whom to ask it.

When responses lack sufficient detail, depth, or clarity, the interviewer asks a *probe* to complete or clarify the answer or to request further examples and evidence. Skillfully done, probes also communicate that you are paying attention to what the conversational partners are saying without uttering "I hear you" a hundred times.

Follow-up questions pursue the implications of answers to the main questions. Follow-ups examine central themes or events, or ask for elaboration about core ideas and concepts.

Main Questions

Before each interview, the researcher prepares several main questions to direct the discussion. Breaking the overall topic into several related questions is done in a way that provides unity to the interview. The wording of a main question should be open enough to encourage interviewees to express their own opinions and experiences, but narrow enough to keep interviewees from wandering too far from the subject at hand.

In preparing main questions for topical interviews, the researcher usually works out a series of queries that together cover specific events or stages of a process. With cultural interviews, main questions often are little more than conversational devices to encourage interviewees to begin describing what is important in their cultural arenas.

You prepare main questions in advance, customizing them to what you think the interviewee might know. But you may not get a chance to ask all of the preplanned main questions. For instance, our colleague Jim prepared 15 main questions for his interviews on civil rights suits with federal judges. In the actual interviews, he rarely reached the fourth question, and sometimes only asked the first one.

Not getting through a list of prepared questions is usually not a problem. The interviewee may answer your questions before you ask them or take off in a direction you did not anticipate but find important. But if you are tracing a series of events or finding out what parts of a program work, you have to ask questions you have prepared on each of these topics or the work is incomplete. To learn how cities handled fiscal stress, Irene had to ask interviewees about a series of key events in the history of the city's finances. She gently moved the interviews along to cover the main questions she had prepared. On those occasions when she still could not get through the questions, she arranged a second interview to finish them or set up an interview with someone else who could answer the remaining questions.

In the next two chapters, we discuss in detail how preparing main questions differs in cultural and topical interviews, but three concerns should be kept in mind, no matter what the purpose of the interview.

First, do the main questions cover the overall subject? When the researcher wants to explore a social or political process, are there main questions on each of the major events and stages? Does the wording encourage a discussion of the separate components of a culture without prejudging what is important and what is not?

Second, do the main questions flow from one to the next? Are the transitions between the main questions smooth? Will they make sense to the interviewees? For instance, in tracing out histories of events, the main questions might follow a chronology. What happened first? What happened next? This is a common way that people share narratives and so should seem logical to the interviewees. The connection between the questions is obvious.

More generally, the separate main questions should cover an overall subject in ways that suggest an underlying focus. Suppose you were interviewing about life in a retirement home and prepared three main questions to cover different parts of life in the home. First you could ask, "How good is the care from the staff?" The second question might be, "What is the social life like at Golden Acres?" A third main question could be, "Do you keep up contact with family and old friends?" Each main question speaks to a major part of life in a retirement home. First you asked about basic care, next about a sense of community, and your last question explored how people handled separation from their past. The interviewee should be able to see the pattern of the questions.

Finally, in choosing main questions, check to make sure the questions match the research design. Do the main questions cover the subjects that emerged from the iterative design? Are the main questions changing appropriately as the research progresses and you learn more? Have the main questions been selected to fit what separate interviewees should know? Have they been worded to accommodate the experiences and perspectives of individual conversational partners?

Probes

Probes perform three main functions in an interview. First, they help specify the level of depth the interviewer wants. Probes signal the interviewees that you want longer and more detailed answers, specific examples, or evidence. Probes encourage the speaker to keep elaborating. Second, probes ask the interviewee to finish up the particular answer currently being given. The interviewer may ask the interviewee to clarify an ambiguity or fill in missing information necessary to understand the answer. The third function of probes is to indicate that the interviewer is paying attention.

You can show interest through attention probes. One form of attention probe is to ask, "Can I quote you on that?" Whether or not you need permission, by asking for it, you are telling the interviewee, "I am listening intently, you phrased that point extremely well, I would like to get it down and use it just the way you said it." The way you take written notes, especially if you are also tape-recording, can also be an attention probe. Each time you mark something down, you communicate, "I heard something that is just too important to forget, that I might want to come back to." Such attention probes teach the interviewee what type of material you find especially informative.

During one interview, Herb asked the interviewee if he could quote him right after the person described a core part of his philosophy of work. A while later, the interviewee offered, "Here is a big quote for you. 'The skillful plagiarism beats inept originality every time.'" The interviewee then explained what the quote meant to him. This conversational partner had figured out from Herb's interest probe which issues Herb wanted to learn about and picked up the format of a summary quote to highlight his points so Herb would not miss them.

You can use continuation probes to signal the interviewee that it is okay to keep elaborating, that what he or she is saying is right on target and you want to listen to all the details. One form of continuation probe is to silently lean forward in a posture of respectful listening. The interviewee reads the body cues and continues without your having to say anything. Brief continuation probes such as, "Go on," or "what happened then?" also indicate that you want to be told more on this subject.

If the interviewee stops in the middle of a narrative, you can repeat part of the last sentence. For example, in presenting a narrative about a crime, the conversational partner might say, "I approached the rich-looking couple and thought about what might be in the lady's purse." The conversational partner then hesitates. You wait for a second, and if the interviewee doesn't continue, you repeat the subject and verb, "You approached . . ." and then you pause. You hope the interviewee will resume the narrative. If you repeat other parts of the sentence, such as "the rich-looking couple" or "in her purse," your probe applies to these phrases and suggests you want to know more about the rich-looking couple or the purse. If the interviewee interrupts him- or herself, resulting in an incomplete thought, you can ask for a completion of that line of thought. "Before we talked about the strike, you were saying that the union was all absorbing . . ." invites either an explanation of "all absorbing" or a completion of the original thought.

Sometimes what the interviewee is saying is simply not clear. It may be garbled grammatically, overburdened with pronouns, ambiguous, or lacking in sufficient detail to give a clear picture. Then you use a clarification probe, a form of conversational repair. "You said she did not want to go to a nursing home. Was that the social worker who said that or your mother?"

Sometimes it is not just grammar that is unclear, but technical vocabulary. Or the steps in a process may not be clearly outlined. When our colleague Jim asked a computer hacker how he got into a university computer, he got the following answer:

> They don't know their own system's security procedures, and we just got the book. We read it, and I ran it, and we got it. He saw us, I guess. We were using an ID of some guy whose account was canceled, and they asked who we were, but we were lucky and social-engineered it and he told me to get out, so I did. So we didn't do anything other than get in, ya know? But, that's what all we wanted.

Jim then used a clarification probe. "Could you run that one by me again? I am afraid I still don't understand how you did that." Herb says in similar situations, "That's kind of technical, but I think I need to understand. Could you explain it again?"

If you are unsure of what someone said—perhaps the person gave you a summary and maybe some key points were left out, or the material was garbled grammatically—you may be able to ask, "What were her exact words, do you remember?" or "What did she actually say to you?"—"I don't remember exactly, but it was something like, 'I would rather be dead.'" In this probe you are asking for evidence (the exact words), but at the same time you get clarification of the meaning.

Elaboration, continuation, clarification, attention, and completion probes are housekeeping probes. They ensure that you are getting a reasonably accurate and understandable answer while encouraging the interviewee to keep talking. They help teach the special rules of conversation that apply to interviews. But probing does more than keep the conversation going, it helps get the depth and dependability you need in qualitative interviews and the freshness of firsthand descriptions by encouraging narratives and stories, and requesting examples and evidence.

If someone gives you a general answer such as, "There is a lot of conflict around here," you don't have enough yet to follow up on, so you probe to encourage the interviewee to continue. You can ask, "What do you mean by 'conflict'?" or "Could you give me an example of a conflict?"

Sometimes you want to know how heavily to rely on a particular answer. You use an evidence probe to find out how the person knows what they are telling you. Evidence probes need to be phrased tactfully and can only be used a limited number of times before you sound like the grand inquisitor. One way is to phrase the evidence probe so it sounds more like a search for detail rather than checking up on how the person knows. For instance, in an interview about a hiring conflict, you can ask whether the interviewee was on the recruitment committee.

How you probe helps define the interpersonal relationship between interviewer and conversational partner. Insufficient probing indicates boredom or inattention; too much probing and the researcher turns into an inquisitor. Fortunately, as the relationship develops, you need to probe less often, because interviewees learn the level of detail and evidence that you want and begin to frame their answers to match.

Follow-Up Questions

Main questions create a scaffolding for the interview, keep the questioning on the topic, and link what is asked in individual interviews to the overall design. Probes clarify and complete the answers, making them intelligible, and signal the interviewees about the expected level of depth. They also show the interviewee that the interviewer is interested in the answers. The purpose of follow-up questions is to get the depth that is a hallmark of qualitative interviewing by pursuing themes that are discovered, elaborating the context of answers, and exploring the implications of what has been said.

Some follow-ups are worked out in the periods between two interviews with the same conversational partner; others are thought of during the interview itself. In either case, follow-ups cannot be prepared prior to the initial interview, because they will be based on the interviewee's responses to the main questions.

After each interview, and after each cluster of interviews, look over your transcripts to figure out what you should follow up on. Look for themes, ideas, concepts, and events and prepare additional questions on those that address your research concerns. Preparing follow-ups between interviews takes work and attention, but you usually have sufficient time to think about which issues should be explored in depth. Following up during an interview is more difficult. With experience, you learn to pay real attention to what the conversational partner is saying and figure out what seems to be missing or what you need to ask to elicit additional depth. The trick is choosing to follow up on only those matters that provide insight on the core matters of concern.

Listen for partial narratives, unexplained lists, and one-sided descriptions of behavior that beg for elaboration. When a conversational partner provides a list of reasons, events, or explanations of the core topic, and then only explores one, you follow up by asking, "Would you talk a bit about some of the other items you mentioned?"

You may follow up when a narrative or example has been left incomplete. For instance, if somebody describes a fight between the public works manager and the budget officer about what project to do next and then goes on and talks about the project, the obvious follow-up is to ask about the fight. Such follow-ups are also suggested when interviewees skip topics that were important in discussions with other people.

Follow-ups cascade, because the answers to one follow-up can suggest new lines of inquiry that you want to follow up on in turn. Consider the following example from our colleague Jim's interviews. In response to a main question about prison life, a prisoner explained that boredom was his worst problem. Jim followed up:

Jim: What kinds of things do you do in prison that keep you from becoming bored?

Prisoner: You can join gangs, play chess with your cellie, go to the [exercise] yard, drink, join the JayCees, get into the education program, or just lay around your cell watching tv, if you don't have a [job] assignment.

Startled, Jim probed for clarification.

Jim: Uh, "drink?" Did you say "Drink?"

Prisoner: Yeah [laughs]. Drink. You know, drink.

Jim: As in "drink, drink?" Like . . .

Prisoner: As in drink, booze, hooch, firewater, joy-juice, alcohol, ya know?

Jim: [laughs].

Prisoner: Got news for ya. Anything you can get on the outside, we can get in here.

Jim then followed up again:

Jim: Amazing. If I were a prisoner, how would I go about getting something to "drink?"

Contradictions or puzzles, statements that sound guarded, incomplete answers, and the use of new words or unfamiliar terms should trigger follow-up questions. In the case of the prisoner and the drink, Jim followed up on the new information because it sounded puzzling. How could someone in prison get liquor, and how could they afford to buy it, assuming that it was available? A similar invitation to follow up occurs when interviewees explain how people should behave. The puzzle is, do they actually behave that way, and what happens when they don't?

Asking good follow-up questions is a matter of trained curiosity, recognizing and pursuing puzzles while exploring emerging themes. Sometimes a theme virtually leaps out at you, as when Jim stumbled across the prison economy. But more often, an unanticipated theme is more subtle and you have to be exposed to it several times before you hear it and it dawns on you what people are saying. Follow-ups to these more subtle themes rarely occur in one interview, but depend upon your taking the time between interviews to study what your interviewees have told you.

Although new words or concepts invite probes or follow-ups, you can't ask about every word you don't understand. If you ask about too many words in a row, the interview ceases to sound or feel like a conversation and you lose focus and depth. You might also appear so ignorant that interviewees feel you are not worth the effort to teach. You sometimes have to request follow-ups without seeming to ask about every word. For example, in one of Jim's interviews with a young computer hacker, Jim was overwhelmed with new vocabulary:

Jim: You said earlier that you were "hacking" last night. What did you do?

Young Hacker: I was running numbers, you know, wardialing 288s, and got a couple of hits. So I cracked into a local dialup, found a PBX and hacked into one of 'em and tried one of 'em. I got in, and ran one and hit. A Unix system. After a few tries, I got root, set myself up, logged out, then hacked out a coupla more. . . .

The interviewee responded with what was to him everyday vocabulary that needed no translation. Jim wanted to know what the interviewee meant but was wary of appearing totally ignorant. So, Jim phrased his follow-up in the following way:

Jim: Now, if you were talking to a reporter, say somebody from the *New York Times* like John Markoff (co-author of *The Hacker Crackdown*), how would you explain to him, so he could explain to the public, what "running numbers" means?

Jim managed to keep the focus on one core term, expecting that an explanation would include definitions of some of the other puzzling phrases without his having to ask a dozen boring questions about vocabulary.

What terms you follow up on depends on the conceptual focus of the study. Suppose you are interviewing students about life in the dorms and find out that loud music is a particular problem. Interviewees mention particular vocalists and musical groups, such as Black Uhuru and Tracy Chapman. If you never heard of Black Uhuru, you should not stop and ask, lest you get into a discussion of contemporary music and lose the thread of the interview. A more appropriate follow-up would be, "Where do you go to study?" or "Is there a quiet floor?" Or "Are there rules against loud music?" Or you could follow up with a question about other problems besides loud music.

Follow-ups are about more than learning the meaning of a core idea or concept, or completing a missing story or narrative. They are the way the researcher explores emerging themes with the conversational partner. When answering such follow-ups, the interviewee becomes a full-fledged research partner. You can ask this conversational partner what he or she thinks of an idea that a different interviewee has suggested. Or you can follow up by asking about themes you think are in the answers this interviewee has already given, but you are not sure about them yet.

For example, when Irene was interviewing in Phoenix, the city manager responded to main questions of why the budget process changed by describing the professionalism of the staff and the political involvement of the citizenry. From her prior research, Irene was surprised that he had not discussed the possibility of financial deficits causing changes in the budget process, because other interviewees had done so. When the manager had finished his answer, she followed up by saying, "I noticed that you never mentioned deficits. Is that a factor in why the budget process changes?" The manager indicated that he thought it was a relatively unimportant source of change, and then he and Irene discussed the reasons why. The discussion stimulated by this follow up caused Irene to rethink an underlying theme.

When you are following up on themes that emerge from the interviewee you are currently talking to, choose what to follow up on depending on what you have learned from other interviews and how well each follow-up helps build the picture you are forming of the research arena.

For example, in the main question of a life history interview, we asked a senior citizen to talk about her early work experience, especially her contact with unions. Her narrative was rich and detailed. She had worked in a clothing factory, because it was the only job that she could get, but she longed for an office job. Eventually she was promoted into the office and loved the work. Then there was a strike. During the strike, she crossed the picket line, but her friends on the factory line protected her and did not call her a scab, because they said, "She is okay, she works in the office." Remembering back all those years, she said, "They really respected anyone who worked in the office." Neither she nor her friends saw promotion to office work as making her the enemy. But her background and her union connections made her suspect to the bosses. Fortunately for her, because she was such a good worker and they knew her already, management let her stay, as long as she promised not to pass any information to the union.

There are a number of ways to follow up on such a complicated narrative, depending upon the themes being explored. The central tension for the woman was between being supported by and admired by union members and being proud of working in the office and winning the support of the bosses. You might want to examine this tension with follow-ups such as, "Were you ever tempted to pass information to the union?" or "How did you feel when you had to cross the picket line?" Or you could follow up by trying to find out what loyalty to the boss meant among the office staff or what "a good worker" meant.

Her answer is so rich with thematic material that it is stunning, and you may not think of all the ways that you want to pursue it at the moment. You might want to come back to some of them later in the interview, such as how she felt about the union after she became an office worker, how she felt about the promotion, whether her pride in doing white-collar work resulted in her looking down on the factory workers, and whether her attitudes were widely shared among the office workers. Any of these would lead to deeper understanding and you choose among them depending upon the overall thrust of your research.

When you get a complex answer like this, filled with new information and possible themes, you stop thinking in terms of single questions, but rather plan clusters of linked follow-ups. To help you keep these in mind, jot down the ideas as they come to you, and then gradually ask them, allowing for full discussion of each one, and sometimes following up on the follow-ups before returning to the original list. Even if you are tape-recording you must jot down these follow-ups and where you are in the process of questioning lest you get lost in the cluster. Both the mental exertion of intently listening to what is being said and the excitement of the answers can make your mind go blank on what you intended to ask next.

Sometimes the initial answer you get isn't as rich as the one in this example; in fact, it may be very lean, though you suspect from other interviews that there is hidden depth. In these circumstances, you follow up in stages, asking about the separate parts of what the person said, beginning first with clarifications of terms and then moving on to the deeper issues involved. The follow-ups here are meant to encourage the person to talk in more depth.

Sometimes the initial question you ask is too abstract or too stressful, and the interviewee cannot come up with a good answer. For instance, we were interviewing a woman about her relationship with her mother and heard her express a feeling of guilt. To follow up, we asked what she felt guilty about. When the woman did not answer this broader question, we asked more specific questions about things she might have felt guilty about. "Do you feel that you should be spending more time with your mother?" "Does she blame you for her illnesses?"

Such follow-ups are meant to encourage the interviewee to start talking. You don't need the answers to these questions specifically, you just made them up to give the interviewee an idea of what an answer might be. She might reject these questions completely, but now tell you what it is she does feel guilty about. In this case, the interviewee responded, "No, it is not time I feel guilty about, it is not having her in my house. And I feel guilty trying to get her to live within her budget, as if I did not want to supplement her income. It makes me feel cheap." Once the interviewee starts to respond in depth, you follow up on the responses, rather than continue to ask the questions you made up that were not based on her answers. For instance, you can continue by asking, "Did she want to live with you?" or "Does she have enough money to live on comfortably?"

Follow-ups generally work better when they are grounded in the immediate topic at hand. When our follow-ups focus narrowly on specific events or themes, our interviewees can usually answer the specific question and then build toward their own generalizations based on particular experiences they have had. They are telling you both what they feel and what they have experienced. If you ask for generalizations first, without focusing on concrete experiences, you may get abstractions back that may not be connected to the interviewee's experiences. For example, in some of Herb's interviews with community developers, he followed up on an answer about funders by asking how the interviewees felt funders responded to the community needs. In response, the interviewees answered that funders did not realize that investments in low-income communities would pay off. That was an okay answer, as far as it went, but it wasn't concrete or grounded and provided few details. Herb changed the way he asked the question, posing a specific example instead of asking a general question. He asked, "What difficulties did LISC [a supplier of funds] create in packaging the project?" The interviewees provided grounded, concrete details about LISC and then described examples of difficulties their organizations had with other funders.

Figuring out what to follow up on is usually more difficult than figuring out how to word a follow-up question. There is one basic principle of wording follow-ups: Try to make sure that your follow-ups correspond to what the conversational partner has said. The following conversation indicates how easy it is to ask a follow-up that doesn't match what the interviewee is telling you:

Interviewer: How did you feel when your father died?.

Answer: I was really torn up. Really bad. I couldn't sleep for a few days, missed a few weeks of classes, and I cried constantly.

Interviewer: Has anybody else in your family died in the past few years?

The follow-up ignores the content of the response and misses the opportunity to explore the consequences and management of grieving. Better follow-ups would stay closer to the material. For example, "What kind of things made you cry?" Or "Did you have anyone to talk to about what you were feeling?" You could even ask about the interviewee's relationship with her dad before he died.

Sometimes the follow-up doesn't match the previous answer closely because the interviewer used a follow-up that was planned in advance without thinking about whether it fit the situation at hand. When the interviewer is continuing a topic with the same conversational partner at a later time, preparing such follow-ups is quite helpful. But be careful not to mechanically use prepared follow-ups in circumstances in which they do not belong.

Herb recently made such a mistake because he was too tired to listen carefully. (This is an argument for pacing your interviews to ensure that you get enough rest between them.) In several previous interviews, developers had complained that they hated the aggravation of convincing multiple funders to cooperate on one project. Herb had worked out a standard follow-up asking how developers handled this aggravation. In the next interview, a person described her main skill as getting funding agencies to cooperate. Herb, too eager to use the prepared follow-up, asked how she handled the aggravation. Herb's follow-up, of course, was nonsensical, and his interviewee told him so in no uncertain terms.

PUTTING IT ALL TOGETHER

Sometimes interviews just happen. You walk into a room, the conversational partner is attuned to your interests, begins talking, and the conversation flows. But you can't count on that occurring; rather you need to plan how to put your questions together to guide the conversational partner through a focused conversation.

Metaphorically, putting together the main questions, probes, and follow-ups is a little like playing golf. You have a series of holes, the separate topics of the discussion, each of which you approach with a main question, a big long drive that you have planned out in advance. Depending on where your drive lands, you follow up with other shots, choosing clubs with different shapes that are most likely to get you close to the green from where you are. If you hit the ball into the rough—that is, get an answer that is vague or incomprehensible—you choose a specialized club, the probe, that helps you get past the difficulty. You continue the probing and following up until you get the ball into the hole. You repeat the process again on the next hole with another preplanned main question, follow-ups, and probes as needed. The holes are connected in a logical order and give structure to the whole game.

The interview is like a golf game in that you think about the overall direction yet maintain flexibility to adapt to what you have heard. Just as the choice of club depends on where your ball lands, your choice of follow-ups and probes depends on what you hear in answer to your main questions. The details of sequencing and wording questions differ between cultural and topical interviews, but the need to maintain overall coherence in the interview remains the same. To do this, you generally plan the overall structure of the interview by figuring out roughly the balance you want between main questions and follow-ups. Then you prepare conversational guides for yourself, such as written protocols, outlines, and checklists, that remind you of what you want to ask without forcing you into a preset pattern.

Framing the Interview

As part of preparing for an interview, the researcher decides how to link the main questions to each other and determines the strategy for following up on what he or she hears. Two patterns of structuring the interview are quite common, although in practice there are a number of variations in between.

With the first approach, the tree-and-branch model, the interview is likened to a tree. The trunk is the core topic; the branches, the main questions. You plan the questions to explore each branch with more or less the same degree of depth. With the second model, the interview is more like a major river that merges different currents into a single stream and then breaks into separate channels, possibly combining again later into a single stream. In this second case, the questions explore one current within the main river and follow it no matter where it goes.

The researcher might use the tree-and-branch model if she or he knows, perhaps from previous interviews, observation, or background reading, that certain main questions must be asked in order to cover the entire subject. The interviewer follows up on the answers to each main question looking for depth and detail, but in doing so balances depth in one part of the subject with coverage of all the parts. The goal is to learn about the individual branches that frame the entire tree but still obtain depth and detail.

In the tree-and-branch model, the main questions establish the overall sequence of what is asked. With the river-and-channel model, the follow-ups are more important. You ask a main question and through it discover one current within the river. Then you follow up on the answer and cascade to further follow-ups to explore related points in detail.

The sequencing of a river-and-channel model is based on the chain of the follow-ups, each building on the previous one, all tied together by your interest in a single theme. The chained follow-ups provide structure and continuity, because they are pursuing a single theme. One consequence, though, is the interview might only follow one thought and end up in a small offshoot of the river.

Each form of framing serves a distinct purpose. The tree-and-branch model is most helpful when the interviewer has an overall topic worked out and wants to paint a complete picture by exploring the separate parts that go together. For instance, if you are trying to understand how a government decision was made, each stage of the decision is an important branch that must be explored. Or if you are interviewing on the consistency of beliefs among members of a subcultural group, you need to explore separately each of the values that help define the overall culture.

The river-and-channel model is most helpful when you want to explore one theme in depth and detail, to understand it well, and are willing to explore the issue to the exclusion of other themes. As an example, assume again you are studying how government decisions get made, but this time you want to explore the theme of agency conflict. Rather than ask about separate stages in decision making, you follow up on the stream describing fights between agencies. You continue on this channel until you understand the basis of the rift. You might begin by asking about competition between agencies on how a job-retraining program should be run and then trace the histories of other issues on which the agencies contended. In those interviews you might never learn the details of the job-retraining program, but you should gather information on a variety of contentions between the quarreling agencies.

Suppose you are studying a cultural group and are interviewing on how families decide how to spend their money. Your interviewees tell you that women manage the money. You switch gears to follow a potential new theme and begin asking about other family situations in which women seem to prevail, such as child rearing or the selection of an apartment or deciding whose family to visit at Thanksgiving or Christmas.

Where you use each type of framing will vary. If a concept or theme is so important that you cannot understand the research arena without knowing what it means, you sequence with the river-and-channel model. When you are interested in learning how the whole is formed from separate parts you frame the questioning with the tree-and-branch model.

How you ask questions differs within each model. A tree-and-branch model covers a topic as a whole and maintains its coherence because each question relates to a part of a broader topic. However, with the tree-and-branch model you have to balance the time for follow-ups for depth and detail with the goal of asking about each main question.

With the river-and-channel model, you often have only one main question that is followed up on in great detail. Structure is maintained by ensuring that each nested follow-up and probe is consistent with an emerging theme and does not digress into secondary issues. You trace out women's domination in housing decisions, but you don't digress into housing policy lest you get bogged down in a shallow bayou.

Protocols, Checklists, and Outlines

The two ways of framing suggest how main questions are joined with follow-ups to form an overall approach to an interview. In addition, to provide structure interviewers prepare *conversational guides* for what they are going to ask. These guides, in the form of protocols, outlines, or checklists, help keep the interviewer focused on the topic and main themes. Conversational guides are not rigid frameworks that are prepared once and for all; rather they are customized for each interview and evolve throughout the work.

The simplest guide is a brief checklist of topics; the most elaborate is a protocol with all the main questions fully written out. In between are outlines that represent the main topics as the main headings; more focused questions as subheadings; and include as lower-level items, specific examples to explore. An outline lacks the precise wording of a protocol but has more order and organization than does a checklist.

Herb guides his questioning with a master outline on which he writes down the topics and ideas to explore; logs whether or not he has done so; and notes with whom, among his various conversational partners, a particular issue should be raised. He updates this list regularly, checking off the pieces of information he has collected in sufficient depth and adding any new items that he now feels should be discussed. Irene is a little less systematic. She doesn't keep a master list but makes a topic outline with major and minor points she wants to raise. She prepares a new outline for each interview after looking over prior interviews and background documents to find out what else she has to learn.

Outlines help you keep in mind the differences between basic themes on the one hand and illustrations on the other hand. The main outline headings suggest overall areas that should be covered whereas lower-level headings point out questions that the researcher thinks might illustrate or refine specific points, though these specific questions need not be asked. Placing the 1993 budget proposal as a main topic suggests that you want to know the what and why of this particular piece of legislation. But if your main topic is how politicians and lobbyists interact, the 1993 budget proposal would be a lower-level item that could be discussed as an illustration but would be no better or worse than, for instance, asking about a crime bill.

Because in qualitative research you are constantly learning what is important to pursue and what can be ignored, there is great flux in the content of the outline in the beginning stages of the work. As the work continues, the main topics become more stable. However, even after the topic list stabilizes, the outline does not become a rigid list of questions that you have to get through. Rather, having an outline reminds you of what you need to find out at a particular point in the study while providing an overall organization that should be comprehensible to the interviewee. It prevents you and the interviewee from getting lost.

Having an outline in hand gives the interviewer confidence when entering an unstructured situation. You have in front of you topics to cover and several different examples that you can pursue, if the interviewee does not provide you with better examples to explore. Outlines emphasize the variety of questions that can give insight to a particular topic. The following excerpt from one of Herb's interview outlines illustrates what they look like:

    I. Organizational Problems
       A. Maintaining Qualified Staff With Low Salaries
         1. Ms. Jones who just quit to work at a bank

    B. Working With a Community Board
       1. Scandal of board member getting priority on apartment
       2. Last fund-raising campaign
    C. Obtaining Funds for Basic Organizational Expenses
  II. Exemplary Projects
    A. The Facade Improvement Project (mentioned in report)

Before the interview, Herb prepared main questions for each of the roman numeral topics, for example, "Could you describe the most interesting (successful, least successful, controversial) project your organization has done?" for roman numeral II above. From his prior research, he knew that if the conversation floundered, he could prompt his interviewee to continue by mentioning more specific examples, such as the facade improvement project included in the outline.

A checklist has a set of items you want to learn about, but they are not yet arranged in a way that makes the same fine distinction between topics, main questions, and examples. Checklists evolve and rapidly change, especially during the earlier stages of a study. For example, before preparing an outline, Herb started his study of community development with a checklist that looked something like the following:

1. Descriptions of the Community Projects
2. Organizational History
3. Relationships With Government

After a few interviews, Herb learned that the organizations he was studying received help from other community groups and joined together to form coalitions to lobby. He also learned that the directors of these community groups had pronounced ideological beliefs about what should be done to improve communities. He modified his checklist by adding these three items:

4. Relationship With Other Community Organizations
5. Coalitions
6. Philosophy (ideologies) of Community Development

Whether you use protocols, outlines, or checklists, the guide is a freehand map to the conversation, pointing out general direction, but not specifying which nooks and crannies will be explored. Guides enable the researcher to balance the need for order with the freedom to explore unanticipated topics. Guides can help prevent getting lost in cascades of follow-ups. In the beginning the guide should be simple and reasonably short, lest you lock in too many assumptions about what you will hear. In addition, the physical guide itself becomes an interviewing prop. Holding a guide makes the researcher look professional and prepared. We have found that it is less threatening to ask questions about counternormative behaviors if the questions are typed on a guide that the interviewee can see. Perhaps by seeing the controversial question in written form, interviewees feel as if they are responding to a scientific instrument and can therefore be more self-revealing.

THE SELF-CORRECTING INTERVIEW

In early parts of most projects, interviews are far from perfect, so you need to build in routines of self-evaluation. Briefly after each interview and at greater length after completing a series of interviews, examine what is going right and wrong. Are you hearing concepts and themes that should be explored? Are you getting enough depth and examples? Are the conversations smooth or do they appear jerky?

In your self-analysis, think about whether you have successfully built a relationship with the interviewee. Look at your introduction. Was your description of the topic too broad or too narrow, giving the interviewee incorrect signals about what you wanted to know? Did you go overboard on describing your credentials and intimidate the interviewee? Did you approach difficult and stressful questions too quickly, rather than slowly build toward them? Were you negligent in not reinforcing the interviewee's sense of competence? Did you notice whether or not your interviewee seemed stressed and did you then tone down the questioning? Was your style too heavy handed or inquisitorial? Did you look or sound bored?

Look at the interviews and see whether or not issues were answered in depth, and if not, try to determine why. Did you carelessly discourage an interviewee from responding at length by interrupting a long reply? Did you forget to use continuation or elaboration probes? Did you accept a generalization and neglect to ask for examples? Did you skip opportunities to follow up on incomplete answers? Did you phrase too many questions in ways that invited yes-or-no reply?

Did you encourage the interviewee to speak his or her mind? Did you inadvertently interrupt what the interviewee said by expressing your own opinions in a strong way? Check to see how you reacted when the interviewees contradicted you—if you got defensive, rather than curious and supportive, try to change how you respond.

If you are hearing themes that don't seem to connect with each other, examine how you sequenced the questions. Are your follow-ups connected directly to interviewee responses? Are you probing when you don't understand? Are you using a conversational guide of some sort to keep you on topic? Are you jotting down notes to yourself to remind you what to follow up on?

Did you ask any questions that did not get answers, or that got truncated answers or strange and evasive responses? If so, what was the problem? You may have asked one question, and the interviewee answered another. What was the question that the interviewee was answering? Was it more important than the one you actually asked? Or did your question mislead because it was based on erroneous information or an incorrect assumption, and the interviewee is politely, but indirectly, informing you of that? Or was the interviewee simply trying to avoid the topic?

Sometimes you might discover that you are failing to hear the indirect speech of your conversational partners. Women, for example, often speak less directly than do men, so their answers seem to be truncated or evasive. Think about what people might be saying indirectly and work out ways of confirming what you think you heard through follow-up questions. A lack of praise in a woman's answer might veil an indirect criticism. Rather than ignore the silence or indirection, follow up to find out what the interviewee thinks is wrong but has not yet stated (Tannen, 1990).

Did you ask a question that just did not resonate at all with the interviewee? For example, did you ask professors about their research and get little or no response? Maybe research work is just something they have to do, but not something about which they feel any enthusiasm. You may need to approach the subject in a different way.

Did you back off when you should have pressed forward, or press forward when you should have backed off? Were your questions too abstract or too long? Did they have too many parts? Was the interviewee afraid of you or fearful of giving you too much information?

If you are not picking up concepts and themes to follow up, you need time to reflect and improve. Stop your interviewing for a while. Go over transcripts of your interviews and summarize what they are about, paragraph by paragraph. Often these summaries will suggest the themes to pursue.

Another way to find themes is to search in the interviews for places where your conversational partners used the word "because" or other close synonyms. As you reread the interviews, look for responses that answer the question "Why?" Such responses suggest themes to follow up on, but their wording may be indirect. An interviewee may talk about professionalism when you ask how changes in the budget process were made. He or she may never say so in so many words, but the underlying theme may be "because we are professionals" we made certain changes. Finally, themes can become apparent when interviewees make wrap-up statements.

This exercise in sorting out themes both helps you to hear better what people are saying and suggests ways of redesigning the interviews to get the depth you need. The themes you hear in the early interviews can become the subject of follow-ups in subsequent interviews.

Though we have mentioned many problems, if you and the interviewees are on the same wavelength, and they know you are on their side, many errors are forgiven. Herb usually interviews people who are aware that he supports what they do and they want to help him to get their story out. They tell him when he misses a theme or go over points many times until they are sure he understands. Herb's biggest fault in interviewing is that he talks too much, especially in his introductions. On one occasion, a ranking official in a major city told Herb to stop talking during the warm-up because the official only had an hour. The official then conversed for the entire time precisely on the target of Herb's research.

Periodic self-evaluation is useful, not only to catch your mistakes, but to remind you of the things you are doing well. Success tells you what to keep on doing, and is a reward for lots of hard work and attention to detail. How do you know you have done a good interview? When you are getting depth and detail, you are doing things right. When conversational partners reach out, hold your shoulder, say "It was fun," and invite you back, you know the interview worked. It is a sign that things are going well when your interviewees anticipate your questions and you don't have to ask them. It is even better when the interviewees suggest lines of questioning for you, or raise questions that you did not think about but are relevant to the topic. It is great when your conversational partners so want you to get it right that they point out subtleties that you would otherwise miss.

Sometimes interviewees set aside a limited amount of time for you but get so involved in answering your questions and exploring the topic that they let themselves run over. Herb recently scheduled a brief follow-up appointment, but when he arrived, the interviewee looked at the appointment book and told his secretary to rearrange the afternoon to allow him enough time with Herb. The interviewee enjoyed the audience Herb provided and talked on the topic for several hours.

You know you are succeeding at a series of interviews when the project log on your wall fills with checkmarks telling you what concepts you heard, what events were explored, what pieces of information that were needed you found out, and what themes were tested and with whom. If you use and amend a topic outline as you move through the research, that outline begins to look more and more like an outline for a final report.

Herb once had the ultimate test of whether his research was coming together. After returning home from an interviewing field trip, he got a phone call for a job interview for the next day. With no time to produce a more formal talk, Herb took his interviewing outline, added a few examples from what his conversational partners had said, and turned that into his talk. The talk was sufficiently coherent and convincing that Herb was offered the job.

Finally, you know that the interviews are working when you feel yourself absorbed and excited as you reread your transcripts and find yourself eager to share what you have learned with others. The interviews are working when you find answers to the questions that you originally posed. In addition, the project is successful if you discover a lot of questions and answers that you did not realize were important when you began the interviewing.

8

Hearing About Culture

*I*n cultural interviewing, researchers learn the rules, norms, values, and understandings that are passed from one generation of group members to the next. Sometimes cultural interviews are done in distant places or among people whose actions are viewed as deviant, to understand behaviors that seem unusual (Fox, 1987; Lozano & Foltz, 1990; Myers, 1992).

But most cultural interviews are about common and ordinary behavior. Researchers study how people meet and marry, raise their children, and take care of their elderly parents. They learn how people shop, cook, and eat; how they make or buy their clothes; how they deal with unemployment and illness. They look at how the young behave in school and how the elderly cope after the loss of a spouse.

Researchers ask about culture to learn how the rules within a group guide the choices that people make. Cultural researchers look at how groups teach their members how to behave and ask what happens to those who violate the rules. Cultural interviewers ask about personal and social histories to discover the kinds of experiences that bring about changes in values and norms.

Although culture is about the ordinary, ordinary does not mean dull. Ordinary events may be both dramatic and important. No matter how common the death of a parent, it is still a traumatic event for those who live through it. Daily events, such as going to school, can be scary for those who are not prepared to learn or for those who have to dodge gunfire at unpredictable moments. And even though people fall in love every day, for those who experience it, falling in love can be a wild and joyous ride.

Ordinary events are important not only to the participants, but to those who want to learn about problems that affect us all. Routine decisions at work may empower employees or repress them, either creating a model of satisfied worker involvement or bringing about endless labor-management strife. The physical danger of the inner city contributes to the formation of gangs; the death of a parent may activate friendship networks and redefine community; union solidarity can cross race and ethnic lines, forging a class consciousness with far-reaching social effects. Ordinary events display the rules of how people act together in conflict and in stress.

SPECIAL CONCERNS OF CULTURAL INTERVIEWS

Before you can conduct cultural interviews, you have to convince people that it is okay to talk about what seem to them to be ordinary matters. Why should people take the time to teach you how they go about their daily business? They might consider many ordinary matters, child-rearing practices, for instance, to be none of your business. At the beginning of the study you have to persuade interviewees to allow you, an outsider, to learn about their cultural arena. Delineating the beliefs, values, and norms that underlie ordinary behavior is a huge undertaking, in part because there is little guidance on where a cultural arena begins and where it ends. To make a study feasible, you have to draw some initial boundaries around the cultural arena in which you do the interviewing.

The Excitement of the Ordinary

For many people, explaining to others what they ordinarily do can be difficult, as such routines are taken for granted and rarely examined or thought about. If you ask people to explain what they buy and why when they go food shopping, they may be momentarily stunned and pause a while before answering. People eat together—but think of the complexity of a simple meal: what foods are served, who sits where, who does the serving and why, or what is discussed and with whom. But to the participants it all seems so ordinary that they do not know what to describe when you ask them to teach you about what goes on at a meal (Counihan, 1992). People follow cultural rules without being aware of them and so find it difficult to explain what for them are taken-for-granted events.

People also wonder why anyone would be interested in what to them is the ordinary and routine. Why should somebody care if women walk in front, beside, or behind their men? For single mothers, managing day care, tracking down late child support payments, and struggling to pay the bills are routine activities, things that just have to be done. Yet a researcher learns from these daily tasks what it means to be a single mother and gains greater understanding of what the feminization of poverty means (Eden, 1991).

At the beginning of a cultural interview, the researcher communicates to the interviewee the importance of the ordinary and why it is of interest to others (Cohen, 1991). You help interviewees understand why others are interested in what to them is routine by asking your conversational partners about the funny, difficult, poignant, or successful things they do. A schoolteacher may describe reaching a frightened child, a waitress may talk about handling an overly aggressive male customer, community developers may talk about how they package funding for a project. These are adventures of everyday life.

Another way of showing people that the ordinary is important is by asking about the choices they routinely make. Asking a student about going to class seems awfully dull, until the interviewer suggests that rather than go to class the conversational partner could have slept late, sunned on the lawn, gone to the library, or read a book. Framing questions in this way communicates that culture is about making choices and being constrained not to make other choices according to underlying norms and expectations.

Another way to help people talk about what to them appears to be ordinary is by encouraging them to think comparatively. "How do you do your job?" is so large and undefined a question that answering it can be difficult. But "How does this job compare to others you have had?" is more specific and much easier to answer.

People might want to share what to them is ordinary if they understand how others will benefit from their experiences. In a study of those with a debilitating disease, you tell interviewees that talking about what they experience can help others who might be afflicted to learn what to do and how to accept the changes in their lives. You show the importance of the details of daily medical routines that the interviewees would probably not talk about in other circumstances.

To those in the cultural arena, what the researcher wants to learn may seem bizarre. A cultural interview is a little like asking a fish what it is like to live in water, that is, what it is like to live in a taken-for-granted, daily environment. Can one fish explain water to another fish? Fortunately, it is usually clear that you are not another fish, that you are an outsider and may not know or understand such things. The downside of being an outsider is that people do not always want to share their intimate lives with you.

Crossing Boundaries

Culture defines who is an insider and who is an outsider. It sets up boundaries between those who should and those who should not be taught the rules. To learn about culture, an interviewer doesn't necessarily need to become an insider but must be allowed to cross the boundary and become accepted as one who can be taught.

To help cross these boundaries, researchers can begin studies of culture with a period of participant observation. William F. Whyte (1955), a researcher who lived in a working-class Italian community for 3 years as part of his study, described the advice his chief conversational partner, Doc, gave him on how to cross the cultural boundary:

> Go easy with that "who," "what," "why," "when," "where" stuff, Bill. You ask those questions, and people will clam up on you. If people accept you, you can just hang around, and you'll learn the answers in the long run without even having to ask the questions. (p. 303)

You usually cannot find out everything you want to know without asking some questions, but you can manage to ask questions in ways that don't overwhelm people. Asking someone to explain his or her culture is like saying, "Tell me everything you know about your life," an intimidating prospect to the hardiest of souls. Go slow. Schedule repeated interviews; don't try to cover everything at once. Take the time to become known among those whom you are studying as someone worthy to be taught and patient enough to learn.

Periods of participant observation help the researcher become familiar with the setting and vocabulary. Some of the culture is learned through observation—who gets the best or worst seats at a ceremony, for instance. Also while observing, researchers may be pulled aside by future interviewees who at that moment want to teach the stranger what is happening (Emerson, 1988). An anthropologist in a small village may be invited to a religious ceremony, an organizational researcher to a staff meeting, or an educational evaluator to a class in which a new methodology is being used.

Through participant observation, you can often learn enough to convince people that you understand what they do and are really not so much an outsider after all. John Van Maanen (1978) describes the police view of outsiders as "assholes" or "know-nothings," that is, people who simply cannot understand their world, so there is no point in even trying to explain. To overcome this barrier, Van Maanen went through police academy; then he was no longer an outsider to the officers he wanted to study.

Another way of showing that you are not a know-nothing is to learn the language of those you want to study. As Whyte (1955) explained, "My effort to learn the language probably did more to establish the sincerity of my interest in the people than anything I could have told them of myself and my work. How could a researcher be planning to 'criticize our people' if he went to the lengths of learning the language?" (p. 296).

Language is not simply a foreign tongue, like French or Italian, but the special cultural vocabulary that allows the researcher to frame meaningful questions. Mastering such language demonstrates to those in the arena that the researcher is not so ignorant that he or she is uneducable. When our colleague Jim began to study hackers, he lacked the technical knowledge to ask meaningful questions. By reading computer journals and bulletin boards, Jim picked up a lot of the argot before attempting interviews. Before interviewing planners and budgeters, Herb and Irene became familiar with their specialized vocabulary by attending numerous city government meetings and reading books written for these technocrats.

Sharing a language is a powerful way of crossing the boundary between insiders and outsiders. Learning the language suggests a willingness to enter into the world of the interviewees and accept their norms and values. It is an effort taken, a goodwill gesture. The phrase, "You speak my language," is a metaphor for being inside.

Defining the Scope of the Study

Without some idea of the boundary of a study, a cultural interviewer might try to understand everything and learn very little in depth and detail. As the work begins, cultural interviewers decide in a rough fashion how broad or narrow the scope of the study is to be. With this decision in mind, researchers are better able to determine what is to be asked and of whom. As they learn more, they focus the study more narrowly to explore key themes, concepts, and ideas.

Studies with the broadest scope portray central themes in a whole society. For example, in *Habits of the Heart,* Bellah, Madsen, Sullivan, Swidler, and Tipton (1985) sketch the core themes of contemporary U.S. culture. The authors questioned people throughout the country from many walks of life on a limited number of core themes. Other holistic, cultural studies focus on arenas smaller than a whole society, such as a particular community, a retirement home, an academic department, a classroom, or an ethnic neighborhood. Some of these studies concentrate on social groups that share a common behavior, ranging from people with purple spiky hair to police officers to cocktail waitresses. What holistic studies share is an effort to learn the norms and values that are central to shaping behavior in a cultural arena (Hamabata, 1986; Liebow, 1993; Terkel, 1992).

Holistic studies ask what norms and values give definition to a cultural arena; cultural studies narrower in scope ask how norms and values affect particular behaviors of concern to others. Researchers of *organizational culture* try to learn what it is in the shared culture of people who work together that explains a perplexing problem or behavior, such as an inability to invent and market new products, or excessive time and energy spent on interdepartmental quarreling (Friedman, 1989; Kleinman, 1983; Schein, 1985; Yanow, 1992).

In a *social problem* study, the purpose of the interviewing is to learn why a problem occurs or how the victims of the problem view the difficulties they face. The researcher interviews homeless people, residents of a nursing home, or the chronically unemployed. The homeless people might describe the dangers of illness and theft in public shelters; the nursing home residents might discuss impersonal treatment and excessive regimentation; participants in a job-training program might elaborate on the set of misunderstandings that prevented them from graduating and getting good jobs. Social problem interviews help people proposing solutions understand problems from the point of view of those who are experiencing them (Gagne, 1992; Kasinitz, 1988; Miller, 1987; Siegel, Levine, Brooks, & Kern, 1989; Snow & Anderson, 1993; Weeks & Berman, 1985; Wharton, 1987; Williams, 1992).

In *life histories,* the researcher examines how people experience and understand life stages—schooling, marriage, first job, sexual encounters, retirement, frailty. Such reports can be compared within and across particular groups. You can contrast the life histories of men with those of women, or those of rich people with those of poor people, to understand how gender or wealth affect what people experience. To learn about the importance of different values, researchers compare life histories of those with different religious beliefs or those from different ethnic backgrounds (Faupel & Klockars, 1987; Ochberg, 1988; Walker, 1990).

With *oral histories,* the interviewers look into the values and norms that operated in the past. What rules were followed in a law office in 1950? What social constraints were faced by a rural schoolmarm in the early 1930s? Oral histories of culture examine how people responded to disruptions in the social or political environment. You might want to know how women adapted as they shifted from the role of breadwinner during World War II to the role of stay-at-home mother after the war. Or you might want to get an insider view of changing political institutions. What was it like to be a civil rights activist in the 1960s? What did it feel like to be a member of a political machine when the values that political machines embodied were in decline (Braungart & Braungart, 1991; Lewin, 1990; Rakove, 1979; Vellela, 1988; Wiggington, 1992; Youth of the Rural Organizing and Cultural Center, 1991)?

Cultural interviews are also a way of exploring particular *careers,* the sets of steps or stages people go through. The goal is to discover how norms and values change as a person passes through different stages of a career. To interview students to learn about their career in school, you

might examine the influence of dorm mates or fellow sorority or fraternity members in changing students' values. Or you could look at the
impact of classes or paid work. Some well-known studies of careers
have examined how interns take on the values of doctors as they go
through their training (Becker, Geer, Hughes, & Strauss, 1961; Fisher,
1987; Karp, 1985).

The scope of the questioning depends to some extent on the type of
study you intend. Holistic cultural studies often cover a large range of
behaviors, norms, and values and focus on the overlap or conflict
between them. Narrower studies concentrate on values and norms reflected in a particular historical period or event, in a stage in a career,
or in the cultural beliefs that affect a specific social or organizational
problem that others want to understand.

You begin the questioning to match the boundaries of the study you
have chosen. But the scope of the questioning can shrink or expand as
you learn from the interviews what concepts, values, beliefs, or norms
you need to comprehend. In settling on a boundary for a study, you make
some trade-offs between breadth and depth. In a broader study, you can
look at more norms and values and how they interact; in a more focused
study, you can go into more depth on a smaller number of norms and
values that explain a given problem.

In general, set the boundaries of a cultural interview with a light hand.
Allow the scope to expand if it becomes clear during the study that you
have not broken off a piece that makes sense by itself or if you have
narrowed the research in a way that does not match the perceptions of
your interviewees. Let your interviewees introduce whatever seems
important to them and later decide what to follow up on. That way you
will not miss important cultural premises, but you can still keep the
study within practical boundaries.

Talking About Culture

To begin an interview by asking about cultural rules can be overwhelming and incomprehensible. Instead, elicit illustrative stories, narratives, and examples and infer the taken-for-granted rules from what
you have heard. Only later in a study do you go back and seek to confirm
with some of your interviewees your tentative understanding of the
rules.

If you begin questioning in a study of conflict in a bureaucratic organization by asking what are the norms here for dealing with conflict, you will leave interviewees puzzled. Rather you begin the questioning by asking, "Have you ever really disagreed with your boss?" You probe for examples of conflicts from different people within the organization and from these examples try to figure out the cultural rules. Then you can ask follow-up questions about these rules to see how they work and when they apply.

For example, if you find out that it is forbidden to argue with someone in a public setting, you might want to find out why—what would happen if people did argue in public. Is it the appearance of harmony that must be preserved? Does the privacy of the conflict allow the participants to start again in a more friendly manner, where a more public stance would have to be defended and maintained? Or does open conflict carry with it the idea of blame for failure to solve the problem harmoniously?

Cultural premises are learned gradually. First you find out what people have experienced and how they understand those experiences, and then later you explore what the underlying premises mean. When we were interviewing in Thailand, many interviewees described the discomfort they felt when approaching higher-ranking officials, so we started asking for situations in which people interacted with those above them in the hierarchy. Our conversational partners repeatedly explained that they felt both awe and motivation or willpower in the presence of their bureaucratic superiors. We interpreted will and awe as core cultural concepts explaining the norms and values of hierarchical relations, and set out in subsequent interviews to explore these concepts in depth (H. J. Rubin, 1973).

Another way to explore a cultural setting is to elicit descriptions of *cultural icons,* that is, depictions of a person, event, myth, saying, or physical artifact that represents a core value, norm, theme, or expectation. A religious saint and a football star are cultural icons, as are specific model years of the Harley-Davidson motorcycle in certain subcultures. An icon can be a physical artifact that evokes cultural values, such as a flag or a wooden cross. Volkswagen Beetles became an icon representing practicality and durability, as opposed to status or elegance. Sometimes icons represent undesirable behavior, such as a small business owner who was treated as an icon of foolishness for a failure to set up a method of checking for theft by employees.

A cultural icon can also be a pithy saying, a statement that summarizes to those in a cultural arena the essence of what their world and environment is all about. In the 1960s in a drug-using hippy subculture, core values were expressed in the iconic statement "tune in, turn on, drop out," suggesting that young people should forget the rat race of competitive society and find contentment through drugs.

Iconic statements are clues to underlying values. Herb was puzzled about how community development workers could maintain their motivation when they faced such enormous community problems. Two iconic statements helped him understand. One interviewee was describing a home built for low-income people that was torched and reflected:

> You're really not engaged in affordable housing if you don't have an arson every now and then. I mean that's like the reality of what's going on in urban neighborhoods. It increasingly is out of your control and so all you can do is work.

In another interview Herb heard the community developer reflect:

> Our biggest success has been that we have been able to change people's attitude about themselves. We don't have enough money or [have] been unable to get enough money. Our biggest measure of success is how have we empowered people so they can take control. You have gotten these folks to make changes in their own community.

These poignant statements encouraged Herb to review his notes, where he found many other similar examples. He had tumbled onto a couple of cultural themes, first, that you have to keep working even if you cannot control the outcomes, and second, helping a small number of people learn to solve their own problems is a considerable achievement that does not necessarily cost much. From such iconic statements, Herb learned how his interviewees adapted to their circumstances and avoided despair.

To get a little deeper into the culture you can explore the coherence or tension between core premises. Among political liberals, free speech is a core value, but so is the protection of the weak, so what happens when free speech degrades those who are vulnerable? Community developers want to help the poor by building homes as inexpensively as possible, yet they need to make enough of a profit to keep their organizations alive. To understand these cultural tensions, you ask for examples of situations in which values seem to conflict, such as when development organizations decide to take a loss in building a home to make the house more affordable to the poor.

CULTURAL INTERVIEWING:
MAIN QUESTIONS, PROBES, AND FOLLOW-UPS

Cultural interviewers are only minimally concerned with covering a set of preplanned main questions. Rather, the purpose of main questions is to encourage people to describe their lives, providing narratives, stories, and examples that the researcher can analyze and follow up on. Often one general main question is sufficient to encourage interviewees to provide such overall descriptions. The researcher draws out shades of meaning in the stories and makes inferences about the rules and themes based on the examples. The next step is to check out these inferences. The bulk of the work is done with follow-ups and probes. In the remainder of this chapter, we describe the purposes and wording of main questions, probes, and follow-ups in cultural interviews.

Main Questions in Cultural Interviewing

Main questions in cultural interviews get people talking about their lives, experiences, or understandings. They specify the arena of concern without limiting the discussion to particular themes or concepts. In oral histories, the opening main question often mentions the time periods you are interested in or crucial symbolic events you want to learn about. For example, "Tell me what it was like to be black in the South before the civil rights movement." In a study of a retirement home, a main question might be, "What did you do yesterday?" An interview to learn about a career in college might begin with, "How does life here at NIU compare to high school?" Each of these main questions specifies an arena but lets the interviewee choose what is important to talk about.

Where do main questions come from? Sometimes they come from events that you are observing along with your conversational partners. Suppose you're studying regional culture in England and have joined people at a cricket match. After a while you look perplexed. "What is going on?" you ask. Your conversational partner explains what is happening on the field. You can watch meetings, ceremonies, and other events, and later on, as the main question, ask your conversational partners to explain what you saw.

In his recent study, Herb attended a luncheon meeting of a coalition of community developers, during which a shouting match occurred between two developers, who were arguing about grant money. Later, Herb interviewed people who had been at this meeting and told them he didn't understand what had happened. Telling them he was puzzled served as a main question. The interviewees took over, described the background of the dispute, and explained what core cultural values were under contention.

Sometimes you can take a tour and use places on the tour to suggest main questions. You may get an excellent and vivid description of the work life of a stripper by accompanying her to the strip joint and listening to her describe what takes place on stage, backstage, in the dressing rooms, and in the parking lot. Each location serves as a main question, "What happens here?" As you listen, you hear data on how strippers manage privacy and safety.

Herb's most memorable tour involved a day on the back of a motorcycle driven by an agricultural extension officer on unpaved lanes in rural Thailand. The tour ended when the motorcycle fell into a stream. Watching the official all day and sharing the hardship of getting to remote locations suggested to Herb questions about the culture of isolation. How do these officials deal with being so far from their clients? How do they deal with the lack of basic resources to carry out the job? Physical tours suggest questions you might want to ask, especially about the activities that interviewees do and see as part of their everyday life and whose importance might not be apparent to them.

When periods of observations are not feasible, you can ask people to provide you with a *verbal grand tour* (Spradley, 1979, pp. 86 ff). Grand tour questions request interviewees to describe an ordinary day or week, or explain how some routine events take place. For instance, for interviews of college students, a grand tour question might be, "Could you tell me about the important things that happen during the school year?" Another way to word grand tour questions is to say, "Tell me about being a prisoner" or "Teach me (or teach me what I would have to know) about being an NIU student." You can bound the grand tour by time (day, week, month, intervals between seeing a doctor) or you can ask about the specific steps or stages in some cultural activity (what happens during a wedding ceremony). An oral history interview could begin with the question, "Could you tell me about your experiences with Dr. King during the civil rights movement?" In a study of organizational culture, the broad-scope main question might be, "What was life like in the housing project before the new director arrived?"

Assuming you have chosen knowledgeable interviewees, these grand tour questions should elicit examples, narratives, and stories. Then you analyze these interviews and glean from them a preliminary sense of cultural themes and vocabulary. These themes suggest what you follow up on in later interviews.

Suppose you are interviewing an Orthodox Jewish woman, who in response to a grand tour question has described what the religious service is like from the women's point of view. She explains that the women sit together behind a screen overlooking the men who are praying together on the main floor. Her answer suggests several cultural themes that you can follow up on in later discussions, including the dominance of men in the religion, the segregation of men and women, and how relationships are formed among the women.

Grand tour questions obtain broad overviews. Sometimes your interests are narrower and you want to restrict the scope of the main question without at the same time limiting what themes or concepts the person describes. You might want to know only what goes on in a classroom, but you don't want to limit the discussion to only academic matters. Or you might want to ask a somewhat narrower main question if you think a really broad one will intimidate your interviewee.

You can narrow down your main question to something more manageable by asking, "Would you tell me about [ ]?" or "Teach me about [ ]," or "Could you walk me through a [ ]?" In each of these questions the [ ] specifies the narrower arena of concern. For example, to learn about the culture of teachers, you might begin with, "Teach me about [how you prepare for classes]," or "Describe to me [a typical class]." You are not specifying what about the classroom is of interest to you (answers might range from teaching tactics to the instructor having fantasies about what to do when the class is over), but you have narrowed the topic to exclude, for instance, events in which the teachers socialize with their colleagues.

You must know enough about the culture to fill in the blank with words that evoke broad cultural understandings, yet at the same time restrict what is said to a narrower arena. You can often figure out what you need to know through observation. Suppose you are interested in the culture of people who work to restore deteriorated communities. In a walk around the neighborhood, you notice a new home in a burned out area. You can frame your main question in terms of this new home. "Teach me about building a home, like the one across the street." In Southeast Asia, we observed large number of young men wearing orange robes and walking up and down the streets in the morning begging bowlfuls of rice. As our main question, we asked people, "Please teach us about the young men in orange with their alms bowls." The subject is focused by the question, but the interviewee is not limited in what he or she can tell you. Some conversational partners told us that the monks begging their food represented Buddhist values; others talked about the status that is conferred by being a monk even for a short period of time.

From observing meetings, Herb heard that community developers who had attended an intensive training period at a place called the Development Training Institute (DTI) seemed to be treated with respect. He located people who had attended the institute, and asked, "Could you walk me through what happened [as you got your training at DTI]?" Such "walk me through" questions encourage conversational partners to discuss matters chronologically with an emphasis on the culturally routine.

Sometimes in talking about a complicated cultural arena, you observe cultural happenings and then ask the tour questions about each stage or crucial event along the way. In learning about weddings, you might ask questions about the bridal supper, the rehearsal, and the ceremony itself; in a study of a career in school, the narrower questions could cover classes, dorm life, social life, or athletic activities.

Although a number of different wordings of main questions are possible and appropriate, some phrasings do not work well and should be avoided. For instance, try *not* to start a cultural interview by requesting an opinion, such as, "How do you like school?" or "Is this a good place to work?" It is tempting to ask your conversational partners for an opinion, as they will probably give you one, but it may not be a thoughtful opinion or a well-balanced one, and the interviewees, feeling the need to appear consistent, may edit from future answers anything that might contradict what they originally said.

If you ask professors if they like teaching (an opinion question), they may describe some recent frustration. They might say, "Students complain constantly about the amount of work and blame the instructor for poor grades." Their answers later in the interview are more likely to be negative to support this initial negative opinion. If you had asked instead for a description of a typical day, you would probably have elicited a more balanced view. The professor might have told you how much he or she enjoyed a good class discussion and how nice it was to chat with students about their work after class. The negative would still be there—the typical day might include a cheating incident—but so would the positive.

Unfortunately, the subject matter might be such that strong opinions are bound to be expressed whether you ask for them or not. If you are tracing a dispute or doing a program evaluation, grand tour questions quickly elicit strong initial opinions that limit whatever else the interviewees might tell you. If you know that strong opinions are going to be expressed, then you should intentionally go for balance by asking for both good and bad things. Your first main question might be, "Tell me some of the good things [or most interesting things] about school." Later, you would ask about some of the bad things. These more focused questions are not as good as the less structured tour questions, because they restrict the scope of what the interviewee can tell you, but they work when people hold strong opinions that they insist on telling you, where tour questions are not usually successful.

Grand tour questions may be too broad, evoking descriptions of a life beyond your concern, whereas the more focused "Tell me about," "Teach me," or "Walk me through" questions might prematurely restrict the discussion to parts of the culture you most readily understand. Too broad is usually better than too narrow until you are familiar enough with the culture to make appropriate decisions about how to narrow the focus. Once you have heard a number of answers to a broader main question, you should be able to narrow the focus without prematurely limiting the range of answers.

Another problem occurs when an interviewee talks for a long time on such a wide variety of subjects that the interviewer feels overwhelmed with the amount of cultural lore. The temptation for the interviewer is to interrupt and try to focus in on some narrower topic. You can focus in later in the interviews, but in the first round of interviewing, you really need to listen to wide-ranging answers and make very few interruptions. If someone goes wildly off the track, discussing baseball when the topic is a religious ritual, you may want to bring him or her back. But generally, it is better in early interviews not to restrict what the interviewee says, because you want to hear a variety of cultural themes and terms in context.

In the initial interviews in Herb's community development project, his conversational partners talked at great length on two distinct themes. One theme dealt with the community developers' problems with bankers and funders; the other theme concerned difficulties the developers had in working with the poor. Herb was tempted to pick one theme and follow it, because he was feeling overwhelmed with the double focus. Instead, he kept on listening and finally understood by hearing data that a core cultural value of the community developers was in spanning the gap between the rich and poor. If he had prematurely focused on one theme or the other, he would have missed how his interviewees saw the relationship between the two themes.

The basic principles of iterative design apply here, namely, that when you begin, you cast your net widely and only gradually narrow down your options as you get more material and understand better what you have.

Probing in Cultural Interviews

A probe can be a brief comment or gesture that the interviewer makes while listening to the answers to keep the conversation going; to encourage the interviewee to continue on the present line of discussion; or to elaborate on a particular incident, case, or example. Probes show that the interviewer is interested and attentive while encouraging the interviewee to provide depth and detail. These functions of probes occur in both cultural and topical interviews and have already been described in Chapter 7.

A second purpose of a probe is to explore the precise meaning of a particular point, concept, or theme that has just been mentioned, to clarify the immediate communication, but in ways that do not distract from the interviewee's narrative or story.

A probe should be brief and presented in a way that allows a quick return to the interviewee's main thrust. Suppose you are losing what the narrative means because you don't understand the term *superchief.* You probe by asking, "Superchief?" When you get the answer, you quickly return to where you were. "That is helpful, thanks. Before I asked about the superchiefs, you were talking about how the decision to expand was made . . . "

Learning when not to probe is almost as important as learning when to probe. First, try not to interrupt when your conversational partners are engaged in telling stories that highlight crucial values or guiding themes. A story may be intensely emotional and have its own, often rehearsed, set of points that are meant to be presented as a whole. Normally, the drama and emotion of a story are clues not to interrupt.

Suppose you were exploring altruism among people who regularly give to charity. To explain why she gave to charity, one interviewee responds with a story. "When I was 22, an old girlfriend who had gone to college out of town moved back. She had always been sickly. She had been back a couple of months, and I had not been to visit her. Then I heard that she had been sick, had been hospitalized, and died." There are many items on which you might want to probe—on the meaning of being sickly, how it feels when a person is out of contact. But you are hearing a cultural story about how someone deals with a terrible guilt. Interrupting such a story with a request for clarification might be interpreted as a lack of respect.

You can sometimes probe without distracting from the interviewee's presentation by asking for a clarifying example after your conversational partner has completed a story or narrative. You would not do this with the story of the sick friend who died, because one hopes something like that happens only once in a lifetime, but with less dramatic narratives or stories, you can sometimes ask for another instance "in which something like that happened." Unlike follow-ups in which you have already drawn the lessons on what the concept or premise means, you use example probes when you feel that you are hearing something important but are not quite sure what it is. You want more examples for later analysis.

After hearing Thai conversational partners talk about their bosses skipping appointments and leaving them in the lurch, we asked for further examples. We mistakenly thought we were probing on bureaucratic snafus. What we got were illustrations of other ways the junior bureaucrats were humiliated, for instance, by being required to act like servants to their bosses. The missed appointment itself wasn't all that important, but it was a cultural symbol of being one-down in a hierarchical society.

Follow-Up Questions in Cultural Interviewing

Although you might do some follow-ups immediately during a cultural interview, it is more common to analyze your first-round interviews and choose the themes and concepts you want to examine in depth before you begin the follow-up questioning. The techniques of following up on themes are a bit different from the techniques for following up on concepts.

Following Up on Cultural Themes. Main questions open up a wide territory; the follow-ups zoom in on particular regions. Based on their interests and the purpose of the research, interviewers pursue a few themes, intentionally excluding others that are less relevant. How do you recognize a theme that needs to be followed up on?

Sometimes, themes just jump out at you because they are repeated both within and between interviews. In Herb's community development project, his interviewees kept telling him, "If we did not do the work no one would," and argued, "We are building communities not houses." In the Thai project, bureaucratic subordinates again and again reported that they were "in awe of the power of those higher up the bureaucracy" but were "dependent on their superiors to give them motivation to attempt difficult tasks." If the interviewees refer to a theme over and over, it probably should be followed up on.

Sometimes when you look at a cluster of interviews together you hear two themes that seem to be in tension with each other, suggesting that you should follow up on both to understand stresses between cultural values. In Herb's first round of interviews, some community developers emphasized the culture of "being a nonprofit business, but a business none the less," whereas others stressed "democratic involvement of community members" in running the projects. The differences in these themes were suggestive of a conflict in the culture, so Herb paid particularly close attention to examples that discussed how making a profit might limit democratic involvement.

Many follow-up questions delve into the taken-for-granted aspects of the culture. But how do you recognize such taken-for-granted items? One way is to look for differences between your own understandings and those of your conversational partners, for instance, when the conversational partners describe outcomes or behaviors as if they were obvious, but to you they are anything but. These situations are red flags indicating what should be followed up on.

Marsha Balshem (1991) was interviewing people about cancer, but what the interviewees were saying made no sense according to her understanding of medical knowledge. She decided to follow up by asking them how they understood medical advice and how they could ignore medical research. They answered that medical research was about others and they were different. Several evoked a cultural icon, the "defiant ancestor":

> The defiant ancestor, a golden age figure of the grandparental or parental generation, was often invoked by community residents during informal discussions . . . and recognized eagerly by others when I myself introduced it. Respondents stated proudly that they themselves had many of the attributes of these ancestors. The defiant ancestor, so goes the story, smoked two packs of cigarettes a day, ate nothing but lard and bread, never went to the doctor, and lived to the age of 93. (Balshem, 1991, p. 162)

By pursuing what the interviewees took for granted, Balshem discovered a cultural icon, or symbol, that explained beliefs about both health and defiance.

Icons, when you hear them, almost always suggest follow-ups. Icons may become apparent through repetition or through the larger-than-life role the icon plays in a narrative. If the name of Dr. Martin Luther King keeps coming up in the interviews, whether the topic is the civil rights movement, or discrimination, or leadership, or selflessness, you infer that you are dealing with an icon, someone who has taken on mythical proportions. Even relatively narrow cultural arenas may have icons. For instance, in computer hacker cultures some people have become heroes by breaking into supposedly secure computers.

Once you have identified an icon, you prepare follow-up questions to find out what the icon means, to help you unravel and understand the culture. In the situation in which Martin Luther King was the icon, you have to figure out what he stands for. Does he represent racial pride? Defiance? Religious belief? Does he represent the goal of full social integration or black achievement and success? In the computer hacker case, you would need to explore why an illegal act like breaking into a computer is admired. Is it the challenge of getting past a barrier and the sense of successful competition to be first that makes a hero? Is it the cleverness or persistence required to break in that is admired? Or is it the defiance that makes a hero?

Icons need not be people or abstract symbols. Specific events can take on iconic values if accounts of them are often repeated and widely understood in a cultural arena. The first time gays in New York City fought back against police harassment, at a gay gathering place called Stonewall, became an iconic event in gay culture. In Herb's and Irene's college years, Sproul Hall became an icon symbolizing the willingness of students to protest.

You can recognize iconic events if they crop up repeatedly in the interviews and each time appear to make a similar point. Herb frequently heard his interviewees discuss a particular successful development project, Irene kept hearing about an easily understandable budget, and our colleague Jim heard about a prisoner who acted as his own attorney and got out of jail. These events did occur: An amazing project provided jobs for the poor; a city changed its budget format so that everyone could understand it; and a prisoner who defended himself was released from prison. But the conversational partners who are telling you these stories are often at a distance from the original event—they are drawing on these examples to make a cultural point. The stories have been repeated so many times that they become a shorthand to suggest a more complicated cultural theme. You follow up to find out what the shorthand stands for.

For instance, a large number of community developers described the same remarkably successful community project. Herb questioned on this iconic project and heard a consistent story, a piece of cultural lore. The story praised the project and the success of the group that had pulled it off, but also mentioned that the community group working on that project was the favorite of the foundations. That group was funded, but others, equally deserving, were not. The story emphasized the cultural importance of clever programs for helping the poor, but it also underscored the theme that the community groups do not succeed all on their own merits. The community developers had created an icon that rationalized their own failures.

Something does not become a cultural icon unless it is needed by the group to help adapt to situations that they routinely confront. Martin Luther King became an icon because blacks facing discrimination needed a symbol of black worth and success; hackers facing federal prosecution make heroes of people who evade detection or successfully defy prosecution. Community developers who face tremendous odds against success develop symbols and stories that help defend them from feelings of defeat and help maintain their sense of possibility. Unraveling the meaning of icons is almost always a core task of the follow-up questions because icons reflect so much of the culture.

Icons, if you can find them, are obvious invitations to follow up. Another obvious invitation to follow up is an example of extremely counternormative behavior. Like icons, counternormative behavior tends to reveal great swatches of the culture once you understand it. In one of Herb's interviews, a community developer presented a narrative that concluded with her telling a banker to "fuck himself." Herb knew how counternormative this behavior was and encouraged her to discuss the event in great detail. Her narrative taught Herb the cultural rules of when it was acceptable to confront the banks.

Recognizing when to follow up takes a lot more skill than wording the follow-up. Any number of wordings of a follow-up will usually do. There are, however, some standard patterns that researchers often follow, and especially when you first begin interviewing, it can be relaxing to have some of these common phrasings at hand. For example, as a follow-up, you mention the issue of concern and ask the interviewee to explain. "I'm interested in how people were chosen for the rewards at that ceremony—could you tell me how the choice was made?"

Another family of follow-up questions are called *minitours* (Spradley, 1979, pp. 88 ff) and worded very much like the grand tour questions, asking for a general description of what happens over time. In addition, though, minitours specify an event, situation, or choice that the researcher has concluded focuses in on core cultural values. For example, you ask a main question to a nursing staff, "What happens on this hospital ward on a typical night?" The answers suggest disagreements about what should be done when a patient requests a painkiller. You can follow up with a minitour question and ask, "What happens when a patient asks for painkillers?" You've made the inference that the decision whether to use a painkiller reflects core cultural values and you want to hear descriptions about how this choice is made.

Another type of follow-up focuses more explicitly on the theme. You ask for illustrations of the theme that the interviewees mentioned frequently in earlier interviews. For instance, in many separate interviews with community developers, Herb heard people brag about how they leveraged a grant, so as a follow-up Herb asked, "Could you give me an example of *how you leveraged* a grant?" In studies in a retirement community, you could request the interviewee to tell you "about a time a when you *just felt sad* about the passing years."

Another phrasing of a follow-up is to ask, "How typical is [ ]?" where the blank is a description of incidents or events that you suspect illustrate core cultural themes. For example, in answering the main questions, many community developers described complicated government rules for removing asbestos; others wondered why requesting a grant from a government agency was so cumbersome. From these responses, Herb inferred the developers shared a cultural belief that "nonprofits are harassed by government officials." As a follow-up question to examine his understanding, Herb asked, "You've mentioned the asbestos problem—is that typical of the way government treats the nonprofits?" The follow-up question was grounded in a particular example, but through using words like "typical" Herb encouraged his conversational partners to draw out a rule or cultural premise.

Another way to follow up on a suspected cultural rule is to ask what happens if this rule is violated. For instance, Herb asked his Thai conversational partners what would happen to someone who did not show proper respect to bureaucratic authority. When Herb suspected a rule of the community developers was to defer to the whims of funders, he asked them to provide examples of what happened when they had a fight with granting agencies or bankers.

Another form of follow-up occurs when you discover several cultural values that seem to be in contention with one another. For example, suppose in interviewing students that you hear "it is important to socialize and make friends," but also learn that another cultural value proclaims "the need to get a good education for a future career." Students may accept both premises at some level so that each can be independently explored through examples, minitours (a night out on the town), and icons (the student who studies all the time). Then you follow up with questions that let you see how the tension between these values is resolved.

One way of exploring the tension is look for the circumstances under which one rather than the other value is evoked and try to ascertain why. Suppose in illustrating the "importance of socializing," the student describes an incident in which he or she skipped studying. You first follow up for richness by asking for another similar incident. Then you ask for an opposite incident, that is, one in which the person studied hard. You repeat this questioning pattern among a number of conversational partners and then from the descriptions try to infer the conditions that lead to partying and those that encourage studying.

The types of follow-ups we have presented assume you have some comprehension of the cultural theme. Other follow-ups test whether you really understand the theme by verifying what you thought you heard, asking for clarifications, or exploring fronts.

With a verification follow-up, you ask if you have understood a cultural theme correctly. Our experience is that when people answer yes, they provide further and more precise examples, and when they disagree, they make a point of providing you with their evidence. Herb thought that a core cultural belief among those in the economic development field was that "their successes depended on factors over which they had no control." Herb asked his conversational partners if he had gotten it right. They agreed that he had and provided him with many further examples of situations for which they were responsible, but over which they had no control (H. J. Rubin, 1988a).

Sometimes you need to clarify a cultural premise, because your understanding of the premise has gotten tangled up in the complexity of real-life details. Herb thought he was hearing community developers explain that the reason they taught people how to become home owners was that ownership was empowering. Yet, every time his interviewees gave him an example, so many other details about the particular client were included that the underlying premise was obscured. So Herb asked his conversational partners to walk him through how they would help a hypothetical client become a home owner. The conversational partners told him the steps in teaching people to become home owners. Without the confusing details of real examples, the theme came through more clearly. Herb would have preferred hearing a real case with a clear cultural premise rather than eliciting a hypothetical example, but that was not an option.

When the interviewees are giving you "front" rather than direct answers, you may want to follow up to help you figure out the underlying themes. Fronts are the images of themselves that interviewees think that the public and other group members expect from them. Gang members may exaggerate their violent exploits or their bravery; police may exaggerate their toughness; accountants may overdo their trustworthiness and reliability.

In cultural interviews, fronts are not falsehoods needing to be discredited; you don't need to find out whether the police officer is truly that tough. Rather, you try to find out why those in the cultural arena feel that being tough is so important, for instance, by asking the police officer for examples of what happened when someone appeared weak. Or you look for the variety of ways that group members try to get the front across. For example, how do accountants convey trustworthiness?

Following Up on Concepts. We have described how to follow up on themes but have not yet done so for the cultural concepts, the building blocks on which cultural themes are based. You have to understand what the concept "community" means before you can figure out what community developers are all about; you need to interpret the concept of "going along to get along" to understand why workers in large organizations seem to do things they know are wrong. Many times, you follow up on a concept by asking for examples in which the word or phrase is used and then inferring from these examples what the concept means.

In follow-up questions on concepts, we seldom ask, "What does [ ] mean?" Such a direct question assumes that the conversational partners know enough about the interviewer's culture to translate their concepts into meanings the interviewer will understand. The conversational partners may *think* they can define the term in ways you can understand and provide a mistranslation instead (Spradley, 1979, pp. 19-21).

To follow up on concepts, the simplest approach is to look quizzical when you hear a concept you want explained. If your puzzled look is not sufficient, then ask the interviewee for examples or associated ideas rather than definitions of the concept itself. Balshem (1991) used this type of follow-up to excellent effect in the following excerpt:

Balshem: When I say *cancer* what does it make you think of?

Answer: Oh, God, I have this terrible thought of cancer—it's like this great big thing that's eating up the whole insides. This big black thing. I just think of it as black. This big black thing that just goes along like a pacman gobbling up your insides. . . . The movie *The Blob,* remember the blob would eat up stuff and kept getting bigger and bigger. Well, that's kind of how I think of cancer. The great big blob of stuff that keeps increasing. (p. 158)

Another way to follow up on concepts is to ask interviewees to illustrate the differences between similar, but not identical concepts. In our Thai study, people used three similar words expressing linked cultural concepts—fear, awe, and a third word that seemed to combine fear and awe. To understand these related concepts, we asked our conversational partners to provide incidents that illustrated each of these terms. From these incidents we inferred the distinctive meanings of the terms.

Another common way of clarifying concepts is by asking someone to provide you with the *characteristics* that are part of the concept. For example, in David Hummon's (1986) work on the culture of community, he wanted to explore cultural reactions to cities of different sizes, so he asked a series of questions like, "Suppose you had a relative who never lived in a *small town* and who was about to move to a *small town.* If he or she wrote you and asked what *small towns* are like in general what would you respond?" (p. 189).

About 25 years ago, in a very influential book called *The Ethnographic Interview,* James Spradley (1979) worked out specific questioning patterns for examining cultural concepts. When used as part of a broader approach to cultural interviewing, the Spradley questions are first rate in eliciting how conversational partners use terms.

One of Spradley's (1979) questions for learning about concepts is, "How would you refer to [the common word or phrase for the term]" (p. 89). For instance, in our recent discussions in a graduated care retirement and nursing facility, we asked people living there how they referred to the building containing the assisted living and nursing care facilities. Their term, "the big house," described the size of the building while obscuring what it represented, namely, continuing decline into helplessness. The fact that the name obscured the function was loaded with cultural freight and suggested a widespread coping mechanism. To make this insight richer, we continued the follow-ups by asking, "What do you think of when I say 'the big house'?"

Spradley (1979) also suggests *verification* questions for finding out if you have understood a term (pp. 126-131). For example, in interviewing community developers, you could ask, "Is talking to people at city hall a form of *advocacy?*" You know developers talk to people at city hall, and you want to check to see if the interviewees would accept the concept "advocacy" to describe what they did.

You may want to learn what a cultural term includes. Spradley (1979) calls this follow-up a *coverage* question. When Herb was trying to figure out what the term *intermediary* meant, he asked, "Is the MacArthur Foundation an *intermediary?*" The answer was no. Then he asked, "Is the Local Initiatives Support Foundation an *intermediary?*" The answer was yes. Then Herb asked whether the City Housing Partnership was an *intermediary*. Some responded yes, some no. By comparing characteristics of the organizations that were, were not, and were maybe intermediaries, Herb figured out what this term meant to his interviewees.

Once boundaries are set around the meaning of a term, Spradley (1979) suggests follow-ups to distinguish between similar terms (pp. 160-172). If you suspect there are differences between two cultural terms, you can ask your conversational partner to agree or disagree. Or you can ask interviewees to describe the difference between two related terms. For instance, Stephen Groce (1989) studied copy and original performance musicians and asked them to describe the differences between "musical artists" and "entertainers" (p. 397).

Another way of getting a more refined set of meanings is to request the interviewee to describe when else he or she would use the term he or she just described. For example, the researcher might say, "You've described *partnering* on the school project. Which of your other projects involve partnering?" Then the researcher could explore what partnering meant in each of these other examples.

To summarize, there are many ways of following up on themes and concepts. In each, you need to make sure the follow-up questions match or flow logically from the interviewees' answers. You need to keep the flow conversational, and you need to get good, rich, and detailed information. Any pattern of follow-up questions that achieves these goals is fine, whether you invent the pattern yourself or imitate what others have done.

CULTURAL UNDERSTANDING
IN TOPICAL INTERVIEWS

In the next chapter, we describe questioning patterns in topical interviews. In some fact-finding topical interviews, the researcher pays little attention to cultural concepts. But understanding what the interviewees are saying during open-ended topical interviews might require knowledge of cultural concepts. If your conversational partner mentions a puzzling term or makes an assumption that you simply cannot interpret, you sometimes have to conduct a mini-cultural interview within the topical interview.

In an ideal world, with endless time to go back to people, you would create a list of cultural concepts and premises that you did not understand and begin a series of cultural interviews. But in doing a topical study, you often do not get a chance to reinterview and diverting the interview to discuss a cultural concept might tax the conversational partner's patience. As a result, you learn to do brief probes on puzzling cultural concepts and premises during a topical interview.

For single words or concepts that are not understood, looking quizzical or repeating the term in a questioning tone often works. The interviewee will explain the concept, sometimes provide an example, and then return to the main flow of the discussion.

For instance, when Herb was doing topical interviews on techniques of building homes or stores in poor neighborhoods, interviewees explained that they were empowering community members. Herb did not understand what empowerment had to do with building a shopping mall or funding housing for low-income people, so he looked befuddled and mumbled the word *empowerment* in a questioning tone. The interviewee explained: "If you have created in the community people with a stake in the community who feel they can shout out now because they are 'ratepayers' in that traditional conservative, American sense, you've moved toward empowerment." Once Herb understood this cultural term, he returned to the topical interview.

Sometimes what you are hearing seems predicated on a cultural assumption that is so puzzling that it has to be explored then and there. Irene had been interviewing a budget official about a technical change, when the budget officer began describing how he reorganized all the programs at city hall to fit the type of budgeting the city had adopted. Knowing that budget offices typically do not have any role in designing reorganizations, Irene immediately asked, "Wait a minute, how could you do that from the budget office?" She risked distracting the interviewee, but without understanding this cultural assumption within the organization, she could not understand how the budget innovation had been implemented.

To conclude, cultural interviews are about learning how people see, understand, and interpret their world. In cultural interviews, the researcher spends most of the time listening to what people say rather than posing detailed and focused questions. Most of the thinking about what to follow up on is done between rather than during the interviews.

By contrast, topical interviews are focused on subjects that the interviewer has chosen, involve more active questioning and rapid exchanges, and are more concerned with matters of fact and less concerned with eliciting shades of meaning than cultural interviews are. Most of the follow-ups are done within rather than between the interviews.

9

Topical Interviewing

*T*opical studies explore what, when, how, and why something happened. An educational administrator might do topical interviews to find out how teachers are responding to a new curriculum. An oral historian might interview topically to find out what happened when the United States rounded up Japanese Americans during World War II. Policy analysts rely on topical interviews to explore what is wrong with welfare programs, why immigration policy is so ineffective, and how health care can be improved.

Often, the goal of topical interviewing is to piece together from different people a coherent narrative that explains puzzling outcomes, for instance, why a dispute occurred or how a controversial decision got made. Irene, in a topical study, examined how a city-manager city—with an emphasis on good management—developed budget deficits; Herb explored how community groups were able to build homes and stores in devastated neighborhoods (H. J. Rubin, 1993, 1994; I. S. Rubin, 1982).

Factual content matters in topical interviews. The researcher checks out details, tries to resolve contradictions, and ascertains how interviewees know what they claim to know. Because those who contribute to the narrative may provide contrasting versions of what occurred, the researcher has to design questions in a way to allow different renditions of the same events to be compared and woven together.

SPECIAL FEATURES OF TOPICAL INTERVIEWS

Researchers more actively guide the questioning in topical interviews than in cultural ones. Prior to the interview, the researcher prepares a set of specific questions based on background research. During the interview, the researcher guides the discussion to keep on target and obtain answers to these questions. The purpose is to avoid omitting a crucial step in a process or a critical event in a decision, lest the resulting narrative be misleading.

Being Prepared

Preparing good questions for topical interviews requires considerable background work, including reading documents or academic studies, undertaking more loosely structured preliminary interviews, and watching events unfold. Extensive background information helps you formulate questions that elicit specific, detailed information. The knowledge that you show in your questioning makes it less likely that interviewees will present idealized or normative accounts, because they recognize that you are prepared.

The background work helps you figure out what questions to ask to cover the entire topic and who has the information that you need. Suppose you are studying how the 1994 crime bill was passed. Your background research should tell you what the major steps were in passage of this legislation, including the gathering of interest group support, the formulation of different proposals, and the winnowing and combining of proposals. These key steps shape the main questions that form the skeleton of the interview.

Such background work is necessary to structure the main questions. What you learn in advance also provides a base to help you formulate meaningful follow-up questions. For instance, in one of Irene's interviews, she asked how a new budget format was working. The interviewee responded that the new format was successful, using as evidence the fact that the budget contained performance measures. Irene knew from her preparation in reading the budget that the budget did not report how close the departments came to meeting the performance measures, but only listed a series of goals. Her interviewee seemed to be claiming more success than the document justified. So she followed up by asking why the performance reports were not published in the budget, where they were published, and how they were used. These follow-ups showed she was informed and elicited richer, more detailed responses than did the initial questions.

Another advantage of background work is learning which interviewees are most likely to know the material you need to find out. If you determine in advance what your interviewees should know, you can tell the interviewees that you want to talk to them because they are knowledgeable in this area. This lets the interviewees know that they have been chosen for a legitimate reason and helps build their confidence that they can comfortably answer the questions you are going to ask.

Your informed questions signal the interviewees that you have done your homework, made an effort, and have not just come to pick their brain. You have gone as far as you can go with the available material and now you need some help. The interviewees are less likely to talk in generalizations or begin with basic background if they can see that you are generally informed about the arena. If you only have a limited time with an interviewee, this ability to signal quickly the appropriate level of depth is important.

For example, in a study of budgeting in Boston, Irene wanted to learn about the financial relationship between the state and the city. She first read about two Massachusetts laws, called the Tregor amendments, that spoke to the ongoing financial relationship between the state and the city. She began a key interview with a main question about the Tregor amendments. The interviewee knew immediately that Irene was informed and answered the question in detail. If Irene had asked for an overall discussion of city-state financial relationships, she would have heard a time-consuming explanation about how the state controlled local finances, which she already knew.

When the interviewer is clearly informed about an issue, the interviewee is less likely to distort information, lest he or she get caught and look foolish. For instance, funders of community development work claim in public statements that the community organizations decide the types of project the funders support. Having done background work on who initiated the ideas for specific projects, Herb knew that the public claim wasn't always true, so in interviews with the funders, he brought up incidents in which the funder set the agenda and did not listen to the community groups. The interviewees explained their reasoning in the particular cases Herb mentioned, and in subsequent answers were more likely to describe how they, rather than the community groups, set the agenda for funded projects. One way of sounding informed is to learn the technical vocabulary of the field. To make questions precise and to understand the answers, words like "tax credit," "affordable housing," "rescission," "plat," "leveraging," or "tax expenditure" have to become part of your vocabulary before you interview community developers, budgeters, or planners. Where do you get such background information? You can pick up vocabulary and learn about events from documents and preliminary interviews with people other than your primary interviewees. Or if possible, become familiar with the background through participant observation. Get a grasp of the topical arena by reading secondary materials such as newspaper accounts, newsletters, court depositions, audits, and consulting reports. Academic literature, legislative updates, and archival materials such as minutes from meetings, resumes, and correspondence describe specific topical arenas, introduce you to the vocabulary, and suggest issues of importance.

You can often find published books and articles that describe the history of a program or the general procedures that are followed in passing a law. Academic literature can also suggest more conceptual issues that you might want to investigate. For example, books on formal organizations talk about the importance of "hierarchy and efficiency"; the literature on community organizations discusses the need for "democracy and participation." The contrast between the two literatures suggests a main question to community developers: "You seem to have lots of community members on your board."—"Yes."—"Well, how do you get things done with so many local bosses?" This question focuses on how organizational efficiency conflicts with community participation.

Before interviewing, we spend many hours reading government regulations and records of hearings, which provide some of the background we need. Herb studied the history of a land-use dispute from files on zoning cases, newspaper reports of acrimonious meetings, and minutes of city council meetings (H. J. Rubin, 1988b). In Irene's study of cutbacks in federal agencies, she read court depositions that contained background detail on agency personnel ceilings because laid-off employees contested their firings in court (I. S. Rubin, 1985).

Sometimes, though, there is little trustworthy written material available. When Herb wanted to know how community groups build homes for the poor, the published documents provided little information about how the projects were carried out. To learn enough to formulate detailed questions, Herb had to do some preliminary interviewing.

He first located people whom newspaper accounts described as informed about the low-income housing field and set up appointments with them. He asked them to help orient him to the field by describing what they and others do. In these preliminary interviews, Herb listened to descriptions of projects but rarely interrupted. His goal was to learn the vocabulary and discover the broader issues in the field. On the basis of this information, he made up his more focused main questions.

Adapting to Time Pressure

One reason topical interviewers prepare so carefully is that some information is available only from one or two specific individuals who might have limited time for an interview and be unwilling to schedule a second conversation. To economize on time, try not to ask these particular interviewees for information that you could get from other people who are under less time pressure or are more willing to talk at length. Figure out the specific information needed from these crucial interviewees and formulate main questions accordingly. In wording questions, communicate early in the interview that you are knowledgeable so that little time is wasted in providing you with background details. Adjust the order of the questions so that if your conversational partner can only answer one or two of the main questions before being called away, you will learn the core information that you are seeking.

You won't have time to build up the interviewees' feeling of competence by first asking a few relatively easy to answer questions. Instead, you have to indicate briefly in ways that the interviewee recognizes that you know that he or she has the experience and knowledge to answer these questions. For example, in a time-constrained interview in Boston, Irene began by telling her informant that she was studying how cities' budgeting changed over the past 20 years and that she had noticed that her interviewee was responsible for introducing a new budgeting system in 1986. By wording the introduction in this way, Irene affirmed the interviewee's competence to answer what she asked.

Care also has to be taken to word sensitive questions delicately and to avoid sensitive topics that are not key to what you need to know. With time constraints, you may not have time to recover from a gaffe, and there may not be enough trust established to smooth over the problem. When in doubt about the sensitivity of a topic, word questions cautiously and indirectly. The interviewee might misunderstand what you want to know, but an indirect approach can sidestep unnecessary antagonisms. For example, rather than ask about a rivalry between two organizations—an issue that may be sensitive—you can ask about the relationship between the two organizations. Or you can word the question indirectly, asking, "Do the planners work with the people in public works?" rather than, "Please describe the fight between the planning agency and the public works department."

Follow-up questions are hard to formulate in these one-shot, time-limited interviews. In some studies, you talk with many people, have time to reflect, then later return and ask follow-up questions. But with one-shot interviews, you don't have the luxury of a time-out. You have to catch openings for a follow-up, formulate a question, and deploy it right on the spot. As you practice interviewing and your hearing skills improve, you develop an ability to come up with good follow-up questions on your feet, but it takes experience.

You cannot prepare follow-ups in advance for answers that you have not yet heard. But you can practice and get ready, so the follow-ups will come more easily. One way is to sensitize yourself by reviewing the interviews you have already done, looking for the places you wish you had followed up, but didn't. You will be more likely to notice those invitations to follow up in future interviews, and some of the themes you did not follow up on may crop up again, giving you a second chance.

In looking over his earlier interviews, Herb noticed how few strings one foundation attached to the grants it gave. Herb wished he had asked why the foundation worked in this unusual way. Later, Herb was interviewing a foundation official, who to Herb's surprise, described how grants were given out, a topic usually not discussed with outsiders. Herb took the opportunity to ask the foundation official how he convinced his board of directors to provide funds with few strings attached.

General background reading comes in handy, too, in thinking on your feet. For instance, Herb had an inkling that one community group had been involved in a financial scandal. So before the interview with the director of the group, Herb read records at city hall on the special provisions attached by city officials to grants to the controversial group. The scandal was too sensitive for Herb to introduce, but when the interviewee raised the subject, Herb was able to follow up with precise questions.

STRUCTURING THE INTERVIEWS:
MAIN QUESTIONS, PROBES, AND FOLLOW-UPS

In topical interviewing, main questions, probes, and follow-ups take on a different emphasis and balance than in cultural interviews. Whereas a cultural interview might be structured around one main question and a long series of follow-ups, a topical interview is more likely to start out with a handful of preplanned main questions that together cover the overall subject. Each of the main questions may stimulate a few probes and follow-up questions, a tree-and-branch model, rather than the cascading stream of follow-ups common in cultural interviews.

This more fixed questioning structure provides the interviewer with a sense of how much time to spend on each portion of the topic. Without this balance between main questions, it is easy to learn a lot about one part of the problem and little or nothing about other related concerns. Learning how a housing project is funded but finding out little or nothing about the clientele or the community response paints an incomplete picture of the efforts to build affordable housing.

The purpose of probes in topical interviewing is similar to that in cultural interviews: to make conversational repairs; to acknowledge that you have understood an answer; and to encourage the interviewee to keep going and to give long, complete, and detailed answers. But in topical interviewing, interviewers are more likely to probe for evidence and sequences of events and less likely to seek multiple examples. In addition, guidance probes, to keep the interviewee on the topic, are more common in topical interviews, reflecting the need to get particular pieces of information in a reasonably limited period of time.

Just as in cultural interviews, follow-up questions in topical interviews seek deeper and more thoughtful answers. But in topical interviews, follow-ups also help to complete a narrative, determine the facts of the matter, resolve apparent contradictions, and get past oversimplifications and formal or normative responses.

Main Questions

Main questions structure the discussion by breaking the subject into specific answerable parts. Main questions are prepared in advance after the researcher has studied available background material or conducted preliminary interviews. Although the main questions structure the interview, you don't have to follow them rigidly. You can modify main questions based on what you learn during the interview.

Preliminary Interviews. If rich background material is not available and participant observation is not possible, researchers try to learn enough to formulate focused main questions by conducting preliminary, less structured, interviews. For these interviews, the researcher seeks out people who are knowledgeable about the topic and are in positions that suggest they are willing to share what they know. People in the field who have received favorable press, or those whose job it is to talk with outsiders, such as coalition heads, staff directors for trade associations or interest groups, scholars who have studied the field, and even public relations officers, can provide a starting place.

The main questions in these preliminary interviews should elicit an overview of the topical arena. For example, you can ask for a step-by-step description of what occurred or how a problem arose. In Herb's preliminary interviews with community developers, he told them he wanted to learn "how you put together a project." In early interviews in evaluation work, you can ask, "What happened here?" or "Overall, what has been your experience with this project or program?"

Sometimes in a preliminary interview, a variant of the "teach me" or "walk me through" question described in the last chapter is appropriate. For instance, "Could you walk me through how you *packaged* a commercial development project" or "Could you tell me what happened to your agency after the *rescission* occurred?" The answers teach the interviewer about the stages of a project or the history of an event. Also, the interviewer learns the technical terms necessary for wording the main questions later.

After conducting several preliminary interviews with community developers, Herb compared what the interviewees said and worked out the core stages in accomplishing projects—getting community support, finding funding, organizing construction—as well as where stresses occurred—working with foundations that were too bossy or finding asbestos in a building being torn down. Then he created main questions to explore these stages and problems.

In conducting these preliminary interviews, the researchers typically do very little follow up, though they may probe a little for clarity and completeness. Following up on individual answers might be tempting, but in the preliminary interviews the purpose is to get the overall picture without omitting important stages or parts.

Focused Main Questions. The core of the topical interview is a set of linked, focused questions that were stimulated by the observations, documents, or preliminary interviews. If you ask more main questions, you will have less time to get depth on each one, so you try to cover the topic with a minimum of main questions. You word these questions broadly enough to encourage the interviewees to express their thinking and knowledge, but narrowly enough to provide you with the specific data that you seek.

Main questions should be worded for the interviewee to easily understand how one relates to another and how each question speaks to an overall topic. If you are interviewing about the causes of municipal financial problems and the first main question is, "What was the role of the unions?" and the second question is, "What was the role of the city council?" the interviewees should understand that you will go down a list of possible actors and plan their answers accordingly.

When reconstructing a history or a political or administrative process, you can use documents and preliminary interviews to create a chronology of events. You can then use your main questions to ask for details on each of these events—who did what, when, and with what intent. However, you may not want to ask each question to each participant, because individuals may not have been involved in every event. You change the wording or focus of the main questions to match what you know about a particular interviewee's role in the activities.

For instance, through interviews Herb reconstructed how open space on the former Danada Farm near suburban Wheaton, Illinois, was transformed into dense housing and malls (H. J. Rubin, 1988b). Before phrasing his main questions, Herb figured out from observations and documents what the key events were in the transformation of the farm-land and then customized the questions for the relevant actors. In the chart below, we've placed the main questions asked to each of the major actors to show both the overlap and differences between the interviews:

Illustrative Focused Main Questions for
Three Actors Involved in the Land Use Dispute

Questions for City Officials	*Questions for Environmental Opposition*	*Questions for County Officials*
Could you trace the annexations that expanded Wheaton until it reached the Danada Farm?		
	Could you tell me how the different environmental organizations (Sierra Club, Prairie Project, the Morton Arboretum) got together to fight more development?	
		Could you trace the history of the open space plan in the county that included the Danada Farm as parkland?
I've heard that the county tried to negotiate an open space and development plan with Wheaton—could you tell me what happened?		I've heard that the county tried to negotiate an open space and development plan with Wheaton—could you tell me what happened?
What happened in the negotiations between the city of Wheaton and the owners of the Danada Farm to rezone it for development when it was annexed to Wheaton?		What happened in the negotiations between the Forest Preserve District and the owners of the Danada Farm to purchase it for open space?

Questions for City Officials	Questions for Environmental Opposition	Questions for County Officials
	Did the Forest Preserve District leak technical information to help the environmentalists in their fight with Wheaton?	Did the Forest Preserve District leak technical information to help the environmentalists in their fight with Wheaton?
I've heard that the zoning hearing on the Danada Farm in August was quite an event—could you tell me what happened that evening?	I've heard that the zoning hearing on the Danada Farm in August was quite an event—could you tell me what happened that evening?	I've heard that the zoning hearing on the Danada Farm in August was quite an event—could you tell me what happened that evening?

You can divide up the topic into main questions in any way that makes sense to the interviewees. You can ask about stages in a process, contributing causes to an outcome, the roles of different actors, or parts of a concept. For example, one of Irene's students was studying how politicians determined if a legislative proposal was feasible. She concluded from preliminary interviews that feasibility had two parts—technical feasibility, that is, whether the proposed program would accomplish its goals at reasonable cost, and political feasibility, whether the proposal had sufficient support from key people. Her main questions were structured around these two aspects of feasibility.

A slightly different logic is used to come up with main questions when the purpose is to evaluate a program or project. From your background work, you build a list of what worked well in the program and a second list of changes that seemed to fail. The list should emphasize program features that could be adopted elsewhere. The main questions are then structured around these lists.

Suppose you were evaluating a job-training program intended to lead people directly to employment, and you found in your background research that an obstacle in the program that was otherwise working was the high cost per person actually employed. Your main questions then would focus on the reasons for the high cost. For instance, if the cost per person employed was due to a high dropout rate, the main questions might be about the difficulties clients had in completing the training.

Your main questions change to match what each interviewee should know. They also change during the study as you learn more.

In Irene's study of Southside, the city-manager city that was running illegal deficits, her main questions traced events mentioned in newspapers and budget documents on deficit financing. She prepared questions such as, "The newspaper said the budget director left that year—what happened? Why did he leave?" Or "The budget was balanced to the penny that year. In my experience, real numbers don't balance to the penny. What happened that year?" Her main questions also asked about the effects on the budget of urban riots, labor strikes, and economic development projects (I. S. Rubin, 1982).

During the early interviewing, she learned about other events that had not been mentioned in the documents or her preliminary interviews. Her informants told her that during the course of the fiscal problems, the city council had reduced the tax rate and at the same time increased public services. Such information spoke to her major research issue, so she added a main question on the effects of tax reduction. In addition, in many interviews people mentioned that the politics in the city council contributed to the deficit. She redesigned her main questions to add another set of questions exploring the roles of different institutional actors, including the mayor, the city manager, the council, the budget officer, and lobby groups such as the chamber of commerce and the downtown banks.

From her preliminary work and redesign she developed a matrix of questions. For each time period, she had a set of crucial events that she felt influenced the deficit, as well as a list of people who were involved. To complete the narrative, Irene asked what each actor was doing during each of the crucial events—when the deficits began, when the city cut back taxes, when the union went out on strike, and when the council voted for a huge economic development project.

She prepared a separate interview for each conversational partner by picking main questions from the matrix that the particular person would be knowledgeable about. She asked the city manager, assistant manager, and firefighters' union representatives about the firefighters' strike and its implications for the deficits. She talked to the council members who were most informed about fiscal affairs and the bureaucratic staff responsible for finances about the increases in spending and the cuts in property taxes. She questioned the city manager about how the council reacted to the legal mandate from the state that required a balanced budget.

In this way, she asked only a handful of main questions to each interviewee and only those questions for which each interviewee had firsthand knowledge. When she combined the answers across all the interviews, she could fill in the events in the matrix to create a narrative explaining the role of each main actor across time.

Probes

Probes encourage the interviewee to expand on the matter at hand, complete an example or narrative, or explain a statement that the interviewer did not understand. For these purposes, the techniques of probing are similar in topical and cultural interviews. You nod at the right moment, say "uh-huh" to encourage interviewees to continue, repeat specific words and then pause for clarification, or use posture to indicate interest and attention.

In addition, certain other types of probes are common in topical interviews. You can use steering probes to return the discussion to the main concerns if the interviewee wanders off. You can probe for specific facts. And you can probe for the information that links the pieces of a narrative, especially those obtained from different interviewees.

Steering probes keep the interview on target by restricting the questioning to those issues that are of most interest. In trying to understand the mechanics of how homes are built in poor communities, Herb probes on costs and the details of construction but doesn't probe on what empowerment means. Interviewees catch on and elaborate on the technical and financial aspects of their building projects.

Sometimes you and the interviewee may get sidetracked into related, but not central, topics. If you feel this is happening, you might want to gently guide the interview back on topic with a steering probe. One common steering probe is to say, "Sorry, I distracted you with that question, you were talking about [ ]" and fill in the blank with the topic just before you both got distracted. A completion probe also gets the discussion back on topic, for example, "Before you started to talk about the cost of warships, you were telling me about the Armed Services Committee . . . " In a discussion about a controversy in the Whittier neighborhood in Minneapolis, Minnesota, the interviewee started providing details on similar fights in other neighborhoods. Herb listened for a while and then interjected, "Sorry, I distracted you with asking about the tensions in the Farview neighborhood. Let's circle back a bit and explore what the tensions were in the fight over the park in Whittier."

Other probes elicit factual detail while the interviewee is presenting a longer narrative. When did an event occur, who was involved, what changed, how much did it cost, what materials were used, what did the instructor talk about, what did she actually say to you? Don't interrupt a narrative to get such details unless you really need them, but responses to such probes can clarify a narrative, help sort out sequences of events, and suggest causes.

In Irene's study of fiscal stress, interviewees suggested a variety of plausible explanations for why the city was running a deficit. Those in management, for instance, blamed the unions, whose obstinacy created a controversial contract settlement. To examine management's interpretation, Irene used *sequence probes* to reconstruct the order of events— when the budget first showed a deficit, when meetings were held, when bargains were reached or contracts renegotiated (I. S. Rubin, 1982). She found that the fiscal stress had started well before the union settlement. From her sequence probes, she concluded that the fiscal stress caused the union militancy rather than the union militancy causing the fiscal stress. When the city manager found that the budget was starting to slide into the red, he tried to weaken the union by breaking off supervisory personnel, declaring them managers and hence ineligible for union status. The labor force fought back by insisting on wage increases and union status for first-line supervisors.

Sometimes you can word a sequence probe directly, "When did that happen?" But people's memories can fail on details, so don't push for a specific date if the interviewee hesitates. Instead, probe for other events that occurred around the same time, events that the interviewees or you can date. After getting three different answers from three interviewees as to when a budget innovation began, Irene finally got one interviewee to remember that the innovation occurred just after he was hired, and of course, he remembered the date that happened.

Sequence probes help you put a narrative together by putting events in order; other probes can help you link together different versions of the same event. Suppose you need to reconstruct what happened at the city council meeting on the 18th of the month. When asked what happened, labor leaders for the city workers remember that their proposal for a pension fund got short shrift, the mayor recalls the obtrusiveness of the television reporters, and city council members recollect a controversial zoning case. But by slowly probing on the details—who spoke first, what was said, where people were seated, whether people came and went or stayed, whether flip charts were shown—your interviewees can reconstruct events and flesh out what happened at the meeting.

If you ask about the flip chart to help people reconstruct the meeting, no one will have any reason to distort the answer. But on the substance of events, there may be considerable differences between versions, so you may need to know how heavily to weigh each response. You probe to learn the basis from which interviewees are speaking. What firsthand experience have they had? What is the evidence for what they say? What bias, if any, are they speaking from? We call the questions that elicit this information *experience*, *evidence*, and *slant probes*.

From experience probes, you learn what the interviewee knows firsthand, and you usually give more weight to information provided by an eyewitness than to indirect reports. In an interview of staff members for Mended Hearts, a self-help group for those recovering from heart surgery, you might probe for experience by saying, "It is my understanding that everyone in the group has undergone open heart surgery. Does that apply to the staff as well as the members?" Or in an interview on cutbacks in government, you could ask, "I know your office was involved in designing the reductions in force—did you personally have anything to do with it?" You can also ask questions like, "Were you at the meeting when he said that?"

People sometimes generalize when they answer questions, but unless they provide specific evidence to back it up, you should not put too much weight on the inferences they have made. To find out if your interviewees have evidence behind their generalizations, you can probe by asking for an example. "You said many of your clients come from multiproblem families—could you give me an example?"

Asking for an example is usually fairly straightforward and doesn't get uncomfortable unless the interviewee cannot provide any examples. But if you are going to probe for evidence other than examples, you have to do it delicately, because it is considered offensive to directly ask people to prove what they say. After hearing a generalization, you can ask, "What occurred that made you think that?" For instance, a professor says, "Students are less well prepared than they used to be when they come to college." You can say, "Do you have some specific instances in mind or are you speaking in general?" If someone tells you something that sounds incredible, you can laugh and say, "You must be joking, that is too wild to be true." That politely invites further evidence or a denial, "No, it's true, I saw it with my own eyes" or "Well, I exaggerated a little for effect." Another approach to asking for evidence is to ask the interviewee exactly what someone said. If a conversational partner tells you, "She told me to start looking for another job," you could ask, "What were her words, do you remember?" or "What did she say, exactly?"

Our experience is that we use evidence probes less often as the interview continues. Many interviewees volunteer how they know something or start to do so after we probe a time or two. One of Irene's interviewees prefaced an answer to a main question with "I don't know what happened from 1970 to 1973, but from 1974 on the city was in fiscal stress. I talked to a lot of people, and that is what they told me." If you ask for evidence once or twice, most interviewees catch on and will tell you from then on how they know.

To piece together a narrative, you interpret what the conversational partners say and the examples they give in light of the slant or bias they display. If interviewees feel badly about something or if an agency has been criticized, the conversational partners might avoiding discussing the topic. Or if they are angry, they may slant the information so that the person or agency they are angry at looks bad. Keep in mind that everyone has a slant. Your role as interviewer is not to judge the interviewees as truthful or not, but rather through the probes to figure out how their slant affects what it is they emphasize.

Probing for slant requires caution. You don't want to sound as if you were charging the interviewees with something immoral. Before you ask anything, see if you can determine slants in the answers already provided. If interviewees present strong opinions without grounding them in experience, you should be suspicious that the answer may be biased. You should also suspect bias if you are given a one-sided presentation, where only weaknesses or only good points are mentioned. It is not hard to pick out the bias from the following passage.

Well, I try not to be hostile toward John but [clears throat] I think he has
a fairly negative attitude towards the neighborhood groups so therefore I
feel that it is my right to respond in kind. Don't you think so? . . . The
people in the state agencies had the same kind of attitudinal problems as
John, which is they didn't know their asses from a hole in the ground when
it came to development.

Herb was cautious in accepting as fact any comments this person made
about John or John's agency.

If slants are more subtle, you may have to probe for them. You can
ask, "How did you feel about [the topic being discussed]?" or "Did [the
event/the person] make you angry?" Sometimes the interviewee will
make a strong statement indicative of an underlying slant or bias—
"They hope that black folk will fail"—and pause for your response. A
quizzical look or a quick "Really?" or "Is that so?" usually will encourage the person to continue and explain or justify their slant. A more
explicit slant probe in this case could be, "Are you saying that downtown *really* wants black folk to fail?" If the answer is still yes, then the
interviewee's attitude toward downtown should probably be considered
slanted—not necessarily wrong, just marked by a strong opinion.

Follow-Up Questions

The basic purposes of follow-up questions are to get richer, more
in-depth answers; to explore newly discovered avenues; and to test and
modify emerging themes. Just as in cultural interviews, follow-ups in
topical interviews ask for details and examples and explore unusual
premises. We have described in previous chapters how to design this
kind of follow up.

In topical interviews, follow-up questions serve other purposes, too.
Through follow-ups, you find missing details to complete a narrative.
Some follow-up questions look for the information necessary to combine different versions of what people say into a single narrative. These
follow-up questions explore the slants of the interviewees or clarify
contradictions in what people said, so that the researcher can decide how
to weigh, assess, and interpret the different perspectives offered by
interviewees.

Filling in Narrative Blanks. Missing pieces of a narrative, steps in an event or a process that are not discussed, or unconfirmed facts stimulate follow-ups. How you word these follow ups differs depending on whether you are following up during one interview or are pursuing in a later discussion what you heard from the person at an earlier time. When you are going over your interview notes and begin to sketch out a possible narrative, you may discover some gaping holes. If you can, you go back to your interviewees to find information to fill these holes. You might find that no one talked about the years after 1980; or that you have no information on the origins of the first 5-year plan; or that although you heard students talk about a curriculum change, you never asked faculty members what occurred. When you go back to interviewees you already interviewed, you can refer to a topic they mentioned earlier and ask them to bring you forward in time—or backward, if what you are missing is an earlier period. For example:

> The last time we chatted, you mentioned the Josephine Housing Project. I found what you said quite interesting because this project shows how community groups have to balance pressure from funders with community social needs. What's happened on Josephine, since we last met?

By framing the question in this way you can fill in blanks of a broader narrative (the history of the Josephine Housing Project) and at the same time go for more depth on the theme that you specified in the follow-up (balancing pressures from funders with community social needs). Or you can ask the interviewee how a particular crisis he or she discussed last time was resolved.

In a single interview, by listening carefully you may be able to detect missing steps or skipped parts of answers that can be followed up on. You word questions by directly asking for the topic to be completed: "After the program started, what happened next?" "Who was on each side of the fight?" "You described the early part of your marriage and the trauma of the divorce, but what occurred right before the papers were filed?" "The department changed the curriculum—how did the students react?"

In wording such follow-ups, you sketch what it is the interviewee has already said in a phrase or two, perhaps by repeating key words or events they've mentioned, such as "after the program started." Then you ask for the missing information, such as, "What happened then?" "Who else was involved?" or "What came next?"

Figuring Out Slant. If brief probes are not sufficient to determine slant, you can use follow-up questions to help you figure out how to put together many interviewees' partial and possibly biased versions of events to form a narrative. Through follow-ups, the researcher tries to understand the experiential or ideological slants people bring to the interviews. Once these slants are understood, it becomes easier to combine what different people say.

With slant follow-ups, the interviewer tries to find out what perspectives people hold in general, rather than exploring the truth of a particular answer. One approach to presenting a slant question is to ask interviewees why they think something happened. "What did the funder gain by yelling at those delivering the service?" or "Why was the state pressing for the death penalty in this case but not in the other?" What you hear in the answers to such questions are opinions, or slants, because there is no way the interviewee can actually know why other people acted the way they did.

You might wonder what slant an interviewee holds towards a funder after you learn that her organization did not receive a grant. You can ask:

Q: How come the Alden Street Association got the money, while the Roberts Lane Development group did not?

A: The funder gives the $50,000 to those organizations that build projects its way, not the community's way.

This answer suggests that the interviewee feels this funder has its own agenda and runs roughshod over the projects the community groups formulate. If you hear several similar answers from the follow-ups, you conclude that the interviewee is cynical toward funders. You now have learned how to interpret her answers to other questions that treat the relationship between funders and community groups. If this interviewee were to tell you that a particular project suggested by a funder was a terrible idea and failed, you might have to give her opinion less weight compared to those of other conversational partners who were less angry.

Another follow-up for slant or underlying values is a *devil's advocate challenge.* A devil's advocate is a person whose job it is to strongly attack ideas to force the presenter to clarify the underlying values. The challenge is not supposed to be seen as personal, just as a way of evoking a discussion. Still, this approach works best if both you and the conversational partner feel comfortable with one another.

After hearing a value-laden statement, you can say, "Let me play devil's advocate for a minute. You argued [repeat the core of what you heard], but someone could conclude just the opposite." The questioning is worded by putting in the brackets either the example or conclusion given by the interviewee, and then drawing a different conclusion and asking how he or she reacts. In one recent interview, an African American community activist kept claiming that it was because of racism that his organization did not receive support from the city. Herb asked permission to play the devil's advocate and then asked, "Are you sure it is race? This neighborhood is quite poor. Maybe it's social class?" The conversational partner acknowledged Herb's argument and then offered further (and to Herb quite convincing) evidence why he felt the motivations were racial.

When you find evidence of slant, it doesn't necessarily mean that you discard the information from the interview; rather, slant guides how you combine different answers when putting together the narrative. For example, people in different positions have an opportunity to see separate parts of a process and come to conclusions based on what they see. Knowing that people see the same events from their own separate angles, you are better able to combine their accounts.

You don't have to pick one point of view and discard the others. You might conclude that builders see a fight over land development in terms of decisions on what types of homes are needed, but planners interpret the conflict as an effort to preserve trees and open space and prevent suburban congestion by stopping further construction. One isn't right and the other wrong; you need both perspectives to see the whole.

Following Up on Contradictions. Sometimes the interviewee's answers contain contradictory implications. Are both implications true, but under different circumstances? Was one response a superficial attempt at an answer and the later response more thought out in depth?

Is there some reasonable explanation why what appears contradictory really isn't? You can follow up to find out.

When Irene asked an interviewee about problems that had occurred because of overly rapid implementation of a budget reform, the person seemed to contradict himself. At one time he stated that substantial improvement was occurring, yet later he claimed that the status quo would "pretty much always be like this." Which did he mean—that improvement would continue or that it would not continue? Later in the interview, Irene followed up by specifically asking how particular government departments would comply with the budget reforms. The interviewee responded:

> Some try to conform, some have linked [the budget process] with personnel evaluation. . . . Some tried to create an operating plan and tried to guarantee it; others pay no attention, they think of it as a punishment. It will be that way, mixed attitudes. There is a correlation between their ability to manage and their attention to the budget. The unsuccessful departments are often not good at budgeting.

By following up, Irene learned that the interviewee really felt that compliance would remain spotty and problematic. The original comment on substantial improvement referred to the first 2 years the program was being implemented, but the improvement had run its course, and the quality of management was not changeable over the long run.

Sometimes what you follow up on are contradictions between your broader understanding of a situation and the immediate responses that you hear. For example, if a nurse tells you that it is hospital policy to undermedicate cancer victims for pain because of the fear of drug addiction, there seems to be a contradiction. Why would the hospital fear drug addiction in a cancer patient, especially one who may be terminally ill? The nurse did not contradict himself, but the hospital policy seems anomalous. By asking follow-up questions on how or why such policies emerge, you can explore how those in the setting handle the dissonances they face.

Sometimes contradictions occur in how people explain the same events. There may be no need to follow up if you understand why people differ in their interpretations. Labor says the offer of the wage was too low and management says it was too high, but both agree on the amount.

There is no need to follow up on the events, although you might want to explore what each considers to be the right amount.

Sometimes, though, when you learn about a splendid and detailed explanation for what happened, and then another interviewee tells you that the event never took place or provides a totally different narrative of what occurred, you need to figure out what is going on. Why are the answers so different? You should word such follow-ups gently, so as not to directly contradict an interviewee. For example, after hearing a rendition of a fight, you could say, "I heard that story a little differently," and then tell the version you heard. The interviewee will usually bend over backward to give you the evidence for his or her interpretation.

With such follow-ups the goal is to learn what was said or occurred and to separate these actual events from how they are interpreted. In his first round of interviewing Herb learned about a controversial meeting but did not know enough to follow up. The funder summarized the meeting as an occasion where information was exchanged, whereas those in the community groups indicated that they had been bullied.

In his follow-ups, rather than allow people to summarize their impressions of what the meeting meant, Herb asked them in detail what was said, when, and by whom. Both sides described the same discussion in very similar words and told Herb about a chart that described a future agenda that had been placed on the wall. Their descriptions of what was on that chart were very similar. The funder claimed that this agenda was meant to stimulate thought on how the movement should proceed. Those in the community groups claimed the purpose of the chart was it was to tell them what to do. By separating out the facts of the matter from the interpretation, Herb was able to understand and to some extent resolve the apparent contradiction.

Sometimes the different perspectives are fundamentally unreconcilable, based on different access to the evidence or conflicting sets of interests. In Herb's study of a land use conflict, environmentalists charged real estate representatives on the city council with corruption; the real estate brokers argued they had to support growth in order to keep taxes down. Unless you discover actual bribes, there is no way to reconcile these views, because each speaks to underlying motivations rather than events that took place. From these two different versions, you can figure out that the environmentalists don't trust the realtors, but you cannot figure out if the realtors are or are not corrupt.

Even though you probably will not resolve the corruption issue, you can still follow up on the conflicting versions. You can try to get more detail about what each of the contending individuals thinks actually happened. You can try to find out their definitions of the matter at hand, in this case, what corruption entails. And you can use some slant probes to find out if environmentalists always think the city council is corrupt. You can also check the facts of the matter, to find out if growth actually does keep taxes low.

You are likely to get opposing versions of events when the people you are talking to are themselves involved in a conflict. Sometimes interviewees are reluctant to talk about conflicts, so you may have to follow up obliquely. You can show a little indirect knowledge on the topic, asking the question in a tentative way, "I've sort of heard how sometimes uh, uh, some groups sort of push their [pause] agendas in trying to get funds. [long pause, searching for words]" This approach is often more effective than a head-on version, such as, "Can you tell me about conflicts you have had with other community groups over funding?"

Sometimes, a conflictual topic can be explored by referring to a small part, rather than the overall dispute. When Herb was trying to explore the conflict between community groups and funders over agenda setting, he was getting nowhere until he decided to ask about a particular policy document that represented one part of the conflict. The interviewees answered this narrower question and then went on to discuss the wider dispute.

GETTING HONEST AND OPEN INFORMATION

You adjust what you hear in a topical interview to accommodate for bias or slant, but you usually assume that people are basically telling you the truth. Yet, especially in the shorter topical interviews, you may not have time to develop a relationship so that you can trust everything that is said, especially on sensitive issues. Every once in a while, an interviewee may seriously distort the truth. More likely, interviewees will give you a party line, or a normative statement, or an evasive answer rather than a boldfaced lie (Lee, 1993).

Approaching Sensitive Issues

Sometimes your instincts tell you to back away from asking about sensitive issues, but your need for the information requires that you follow up. With established, ongoing interview relationships, we can usually ask what we need to know without risking a lie or a termination of the interview. In more ephemeral relationships, we try to ask sensitive questions in ways that avoid directly threatening the interviewee to reduce the chance that he or she will lie.

One approach is to summarize what you think you have learned, but somewhat misstate some of the details of the situation. That way, you show a little knowledge, so that conversational partners don't feel that they are "washing dirty linen," that is, gossiping and telling negative stories to a stranger. When they discover your misunderstanding, interviewees generally try to correct your mistake by providing their version of the events:

Herb: If I remember correctly, when [organization name] got into trouble, [the national funder] was brought in by the City.

Interviewee: Well, no [the national funder] caused the trouble.

Herb: Oh?

Interviewee: That's what caused the trouble for [the organization]. When [the national funder] came in and they were going to do this project and [name] was trying to figure out every way in the world . . . to destroy everything because he didn't want . . . he basically doesn't want housing to occur. He wants to keep everything barefoot and pregnant and over the line, so he can be the king of it. It's that simple, even though you'll hear some people [talk] about how wonderful he is. He isn't. And so they were actually going to do some housing. Well, [name] managed to lean on [national funder] and make a bunch of allegations.

Another relatively gentle way of persisting at getting sensitive material is to "throw out the rabbit" (the phrase describes a form of sermon in African American churches). Throwing out the rabbit involves a series of nonthreatening questions that allude to sensitive subject matter without directly asking about it. For instance, in one interview, a person who had usually been forthcoming skirted the issue of his organization's relationship with a city council member. Herb suspected that he had accidentally touched upon something sensitive, changed his questioning pattern, and began to throw out the rabbit. Each time the conversational partner mentioned city participation in any neighborhood project—tree planting, stop signs, a major strip shopping center—Herb probed with a question on what the particular city council member did. Each time, Herb got a short, direct answer but with little detail. Herb was patient and continued to ask about the city council member's role on different projects, without pushing for the detail that the interviewee seemed reluctant to provide.

Later the conversation turned to how the community group handled zoning cases. This time, without Herb having to ask about the council member, his conversational partner explained that the council member took bribes in rezoning cases. By contesting controversial zoning cases, the community organization made it more difficult for the official to fix the outcomes and thus lowered the income of this elected official. The reason for the interviewee's stress and the brief answers became apparent without Herb having to push and ask why. The rabbit was caught.

Another approach to following up on sensitive issues is for the interviewer to raise some other delicate issue him- or herself as a way of breaking the ice. In one of his interviews, Herb felt that the informant was reluctant to talk about corruption in a city housing program, so for the moment he steered away from the matter. Later in the interview, they were discussing a complicated tax program that benefited the rich more than it did the poor. Rather than let the interviewee draw out the implication of this class bias, Herb took a chance and interjected his opinion. The conversation went as follows:

Interviewee: We've got programs that . . . [are] less restricted and more money. Why would we deal with your program for less money and more headaches? That's backwards.

Herb: Because it gives tax credits to the [rich] and that's their purpose.

Interviewee: Thank you, thank you.

Herb was betting that if he could discuss matters with this degree of openness, then so could the interviewee. The interviewee acknowledged Herb's honesty with the "thank you, thank you," and then, the next time the city housing program was mentioned, elaborated on the kickback arrangements that were involved. It was as if Herb had said, when talking about the tax credits, "I am not naive, I am not going to be shocked, I know not everything is as it is supposed to be, and such information will not turn me against you, your group, or the movement." In doing so, Herb freed his conversational partner to talk more openly.

Such complex follow-ups require advance thought. You don't want to force your interviewee to talk unnecessarily about something sensitive. But when you have to follow up on a sensitive matter, you want to do so in way that you do not cause the interviewee to shut down on you and take evasive action, or worse, lie.

Getting Past Formalistic Statements

In most interviews, conversational partners are helpful and want you to understand their answers. But on occasion, what you hear in response to the main questions are formalistic, or normative, replies that obscure the way things actually occurred.

To get behind formalistic statements, first try to understand why interviewees might give such replies. They may be bored and want to get rid of you or not want to make the effort to think through the question you asked. Or they may have been instructed to give a formalistic reply because the real answer is not something they can make public. Electric company spokespersons may insist that the nuclear plant accident never put citizens in any health danger, because to admit otherwise might force costly repairs and lawsuits for health damage. Police and court employees are particularly likely to give formalistic answers, because if they do not follow appropriate procedures, they can invalidate their own work and that of others. They want to be seen as methodically following procedures whether they do so or not. Similarly, scientists might give normative answers about how they do their research, because actual procedures may seem too casual and threaten their credibility and possibly their funding (Thomas & Marquart, 1988).

If you ask someone how he or she carries out an activity that is supposed to be structured by written rules—say, how a policeman subdues a perpetrator—the interviewee is likely to give an answer that comes directly out of a training manual. Rather, what you want to ask is, "Please think of a recent example in which you subdued a perpetrator. Could you tell me what happened from beginning to end?"

Another approach is to work out questions that simply cannot be answered from anything mentioned in the procedures handbook or occupational manual. It is not that people want to lie, they just feel more comfortable quoting the rules. When our colleague Jim was asking court officials to discuss how they carried out hearings on parole requests, all he got back were descriptions of the formal procedures. About to give up, Jim switched his line of questioning to topics not covered in the manuals and asked the officials how they felt about the convicts. To this question, the interviewees responded directly and openly. Then the officials discussed how their negative feelings toward the prisoners influenced the way they conducted hearings.

A similar situation occurred when a student was interviewing campus security police on how they reported crime on campus. The answers only spoke to the rules the officers were supposed to follow in writing incident reports. Once she realized that the interviewees were afraid to indicate they had not followed the rules, the researcher questioned indirectly. She asked about which police force, the campus police, county, or city, had responsibility for handling different types of crime and how the boundaries of responsibility were negotiated. This was something for which the security officials had no handbook answers, so they answered openly, in ways that also taught the interviewee how incident reports were written, irrespective of the formal rules (cf. Heinsler, Kleinman, & Stenross, 1990).

Another approach to a formalistic answer is to back off and later follow up by reversing the way you approach a topic. If you originally asked about a general problem and got no meaningful answer, you can later ask about a concrete incident of that type of problem. Or conversely, if people have described a specific project in harmonious terms and you suspect that you are getting an overly optimistic report, later in the interview you can ask about stresses in the general process.

Only if these more polite and indirect approaches are failing would you want to risk a more challenging opening. "I really want to talk to you about the role of faulty welds in the coolant system in the recent shutdown of the plant, and whether officials knew about the welds. That is what some folks are saying, and I would like to get your side." That is challenging wording, but it may be necessary if the interviewee has been giving nothing but bland statements. He or she may respond in order to find out how much you know and in doing so confirm or disconfirm your suspicions. Or you may get a detailed rebuttal of the charges. Once conversational partners start to explain, the tendency is for them to get it right, especially if you have already shown that you are sympathetic and trustworthy.

Dealing With Falsehood and Distortions

Although you may sometimes have to get past a front or party line, and you may occasionally listen to a lie or distortion, the problem of penetrating blatant lies is not usually very serious in qualitative interviews. In many projects you get to know your interviewees well, and they get to know you well enough to be forthcoming. And because you can compare what people say in a series of interviews, if people do lie, you can figure it out without a verbal confrontation. Further, because people know you are talking with others there is a tendency to be reasonably truthful.

When you catch lies, don't get upset over being deceived. After all, you may have caused the lie yourself by inappropriately pressing for answers when an interviewee was still fearful, or you might have put too much pressure on someone to resolve an apparent contradiction. In any case, try not to give in to the feeling that you have been betrayed. If you react at that emotional level, you are likely not to get any additional information and might end the relationship. Back off and rethink.

Rather than get upset about lies, think about why the person may have lied. Lies, evasions, and inconsistencies can provide useful information. What was so important about that point that they felt they could not tell the truth about it? Was it a more stressful event than they let on? Do they feel guilty about something? A lie or distortion usually means that interviewees care deeply about something; you might want to figure out what that was.

One general strategy for dealing with the possibility of lies and evasions is to hold back questions that you think might make the person distort an answer until the interviewing relationship is pretty solid.

Another way is to make sure the interviewee knows that you are informed enough to test the answers you get. To prevent getting a normative statement in the first place, phrase your questions in ways that show that you are familiar with the way things actually work. Irene almost always talks with subordinates and technical staff before interviewing bosses and political appointees, and then from what she learns, words her questions to send the signals that say, "I already know quite a bit, if you say something phony I will pick it up." Being seen around as a patient observer is another way to encourage people not to distort answers.

To help signal that you are knowledgeable and to ward off deceptions, reveal that you are knowledgeable early in the interview. You can ask a ranking official about layoffs in a federal agency by saying, "The unions have argued that there was no need for a reduction in force, but that it was carried out anyway. What could they mean by that? What *was* the reason for the reduction in force?" By mentioning that you have talked to union representatives and implying that you have access to their documents, you suggest that you are not ignorant and reduce the likelihood of getting a misleading answer.

The interviews in which truth is most routinely problematic are evaluation interviews. If people have to talk to you and the consequences of being fully honest may be a cut in their program's budget, a reduction in responsibility, or even program termination and job loss, they may well lie or distort information.

In such a situation, you need to provide the interviewees with reasons to cooperate. You may be able to offer to relate the strengths of the program to the funder or help interviewees figure out how to portray themselves to best advantage. You might argue that a fair evaluation by you—who basically support the program—may stave off a more negative evaluator later. Or you might be able to include in the evaluation the interviewee's accounts of how funding cuts have affected the ability of the program to function, indirectly laying at the feet of the sponsors any major troubles that the interviews uncover.

When interviewees have a high stake in making themselves look good, don't box them into conclusions they would be uncomfortable with, because that may make them lie. Thus ask what obstacles a program has run into, rather than why things don't work. Wording questions this way doesn't necessarily imply the problems were not solved or that the interviewees were at fault. Another approach is to be quite clear about how the information from evaluation interviews will be used and whether the interviewees will be quoted or if they can go off the record and provide background information without it being attributed to them.

Now and then people do lie, distort, exaggerate, and otherwise try to keep us from finding out what we need to know, but this occasional problem should not be blown out of proportion. Not only does it not happen very often, but the very strength of qualitative interviewing, especially when combined with observation and considerable background research, is in checking and double-checking everything. The analysis carefully weighs the strength of evidence presented and discounts for bias. In addition, the overlapping of narratives between interviewees provides a set of checks, and comparisons of documentary and interview material allow an additional way to verify information. Qualitative interviews emphasize context, and context suggests clues to the integrity of answers. The design of qualitative interviewing provides the tools for encouraging people not to lie, for detecting bias, and for compensating for bias when it does occur.

10

What Did You Hear?

Data Analysis

*D*ata analysis is exciting because you discover themes and concepts embedded throughout your interviews. As you continue with the data analysis, you weave these themes and concepts into a broader explanation of theoretical or practical import to guide your final report. Data analysis is the final stage of listening to hear the meaning of what is said. (Cf. Antaki, 1988; Antaki & Leudar, 1992; Charmaz, 1983; Glaser & Strauss, 1967; Mumby, 1993; Riessman, 1993; Spradley, 1979; Strauss, 1987; West, 1990.)

Data analysis begins while the interviewing is still under way. After completing each interview and then again after finishing a larger group of interviews, you examine the data you have heard, pull out the concepts and themes that describe the world of the interviewees, and decide which areas should be examined in more detail. This preliminary analysis tells you how to redesign your questions to focus in on central themes as you continue interviewing. After the interviewing is complete, you begin a more detailed and fine-grained analysis of what your conversational partners told you. In this formal analysis, you discover additional themes and concepts and build toward an overall explanation.

To begin the final data analysis, put into one category all the material from all your interviews that speaks to one theme or concept. Compare material within the categories to look for variations and nuances in meanings. Compare across the categories to discover connections between themes. The goal is to integrate the themes and concepts into a theory that offers an accurate, detailed, yet subtle interpretation of your research arena. The analysis is complete when you feel you can share with others what your interpretation means for policymaking, for theory, and for understanding the social and political world.

The analysis phase is exciting because of the continuing sense of discovery, but analysis can be intimidating because of the sheer amount of interview data that has to be understood. For each hour spent interviewing, you end up with about 10,000 words to read and understand. The researcher has so many ideas, so many bits and pieces, he or she may despair of ever putting them together. But if the research has been well designed and you approach the analysis stage with patience and at least occasional inspiration, the pieces will come together.

In this chapter we present the logic we use to analyze and weave together the ideas, concepts, and themes in the interviews. We describe how we code—that is, organize what people have told us—and how we look at the coded data so that the ideas jump out at us. We also discuss how we combine ideas to gradually build a theory grounded in the data we heard, and how we interpret what we have discovered in light of other theories in our field. You will probably come up with your own patterns for analyzing interview data, but in the beginning, it can be helpful to see how someone else does it.

THE STEPS OF ANALYSIS

In his present study of community developers, Herb has collected over 2 million words of interview data, along with 12 boxes of documents. He reads the interviews, paragraph by paragraph and word by word, marking off each time a particular idea or concept is mentioned or explained, and indicating in a code the subject of each paragraph. Then he groups together responses describing the same idea or process and examines everything he has put in the same category.

This is detailed work, but he is rarely bored because so many of the examples are illuminating and periodically he gets an insight by seeing quotations and descriptions from separate interviews side by side. If the idea seems particularly exciting, he may leap away from his computer and grab Irene or call another colleague to share his thoughts about what the data mean.

When he takes a break from the coding, Herb has lunch with colleagues in the university cafeteria. At these meals, the topic of urban poverty sometimes comes up (along with complaints about salaries, deans, and parking spaces). If someone at the table complains that poor people don't want an honest job, Herb jumps right in and tells a story that came from his interviews. He describes how a community group helped women on welfare get training as certified day care providers and that the women ended up with jobs that benefited themselves and their communities.

Herb's activities illustrate the process of data analysis. First, Herb *coded* the data, thinking about what he was doing as he was doing it, letting interpretations come to him as he examined the data response by response. After he divided the data into smaller categories, he began reassembling the information into themes and arguments. Then he worked on figuring out the *theoretical or policy implications* of the data—what broader questions he could answer and what insights he could provide. He chose what themes to emphasize in part based on his audience and what they find stimulating, useful, or challenging.

We start the coding process by rereading the interviews, so we have their general content clearly in mind. When we reread, we also think about the themes, concepts, and ideas we were trying to explore in each interview. Some of these efforts panned out; others we dropped for lack of support. We come up with a starting point for our coding categories by reconstructing which themes, concepts, and ideas we were able to successfully examine. We go back to the interviews, and this time mark off these concepts, themes, and ideas each time they occur in an interview. As we do this coding, we discover other themes, concepts, and ideas and designate new coding categories to include them. Whenever we add new coding categories, we have to go back to the original interviews and look for and mark each place that is an example of the material that now belongs in the new categories.

When the coding is complete, the data are grouped in categories that allow us compare what different people said, what themes were discussed, and how concepts were understood. Through examining the information within each category, we come up with overall descriptions of the cultural arena or explanations of the topic we are studying. We then seek out the broader significance by asking if our data support, modify, or contradict an existing theory or policy. Which themes we emphasize in the analysis depends in part on the audience for the report we are writing. If he were writing for a government housing agency, Herb would try to answer the policy question, "How do community development organizations provide homes for the poor?" If he were writing a scholarly article intended for academics, he would be more likely emphasize different ways the word *empowerment* is used. When he was talking to the lunch crowd, he highlighted employment for welfare mothers.

HOW DO YOU HEAR AND RECOGNIZE WHAT THE DATA SAY?

The purpose of the data analysis is to organize the interviews to present a narrative that explains what happened or provide a description of the norms and values that underlie cultural behavior. Researchers have developed many ways of coding to help them get at the meaning of their data more easily. For example, both Spradley (1979) and Strauss (1987) have devised formal systems for the analysis of qualitative data. Each approach involves techniques for finding and marking the underlying ideas in the data, grouping similar information together, and relating different ideas and themes to one another.

Our approach to analyzing data parallels Spradley's (1979) and Strauss's (1987) systems but accommodates the particular type of research we do. We each read and reread the interviews to note core ideas and concepts, recognize emotive stories, and find themes. We code the material to group similar ideas together and figure out how the themes relate to each other. To reflect the distinct nature of the material we collect, each of us uses different coding techniques that vary in detail from Spradley's (1979) and Strauss's (1987) approaches.

Recognizing Concepts

Conversational partners refer to the ideas or concepts through which they understand their worlds by using a specialized vocabulary or giving a particular tilt to a more common word or phrase. As you begin the data analysis, you look for these explanatory concepts by picking out the words the interviewees frequently use that sound different from your ordinary vocabulary. Not every strange word, though, is a label for an important concept.

Sometimes the vividness of the vocabulary suggests that an important concept may be involved. Our colleague Jim shared with us the following excerpt from a conversation between paramedics:

> It was slow tonight. Some drive-bys and a few carry-outs . . . a cold one, a coupla bleeders and a blue-icer.

In describing the evening's routine, the speaker was not describing grabbing a beer and a hamburger in a drive-through MacDonalds. He was using the vernacular of his profession to explain that it was slow evening, and he and his partner made a few routine stops and also transported ("carry-outs") several people to a hospital. Two of them were bleeding trauma victims. One of the passengers ("a cold one") had died; another one was a choking victim ("blue-icer"). There are a number of strange words in this passage, but the main concept is "slow night," and it is defined by the small number of "drive-bys" and "carry-outs." The other odd terms, "cold one," "bleeders," and "blue-icer," do not seem to be important ideas in themselves, but taken together, these words suggest that the paramedics have distanced themselves from the depressing nature of their work by giving nicknames to types of serious injuries. We might call this concept "nicknaming tragedies," or "distancing from bodily trauma."

A second straightforward way of noticing concepts is to look for nouns or noun phrases that are repeated frequently and seem to be expressing an important idea for the conversational partners. If the word "planning" comes up a lot, it may represent how the interviewees define what they do; if the phrase "lack of time" or "pressed for time" shows up in different interviews, "time pressure" may be a label for an important concept.

You can sometimes find additional concepts by looking for the pair, the mate, or the opposite of the concept you have just discovered. If a student has mentioned a "fair professor" in an interview, and you identified that phrase as a label for an underlying concept, look through your interviews and see if anyone discussed or defined an "unfair professor." Herb frequently heard the phrase "bricks and mortar" in his interviews, referring to the underlying concept of building homes, offices, and factories. "Bricks and mortar" was a label for projects that had a physical presence, so Herb, in looking for its opposite, examined the interviews for references to activities that resulted in a less visible product. Some of his conversational partners talked about providing social service support, that is, helping people maintain their homes or learn how to run businesses. "Social service support" was a matched idea to the concept of "bricks and mortar" projects.

Sometimes people describe a core idea but don't label it with a single word or phrase, so you then create a label yourself for the concept. In her study of how cities' budget processes changed, Irene found that people measured the success of projects not in terms of how much the projects were needed but by how much they were demanded by the citizens. She labeled this idea "project popularity."

When looking for concepts and core ideas that interviewees have not labeled with a specific word, ask yourself first, what is the interviewee talking about? Then, is this idea important? If it is important, can I summarize this idea with a word or phrase that suggests the meaning of the underlying idea? If the answer to that question is also yes, you have yourself a concept.

Hearing Stories

When you are looking for underlying meanings and themes, it can be useful to pick out and analyze stories. Stories, as we use the term, are refined versions of events that may have been condensed or altered to make a point indirectly. Narratives are straightforward efforts to answer the question, "What happened?" But a story is often thought out in advance and designed to make a point, usually one that cannot be made in a direct way. Interviewees do not always provide stories, but when they do, you should pay attention, because stories often communicate significant themes that explain a topical or cultural arena. Because interviewees seldom preface stories with, "I am going to tell you a story," you have to learn to recognize them. Stories have some or all the following characteristics:

1. Stories are told smoothly, with little fumbling or backtracking. The interviewees may have told them many times before, so they are familiar with their main lines.
2. Stories are often told as adventures, such as how my grandparents came from the old country without any money and started a business; or how Herb and Irene got, and got rid of, Teddy the Himalayan black bear.
3. Longer stories are carefully structured. They may begin with a time or place setting, introduce characters, describe some event or complexity, and then offer a resolution. Not every story has all these parts, but it would not be much of a story if it did not contain a dramatic event.
4. Stories are often marked by haunting symbols—condensed, summary images that convey a great deal of emotion and multiple meanings.
5. Stories might be marked by a change in speaking tone. Short incomplete sentences are replaced by fully elaborated ideas, or the interviewee sits back, takes center stage, and begins a long description.
6. Sometimes the researcher asks a question and gets an extended response that seems not to speak to the question. The disjunction between question and response can be a clue that the interviewee is telling a story.

Herb experienced an example of this last way of recognizing a story (H. J. Rubin, 1988a). Herb had asked the interviewee what his background was and if he had been trained as an economic development practitioner. The interviewee talked about the sequence of positions he had held and the increasing enjoyment he experienced as he got closer to the type of work he now did. Then he interrupted what he was saying and said:

I really enjoy it when there is a success in getting a business to expand or to locate in this community. I have a little scrap book here from Kankakee which I keep . . . where I have pictures of the buildings and the very briefest outline that you have ever seen of what the project was . . .

He pulled out the pictures and showed them to Herb, one by one, describing with excitement the victories shown in each picture, and then returned to talking about the list of jobs he had held. The personal nature of the story—I keep a scrapbook of the buildings—and his joy in the victories called attention to the story, in comparison to the impersonal list of positions he had held.

Once you notice a story, try to figure out what lessons it is meant to communicate. In almost any kind of interview, people can use stories to answer difficult or threatening questions indirectly; in cultural studies, stories often present moral themes.

Irene was having trouble getting answers to questions on the problems in a city's budget process. Department heads kept saying everything was fine. Then one of her interviewees, after saying the budget process worked well, told Irene a story. The story began with a description of an old fire station being shut down without any farewell party. The story continued with the interviewee describing how when the new fire station was opened, the firefighters refused to participate in its housewarming, even though the new building was physically much better than the old. The interviewee then pulled the moral out of the story—that the budget process that forced the closing of the old building paid no attention to the human side of work life. The story had a poignant image in it, of an old building that had seen several generations of firefighters, that had been full of life and living, torn down without a farewell. The story was a way of talking about emotions in an environment that did not recognize the legitimacy of emotions. It said the budget process did not have a heart.

Stories are often intentionally indirect, so you may have to figure out their meaning yourself. It may help to ask yourself, why did the interviewee choose to tell a story now, in answer to this question? Is the material emotionally intense? Is it embarrassing? Is it in some sense dangerous or forbidden? Is it a modified version of events that allows the interviewee to live with an uncomfortable or mixed background of some sort?

Elliot Mishler (1986, pp. 233-255) reports that he was having trouble getting a husband to describe the low points in his marriage. Instead of answering questions about the marriage, the interviewee launched into a long story, involving financial problems, too many bills for hospital care, and the offer of a physician to reduce the interviewee's bill. The climax of the story was when the interviewee rejected the doctor's offer and paid off the bill.

Mishler (1986) had asked about the low times in the marriage, but instead got a story about the interviewee paying bills. The disjunction between the question and the answer made Mishler guess that something about the question was so painful that it simply could not be confronted, and the interviewee had replaced the pain with a more comfortable interpretation. From a later interview with the wife of the couple,

Mishler learned that at the time of the story the husband had been an alcoholic. He had lost his job and the financial difficulties were caused by him.

Oral history interviews may be laced with stories that are intended to set a tone to help interpret the rest of the material. In stories, people may describe themselves in ways that would be inappropriate to say directly. Rather than tell the interviewer, "I am an iconoclast," the conversational partner tells a story in which he or she stood out from the crowd.

Hearing Themes

Themes offer descriptions of how people do or should behave. "Everyone is out for themselves" or "Good people care for their parents and help those in need." Themes may tell people how not to behave—"Planning ahead is foolish as it is all fate anyway." Themes may describe whom to trust or not trust. For example, among prisoners, "The only good guard is a dead one." Themes provide explanations for how or why things happen. "People are poor because they are lazy" or "People are poor because companies buy equipment and lay off workers." Or as in Irene's work, "Cities in fiscal trouble may hide the extent of their financial difficulty, making problems worse."

When you hear themes, ask yourself which ones go together. Related themes help you build toward a broader description or an overall theory. If you hear about discrimination against African Americans in hiring, about poor quality inner-city schools, about residential segregation, and about the difficult time that interracial couples have in raising their children, you might put these themes together as a start of a theory about the effects of discrimination. Community developers complain about building codes delaying the refurbishment of apartments for the poor; they also complain about governmental slowness in dispersing grant money. These two themes can be combined into one larger one: "Although necessary for development work, government is often an obstacle not a help."

Some themes are explicitly stated by conversational partners. In a study of African American teenagers, the interviewees may tell you, "Gang membership is a form of self-defense." Faculty in research universities may tell you, "We don't get promoted if we don't publish." Where themes are not explicitly stated, you can often deduce them from several illustrations. Look through your interviews for the places that women are mentioned, and when you find that they are described as serving food, taking orders from men, or chauffeuring their children about, you start to suspect a theme about the subordinate role of women.

By combining information from different interviews, the researcher creates descriptive themes that no individual interviewee mentioned. From one set of interviews, you learn that government officials want to increase the local tax base by encouraging new construction. A second set of interviewees explain that builders define their task as satisfying the demand for new homes. A third set of interviews makes clear that officials in park districts believe that they should only purchase small amounts of recreational space for residents who live nearby. When these separate ideas are put together, the theme emerges of inevitable destruction of farms and wetlands and a continuous expansion of suburbs because no one has incentives to preserve open space.

How do you pick out the themes from the interviews? Sometimes people repeat their own themes or emphasize them, to be sure that you haven't missed them, or they tell a story to underscore a theme. Look for places in the interviews where interviewees tried to call your attention to a major point or argument.

In coding the interviews, you can mark each passage with a brief summary of what the person was telling you. Some of these summaries that you make suggest themes, because they seem to fit a common pattern—of the poor losing out, of women being subordinate, or of authors being moody. You then check out the theme suggested by your coding by reexamining the interviews for further examples that confirm or disconfirm your tentative new theme.

Sometimes potential themes just leap out from the interviews. Consider this rich segment from an interview Jim conducted with a prisoner:

Q: How did you decide on where you would get a tattoo?

A: Well, in the joint [prison] I was limited. There was a couple of artists, and you didn't have a lot to pick from. And you couldn't travel where you wanted, so you were limited there. There was some that was recommended, and other shops across the U.S., there were people that would recommend them and friends that do it for reasons of, ah, brotherhood. If their work was good, they could do it.

This segment suggests a theme of the prisoner being physically bound in one place, yet connected to a nationwide net of others like himself. The idea of physical constraints was mentioned four times: "I was limited," "You didn't have a lot to pick from," "You couldn't travel," and "So you were limited there." The researcher would have to be very distracted not to notice this portion of the theme. The second portion of the theme was mentioned three times, "Some that were recommended," "People that would recommend them," and "Friends that do it for brotherhood." These three comments describe a network of helpers, people to tell the prisoner where to go to get free help—to find people who do things for reasons of brotherhood. Interestingly, though, the theme is nuanced as the last sentence implies that the prisoner did not have to use this free service. Quality counted when prisoners were looking for tattoos.

Iconic statements, pithy summaries of how the interviewees interpret their world, also suggest themes. A community developer was reflecting on why he was about to start on a tough project, one that could easily fail:

> It is a tough row to hoe these days, especially since financing has just dried up, but . . . it is tough . . . that is why we are doing it. That is why not-for-profits do it, because it is tough, because the for-profits won't do it. Well, you've been doing this since Christmas so you've heard the same sob story over and over.

The theme is that not-for-profits step in where others despair. Just in case Herb did not catch it, the interviewee reminded Herb how widespread this feeling was.

Iconic statements suggest striking thematic resolutions of puzzles. Herb had been worrying about the extent to which his community organizations felt they were subject to the whims of their funders. Herb noticed the following statement:

> We don't just take their money and do what they say. Just because they gave you the money, you jump every time . . . [development groups] play that game of not biting the hand that feeds them. Shit, bite it once in a while. At least, nibble at it.

This statement suggested to Herb the theme, "Ideally, you do fight back but even rebellion must be done with some caution." He then reread other interviews and noticed many other examples, although less vividly stated, of how community organizations balanced doing projects they wanted with satisfying the demands of the funders. Because dramatic statements often suggest important themes, Herb keeps a computer file of "sexy quotes" that he groups into different thematic categories. One such quote describing the Local Initiatives Support Corporation (LISC), a funder of community projects, was provided by a radical community leader. In rejecting LISC, this person yelled "Shoot the fucking intermediaries, especially LISC . . . who'd rather you don't mess up your development work with involving low-income people." The vehemence of the statement focused Herb's attention on the tensions between "working with such funders" and the importance of "involving low-income people" in community projects, suggesting a core thematic tension in community development work.

Both compatible and contradictory concepts can help build themes. An example of merging compatible concepts occurred in Herb's study of economic development officials. Herb had heard the interviewees complain about "uncontrollability of the work environment" and spending excessive time on ineffective "busywork," such as sending out brochures. Herb put these two concepts together to suggest a broader theme, that the "inability to control outcomes led economic development practitioners to increase the amount of busywork they did." An example of merging contradictory concepts into a single theme could use the previously mentioned "bricks and mortar" and "social services." One theme could be that the social services made the bricks-and-mortar projects viable for the poor. Another theme using the two concepts emphasizes the tension between them, namely that funders have a bias toward bricks and mortar and are reluctant to pay for the social services that make the projects functional.

Another way of finding themes is to look for similarities in how people who are in different circumstances interpret their world. For example, Herb found that community groups in rural areas that were isolated from one another, and those in big cities sometimes located only blocks apart, complained about too much competition in their field, suggesting to Herb that he should explore the theme of rivalry among development organizations.

If you think you have a set of connected themes, you examine the interviews for confirming and disconfirming evidence to ensure that the linkages are grounded in the data. Toward the end of her analysis of the interviews in the city-manager city that ran a deficit, Irene began to conclude that political factors were more important than economic ones in contributing to fiscal stress. She reexamined her material to see how much support there was for this theme. She noticed that politicians repeatedly emphasized bricks-and-mortar projects and wondered if political pressures to build construction projects increased the city's fiscal stress. With this question in mind, she read her interviews again, and noticed that council members had told her they rarely criticized each other's bricks-and-mortar projects. These projects were too expensive for the city, but political norms of back-scratching allowed several to be funded at the time when the deficit was growing.

CODING INTERVIEW DATA

Coding is the process of grouping interviewees' responses into categories that bring together the similar ideas, concepts, or themes you have discovered, or steps or stages in a process. You can code for names, evidence, or time sequences. You can also code for hesitations, blocking, signs of emotion, and indications of fear or amusement. In fact, you can code on anything you think may later help you analyze the data. You can use several schemes in combination if you wish. And you can recode the data as often as you please.

In a very practical way, coding is affected by the precision of the interview data. With tape-recorded interviews, you can analyze the length of pauses, the order of wording, and the exact words that were used. If you have taken notes by hand, paraphrasing in places for speed, you have to be cautious about analyzing the interviewee's word choices, as what you have written down may be your paraphrase and not the interviewee's words at all.

The coding categories you choose reflect the interests of the intended audience for the report. If your report will go to policymakers who are concerned about designing counseling programs to help reduce the number of teenage pregnancies, you might set up coding categories that group discussions of concepts such as femininity and masculinity, independence, adulthood, and responsibility. If you were coding the same data for public administrators, you would be more likely to code into categories that reflect the public administrators' perspective such as discussions of how the father helps support the child, the role of social service agencies, and the availability of day care so the young mother can stay in school.

Coding proceeds in stages. First, you set up a few main coding categories, suggested by the original reading of the interviews and the intended purposes of the report. You can make yourself a list as you go through your interviews. Okay, you might say, here is an illustration of "frustration," which was an important idea I was looking at in some of the interviews. I will look for that one throughout my notes or transcripts. Oh, and yes, there is "uncontrollability of the work," I remember when I was looking for that one, that was important too. You can start out with a relatively small list of these categories.

As you go through the interviews, you can put in brackets, or underline, or otherwise mark off each word, phrase, sentence, paragraph, or extended story or example that you are using as a single coding unit that fits the coding categories you are listing. For instance, each time Irene ran across an example of how a city department got a request for funds approved, she coded the passage as an illustration of "successful departmental budget strategies," even when the example ran several pages in her notes. Sometimes a single sentence or paragraph might be coded into several categories. For example, one paragraph might illustrate the concept of "empowerment" and also contain a discussion on "problems of inadequate funding."

After you have designated the beginning and end of the coding unit in some way, you mark the unit with an indicator for the coding category into which you are putting the material. You can identify the category by putting a word in the margins, such as writing down "empowerment" or "the dispute over the south highway," or you can use a numerical coding system, where each number is a shorthand for a coding category.

As you sort the data into the categories you chose, you might find that important information doesn't fit into these categories or that one of your categories blurs two or more separate concepts, themes, or stages. Then you have to add new categories to fit the data. Whenever you change or add coding categories, you have to go back and recode the material already examined. When you first start coding, you are simultaneously placing data into preliminary coding categories and deciding whether these preliminary categories provide a good fit to the data. If the fit is inadequate, you change the coding categories to reflect what you discover in your data.

Because you have to start the coding again each time you make major changes in the coding categories, if you are dealing with a large data set, you might want to choose a sample of your interviews and work out the coding categories on them first. If this sample is reasonably representative of your interviews, you should not have to make many adjustments to your coding categories later and can avoid a lot of recoding. Before trying to code his massive interview set on community developers, Herb chose a group of interviews that represented the variation he had built into the design, that is, people from rural areas, others from bigger cities, one from a group that worked on housing, one from a group that was engaged in advocacy, one from a funder, and one from an "intermediary" between the funders and the community groups. Herb then worked out his coding categories on this sample and had to make very few changes when he applied these coding categories to the rest of his interviews.

When designing and applying your coding categories, you have to keep your mind engaged; avoid turning coding into an automated task. If you pay close attention as you code, you will hear much more meaning in your data than you can when you just read the interviews. You may see connections between what different people have told you, or you may read different examples of the same concept and suddenly notice that the examples point out nuances you need to pay attention to. Coding encourages hearing the meaning in the data.

Herb, for instance, noticed as he coded the word *empowerment* that some of his interviewees were using it to include ownership of property. That usage gave empowerment a more conservative twist and made Herb think more carefully about what some of his community developers were trying to achieve.

After you have marked up the interviews with coding categories, you put all the material with the same codes together. We used to physically group the data into the categories by photocopying the interviews, cutting the copies into pieces, and putting each designated coding unit in the proper pile, but now we use the computer to move material around, as it instantly joins together items in the same category. Be sure to make copies of the original interviews, and do your physical or electronic regrouping only on the copies.

The computer helps in grouping the coded data; it is fast and efficient and saves many, many hours of tedious work (Tesch, 1990). But the computer cannot do the creative part of coding, such as setting up and modifying the categories and figuring out in what categories each segment of an interview belongs. Nor can the computer label ideas as concepts or recognize themes, compare the separate concepts, find subtleties in meaning, or follow up on comparisons or nuances. Computers can take much of the drudgery out of coding a large data set, but any claims for a computer software package that it can think for you are exaggerated.

Once you have all the material that belongs together in the same place, you can analyze the material within and across categories. Examining the material in individual categories allows you to refine what a concept means, compare examples of a theme, or piece together the separate events in a narrative. Comparing material across categories allows you to figure out which themes seem to go together or contradict each other.

Mechanics of Coding

You code for themes, concepts, and ideas, but you can also code for the names of agencies or people, major projects, dates, stages or steps of a process, or just about anything that you think might be useful in tying things together. In addition to coding for ideas, Irene also marks where interviewees are speaking from firsthand experience because she finds it useful in deciding how much weight to give each piece of information when she is putting a narrative together.

After you have set up the major coding categories, make a copy of the text and then mark each word, phrase, sentence, paragraph, or example that belongs in each coding category. Sometimes the interviewee uses a word or phrase such as "empowerment" that indicates a concept. At other times, you have to recognize that a concept is described but not named. The phrases "I feel in charge" and "They had to hear me out" are expressions of empowerment and need to be labeled as such, even though the word *empowerment* is not used. Or if you are coding for people's names, you may find references to them that do not mention their names. You have to recognize that the phrase "the crooked politician" refers to Mr. R. N. and mark the phrase accordingly.

Some Examples of Coding

The following illustration is from one of Herb's interviews on neighborhood-based economic development:

> ... like one of the things that is going on right now, not in our neighborhood, but another neighborhood. It's as if there is a backlash toward Section 8 tenants. Because people feel that they [the Section 8 tenants] are not screened properly and that they are supervised or managed [poorly] and that there are a lot of Section 8 people in our neighborhood. It's mostly over here, because some of the neighborhood activists decided, "no more poor people." And what they are really saying is no more hell raisers, you know, no more children without supervision, no more substandard housing, no more loud parties late at night, no more drive-by shooting, no more drugs. And that is seen as a direct marriage relationship to poor people today. Even though that may only be 5% of the population, or whatever, you know it's still—that prejudice exists.

First, you code on the concept of "backlash" and the term "Section 8," the name of a subsidized housing program. This passage argues that some people think that Section 8 is poorly managed and that the poor people who participate in the program are not properly screened, allowing troublemakers into the neighborhood.

The paragraph suggests at least three themes: (a) people assume that all poor people cause trouble; (b) some neighborhood activists, to improve their neighborhoods, want to prevent any more poor people from coming to their neighborhoods; and (c) the unintended consequence of some neighborhoods keeping the poor out is that other neighborhoods get a disproportionate number of poor people. The entire paragraph illustrates "problems in doing community development work" as well as "tense interaction between neighborhoods," so you might also want to code the paragraph for these ideas. If you are going to write out themes and concepts next to the interview material, you should probably leave some extra space between the paragraphs, or split the page into columns, with the text on one side and your codings on the other. If you are just going to use numbers or letters to designate the coding categories, you may be able to do all the markings in the margins.

The following example from Irene's recent study of city budget processes shows the completed coding of an interview with the budget director of Rochester, New York—Al Sette. We present the coding in brackets in italics. The notes have been lightly edited. We then describe the logic that resulted in this marked-up version. Irene began the interview by asking how budgeting had changed over the previous 20 years.

6. *Sette:* Over 20 years? The document has become much more open
7. *[openness]* in the last 10 years in terms of information being put
8. out and the size. From 1970 to 1980, *[dates]* the budget
9. doubled in size. That is without the school district.
10. The 1969-1970 *[dates]* budget was difficult to follow, it
11. tells you nothing, it emphasizes line items *[line*
12. *items],* and the previous year's budget and the upcoming
13. year's. There is nothing on programs, *[program*
14. *budgeting]* or in the program format until the 1970s.
15. *[date]* We did not start a program budget until some
16. time in the 1970s, before I got on board. *[lack of first-*
17. *hand knowledge]*
20. Most of our work recently *[time]* has been to halt the
21. growth in the size of the document without sacrificing
22. information *[size versus information]* and continue
23. refinements of the performance *[performance*
24. *budgeting]* indicators. The line departments do not even
25. know what they *[performance indicators]* are. [The forms
26. were] getting cluttered, they did not know why we do
27. it. [require all that performance data] If they got 20
28. complaints and responded to 20, that is what they
29. reported. *[departments don't understand performance*
30. *measures]* Then, it gets hard to measure efficiency. To
31. be honest with ourselves, we don't
32. have good result indicators. We probably won't have
33. them, the resources to develop them aren't there.
34. *[reason: no resources]*
35. [Re]election is the result, citizens showed that.
36. *[political performance reporting]* For example, you get
37. 25 calls for potholes, you filled them, you used x tons
38. of fill, each cost 100 dollars, but so what. You filled
39. 25 potholes. That is what matters to citizens.
40. *[accountability]* In the '70s, *[date]* we wanted all
41. types of indicators, demand, efficiency, results, but

42. you would have repetition in all the categories.
43. *[failure of performance measures]*
44. Are the citizens pleased with the pothole filling?
45. *[accountability]* Periodically, every 10 years, we sur-
46. vey them, but that is not ongoing. We don't do that.
47. *[lack of performance measures]* Impact indices take a lot
48. of research. *[reason for lack of performance measures]*
49. And we may not be ready to share. *[reason for lack of*
50. *performance measures]* Citizens think we do a lousy job
51. at that. We got rid of a lot of junk. *[budget*
52. *simplification]* Some indicators, departments like,
53. others are the basis of decision making. We use
54. indicators to report to the mayor on progress. *[reasons*
55. *for keeping some performance measures]*
56. *Irene:* When did the change take place?
57. Was it anything to do with the mayor?
58. *Sette:* It's been gradual. I did not sit in on the
59. budgets in the 1970s. *[lack of firsthand knowledge]* In
60. the 1970s, *[date]* there was program evaluation on the
61. federal budget. *[program evaluation] [federal*
62. *government as source of change]* That is what we did.
63. (It created a great deal of anxiety.) Then we lost fed-
64. eral funds, evaluation disappeared. *[implied reason for*
65. *ending program evaluation: departmental anxiety]*
71. *Irene:* Was it in place by the early 1980s? *[time]*
72. *Sette:* The shift was in place, it began because of the
73. format, but it was enhanced by the upgrading of the per-
74. formance measures, they became more meaningful and more
75. focused. *[performance measures improved]*
76. The council now had a new role of watchdog. *[council's*
77. *role changes]* That has been since 1986 [when the form
78. of government changed]. *[time][consequences of the*
79. *change in government]* It's a difficult role. Under
80. the city manager form, there wasn't the same kind of
81. oversight. It was more like a board with an executive
82. director. . . . I sense that the
83. increased importance on performance *[performance*
84. *measurement]* is in part due to the new form and the new

85. role of the council, it added impetus to a process
86. already under way. *[consequences of the change in*
87. *government]*
88. Can do it with the budget process. But on the other
89. hand, only time will tell. *[permanence of the changes*
90. *questioned]* There are things in the budget that are
91. unflattering, but whether that will continue, I don't
92. know. *[perception of political nature of the threat to*
93. *the permanence of changes—politicians vulnerable to*
94. *unflattering statements]* If it is politicized, *[politicization]*
95. other than what the charter requires, we don't have to present
96. it this way.
97. *[disjuncture, brief story]* We got a GFOA [Government
98. Finance Officers Association] award 5 years running.
99. A lot of cities don't care [about whether they get the
100. award or not]. [The award] equals professionalism.
101. *[professionalism]* Less professionalism was one of the
102. arguments against the mayor form. But we didn't go
103. down the tubes. *[point of the story: professionalism*
104. *linked with budget reform, opposed to change in*
105. *governmental form which was associated with political values]*

First, Irene used the dates she coded to put events roughly in order, creating a brief narrative. The narrative indicated important events as well as explanations of what happened. She noted the formal changes in budgeting started about 1970, as the budget shifted from straight line items (how much for pencils, how much for wages) to a program budget (how much for crime suppression, how much for road maintenance) (lines 11-14). The city also added performance budgeting, but it did so in a rather mechanical manner, in ways that the departments did not understand as the departments used the same indicators to measure all the different standards (lines 23-30). The last stage of the narrative shows the budget getting bulky with unusable information (lines 8-9), so in recent years, the effort has been to cut back on the size, keeping the usable information and dropping the rest (lines 20-24). To trace the themes in the narrative, Irene marked statements in which the interviewee discussed why he thought the changes occurred. The reason that the demand, workload, and output measures were all the same was that *the departments did not understand the differences between them* (lines 29-30). Whether due to ignorance or fear—the reasons suggested by the interviewee—the departments treated the new requirements formalistically, reporting on the number of hours they put in rather than what they accomplished. And they got away with doing so.

A second explanation for the events is that the budget office and the mayor cut back on the bulk of the budget, simplifying it, and taking the useless information (the formalistic stuff) out because the budget had become so large it was unreadable (lines 20-22). Rather than push ahead with implementation and make the system workable, the budget office and the mayor ratified the departments' rejection of the system and retained only those measures the departments understood or that the mayor was interested in monitoring (lines 52-55). Sette offered other reasons for not pressing the performance measures on the departments. One was that *they took a lot of research;* the second reason was that *the city did not have or was not willing to commit the resources* to developing good outcome measures; and the third reason was that *performance measures made the politicians vulnerable.* "We may not be ready to share," Sette argued—that is, we are not ready to make the outcomes of performance measures public (lines 31-33, 47-49).

When she coded the rest of her interviews, Irene concluded that "degree of political reform" was an important concept. Because the city-manager form of government is considered more reformed than the mayor-council form, she decided to look at the Sette interview again, to see if Rochester's recent change from the council-manager to mayor-council form had an impact on budgeting.

Sette addressed the impact of the change of form of government, indicating that many people feared the mayor-council form would be less professional than the council-manager form (lines 101-102), but then Sette said that the city won an award from the Government Finance Officers Association, implying that the budget was still professional. Sette was getting emotional about this topic and talked about professionalism in the form of a brief story, with the moral that the issue was being resolved in favor of openness and professionalism, but he wasn't sure this outcome would last. He repeated this theme of the uncertainty of the outcome several times (lines 88-89, 94-96).

In this second round of coding, Irene began to understand the antagonism between the concepts "politicization" and "professionalism" and looked back at the interview for illustrations of this tension. Getting elected (or reelected)—an indication of politicization—Sette said, was "the result" (line 35) of programs. It did not matter much how well a job was done. Voters cared about the number of potholes filled, not how much hot patch mix was used to fill them. According to Sette what had changed with the shift to a mayor-council form was that budgetary reporting was now used to satisfy political demands, with reelection the explicit goal, a concept Irene labeled "political performance reporting." Having discovered this new concept, she then went back over all her other interviews to code for examples of it.

This example from Irene's coded notes suggests some common procedures in coding. Initially, the coding relies on the clearer statements and the themes that are repeated several times. But what you learn from coding later interviews often gives new insights into the murkier parts of earlier interviews. You go back over the material you have already coded to check out themes as they come up and to eliminate themes that only occur in one or two interviews. Finally, as the analysis proceeds, you link concepts to each other, look for examples of them together and apart, and work toward a broader understanding of what is going on in your data.

Irene works out categories inductively as she codes, but Herb separates the steps more sharply. In setting up his preliminary categories, Herb follows Spradley's (1979) idea of *domain analysis* by asking himself which ideas or concepts go together to form a cluster of related terms and processes. Each cluster then becomes a major coding category; the individual ideas and themes are treated as subcategories. He organizes these categories into groupings of ideas that are thematically related, a process that Strauss (1987) labeled *axial coding*. For instance, Herb noted that the stages of creating a community project—having the original dream, getting the financing, getting knowledgeable help—are distinguishable, yet closely related, because each stage must be done successfully before the project is complete.

Herb then tests his coding ideas on a sample of his interviews. Usually, this has to be repeated several times as he notices new associations and discovers missing ideas. He then organizes his coding categories into a numbered outline that shows the relationships between the core ideas, concepts, and themes. He marks up the interviews and designates coding categories by using the numbers from the outline, an approach that facilitates later computer retrieval. We've reproduced a small part of his most recent coding sheet:

III. Theoretical Questions and Approaches
   A. Alternative philosophies
   B. Interstitial organizations
   C. Coalition approaches; theories of embeddedness
   D. Nature of community and communitarianism
   E. Philosophies of change with the pragmatics of survival
IV. Projects
   A. Literature and secondary reports, macro-signs of success
   B. Projects by types
   C. Projects as stages
      1. Stages
         a. Predevelopment dreaming
         b. Financial overviews—typical packaging
         c. Multiple partnering as financing
         d. Community linkages
         e. Client, enabling the client, the dysfunctional client
         f. The traumas of construction
      2. Projects as repeated processes
         a. Physical developmental processes
            (1) Restructurings . . . The Endless Redoing It theme
            (2) Bootstrapping and leveraging between projects
            (3) Funding as leveraging and bootstrapping within projects
            (4) Consultants
         b. Core linkage processes
            (1) Maintaining the social . . . through linkages to other activities
            (2) . . . remembering the client training, teaching, keeping rents affordable
            (3) . . . projects as publicized for their own organization and the movement as a whole; . . . fitting into the political nexus
         c. Project and housing management as a pain/general management
         d. Involvement and identity—for the directors
         e. As packaging intermediaries
      3. Banks

V. Projects as Philosophy
   A. Goals as philosophy ( )
      1. Empowerment theme and empowerment as symbolism theme
      2. Grand motivational theme
      3. Holistic development
      4. Shared stake
   B. Development from below philosophy
      1. Partnerships: Ideologies of partnerships
      2. Networking ideology
      3. Niches/catalysts
      4. Social costs versus economic costs
      5. Exemplary copying, inspired by the funders
   C. Projects within the community
      1. Community autarchy as money and control as power—Assets for the poor
      2. Community as conceptualization of what is being rebuilt
      3. Community as involvement
      4. Accomplishing goals for individuals within the geographic community
   D. Tensions between ideology and financial imperatives
      1. Tensions of the organization
      2. Tensions in doing, legitimating, the project
      3. Client empowering versus reality that you are handling clients with incapacity including community businesses
      4. Projects as process or as outcomes
      5. Project types as themes of hope
      6. People versus place

All these categories represent information grounded within the interview data. The categories were chosen after extensive reading and rereading of the interview transcripts. With a coding sheet like this, Herb can simultaneously code for themes, concepts, processes, examples, and stories while keeping in mind the relationships between the categories.

Category IIID was used to mark off every time an interviewee talked about what community means; VA1 designates descriptive examples and definitions of empowerment. The separate categories grouped together under IVC1 include the stages of doing a development project, with predevelopment dreaming coded as IVC1a; financing, IVC1b; and getting a partner to help with the project, IVC1c. Once the data are coded in this way, it is easy to compare, for example, how projects are financed by looking at the entries under IVC1b across all the interviews. To present a holistic picture of how projects are accomplished, you would examine all the information under category IVC.

For instance, one coded passage in Herb's notes looks like this:

ivc2b3
vc3
ivc1e
va1

I think one of the most powerful demonstrations that I've seen here has been the building of our adult learners program. We started from nothing and we've got a base of 50 students and 70 volunteer tutors who are working on changing lives and that's really what's going on in this program. It's just been just incredible. It's a community of learners on both sides, both the volunteer tutors and the adults who are learning, really learning, how to read and write. And the stereotypes, my own stereotypes, have been blown away. Most of these people are employed. They are active members of the community. They are not low income people.

The learners. Well, we've got like 3 years of data now and we can tell ya, you know, if people want the objective measures . . . we're trying to educate funders. But we still have to demonstrate grade level gain or getting people over that 6th grade literacy mark and all that stuff and we can do it. But what really goes on is the change in self-esteem and self-confidence and we started groups now of both student groups and tutor groups and we're very much interested in really doing a [word missing] and empowerment and we want to figure out ways to get that group cause it's an incredible resource and organizational builder. And they are all from this community and we're working on getting that group more involved in different aspects of community development. And that's really what we want to do over the next year.

The overall passage is about the types of projects that community groups do, and how they can move from one successful project to another, so the passage is coded ivc2b3. It is also about how a project mobilizes and involves a community, a theme coded under vc3. The interviewee describes with enthusiasm how the project helps the clients, who are learning, "really learning," to read and write, a set of impressions coded under category ivc1e. Finally, the paragraph mentions the concept of empowerment, which is category va1. In this case empowerment means that people who learn how to read and write learn to control other aspects of their lives.

Once data are encoded in this fashion, the researcher can ask the computer to create and present a file of all references to "empowerment" or to "financing projects" or category "ivc2b3," or the researcher can ask the computer for any combination of items. The files that the computer creates (or that you create by hand) become the raw data for your analysis.

For a recent paper, Herb asked his computer to find all references to empowerment or empowering as well as category va1 in the 8,000 pages of notes from his community development interviews. A file with 520 references appeared in under 20 seconds. Herb then studied this file to find out what the concept empowerment meant to different interviewees. He was also able to check to see if his interviewees routinely brought up any other ideas when they discussed the concept of empowerment, suggesting further concerns to explore.

THE FINAL STAGES OF ANALYSIS

In the final stages of analysis, you organize the data in ways that help you formulate themes, refine concepts, and link them together to create a clear description or explanation of a culture or a topic. This material is then interpreted in terms of the literature and theories in the researcher's field.

Building Toward Overarching Themes

The coding process fragments the interviews into separate categories of themes, concepts, events, or stages. Coding forces you to look at each detail, each quote, to see what it adds to your understanding. Once you find the individual concepts and themes, you have to put them together to build an integrated explanation. You follow a two-stage process of thinking about the data. In the first, you examine and compare the material within categories. In the second, you compare material across categories.

Within one category, you ask yourself, how uniform are the examples? Do the illustrations suggest some nuance of meaning in concept or theme? Is what was coded as one concept actually two related concepts? "Community" might mean both ethnic affiliation and neighborhood. Are some actors defining a term one way and others a different way? You may find, for example, that marriage means something different to men than it does to women. Is there some systematic variation in how people understand an idea—people in big cities said one thing and people in small towns said something different?

If you have coded for events, a single coding category should contain different perspectives on each particular event. For instance, Herb coded into one category what politicians, environmentalists, and developers said about how a particular parcel of land should be used. These different perspectives can help you understand conflicts or different understandings of the same topic.

You can use the information within one coding category to compare separate versions of an event or combine the separate parts of an event into one narrative. In that coding category, you have put together different people's renditions of events and backup documentation. You ask yourself a series of questions: Are the interviewees' descriptions different because they saw the process from distinct angles, or do they blatantly contradict each other? Does one say that the idea for the project came from the community and another say it came from the foundations? Is there any logical way of reconciling the contradictory positions? For example, if one interviewee says a particular health care proposal had the President's backing and another one said it didn't, could they be referring to different time periods or different incarnations of the proposal?

If the contradiction won't go away and it is important to find out which version to rely on, then see if other internal evidence helps. Were both interviewees in position to know or would one have had to depend on rumor or secondhand information? Did either produce documentation, a letter or written plan, to support his or her point? Which one gave concrete evidence, on this as well as other points? Might one interviewee have been trapped by his or her own argumentation to distort a bit of evidence to fit into a broader pattern? Can you interpret what they say based on the slant probes that you used?

If you coded for time sequence, by looking at a file that contains all those sequence markers you can put together a time line that can organize a narrative. Irene did that first when she was analyzing Al Sette's interview. You can reconstruct the events that led to a divorce or the sequence of events that led to deficits in a city-manager city or the events that led to the dissolution of the Soviet Union. If you have constructed time lines for a number of divorced couples, how similar are they? Do the same events occur in roughly the same order in different marriages?

These reconstructions let people understand what happened, but they also stimulate important theoretical and practical concerns about why things occurred. For example, they raise the question whether some of the events were more crucial to the outcome than others. What allows or causes a marriage or a nation to dissolve? Where in the sequence leading to divorce do minor disagreements become frequent or violent? How important is being together or being left alone in causing a marriage to end?

Because events that follow other events cannot logically have caused them, time sequences can help provide evidence on why things occurred the way they did. In Irene's study of the city-manager city running deficits, the expensive settlements with the unions occurred after the onset of fiscal stress, refuting previous arguments that union settlements caused fiscal stress (I. S. Rubin, 1982).

If you code on people's names or on program names, sometimes you will get an unexpected result when you look at the material you put in the same coding category. In Herb's study of the conflict between the environmentalists and developers, one way he coded was on people's names. By doing so he discovered that the same person who had been a senior government official a decade ago was now on the payroll of the major developer. Herb saw the glimmerings of a theme and began to understand why the developers were so effective at dealing with government agencies—they had former government employees on their staff.

After you have analyzed the material inside each of the coding categories, you look for linkages across coding categories. Sometimes, you can see linkages easily, because the interviewee raises concepts or themes together and describes their relationship. In Irene's interview with Al Sette, Sette linked the concepts of openness and professionalism and argued that professionalism and politicization were opposites. Analysis across your coding categories lets you look for linkages that are much less obvious by putting related ideas in proximity to each other that were not raised at the same time or by the same interviewee. In Irene's study of how budgeting in cities changes over time, one of the themes that came up in cities with a strong-mayor form of government was that mayors are reluctant to make some kinds of budget information public. A theme that was prominent in cities that had a city manager form of government was that city managers were eager to get budgeting information out to the public. One immediate conclusion from putting these themes back to back is that the form of government affects the adoption and use of budget reforms.

One of Herb's coded categories described the pressure tactics the community organizations used on those who paid for projects; another category suggested that these same community organizations deferred to the whims of their funders. Putting these two themes side by side made Herb question how the community organizations could be aggressive and deferential at the same time. Herb reread everything that he had coded into the pressure category and observed that many of the pressure tactics were indirect. Rather than the community organizations themselves leading a pressure campaign, they asked supportive funders to talk to other funders on their behalf or they established coalitions whose sole purpose was to take the heat if funders got angry at being pressured.

You can string together two, three, four, or even more themes and concepts, thinking through the implications each time you add one more to your existing synthesis. You can start with any of your themes or concepts and ask how they relate to each of the other themes and concepts that you have worked out. You should aim to come up with a number of themes that are linked together and collectively describe or analyze your research arena.

PREPARING THE THEMES FOR THE FINAL REPORT

A goal of analysis is to find themes that both explain the research arena and fit together in a way that a reader can understand. Sometimes you can find an overarching theme that ties the individual pieces together. For example, one of Herb's community developers explained why he kept at the difficult and frustrating work of building homes for the poor by saying, "If we don't do it, nobody's going to do it." Herb's first reaction was stunned silence. Then he thought about how many of his other interviewees had expressed similar sentiments, but less dramatically, and understood that he could integrate much of what he learned using this statement as an overarching theme.

Sometimes to create an integrative theme you step back and examine the smaller themes to see what, if anything, ties them together. Herb had discovered many smaller themes in his interviews. His interviewees explained (a) how their agencies helped the poor, (b) what actions they took to reverse neighborhood deterioration, and (c) how difficult it was to work with government agencies that did not trust community groups and how frustrating it was to try to get support from bankers who did not understand nonprofits. Each of these separate themes would constitute a section of his report, replete with numerous examples.

Herb asked himself what, if anything, tied these three separate themes together. He thought about what the community organization was doing in each case—that is, helping individuals from different walks of life to work together. Herb came up with a possible integrative theme that "community development organizations work in the niche to span social and bureaucratic gaps that other organizations ignore." The community development organizations linked the poor to employers, to bankers, to stores, and to the economy more broadly. The idea of a niche organization became one of Herb's integrative themes.

Once you have developed your overarching themes, you need to think about the implications. Why is your work important, why should anyone pay any attention to it? By comparing what you have found to broader theories or policy concerns in your profession, you answer questions such as "Who cares?" and "So what?" Do your findings differ from those of other writers? If so, what accounts for the differences? Do your findings suggest new theories or policy approaches to solve a social problem?

In preparing a book on the city-manager city that ran illegal deficits, Irene was guided by three contending theories that explain why cities get into financial trouble. The theories differed in their emphasis on demographic shifts, economic change, and political practices. Irene first examined where her data supported and refuted these three arguments, and then showed how her findings suggested modifications, extensions, or revisions in all three theories. By presenting the results of her grounded interview data in comparison to these broader theories, she established the theoretical significance of her study and let readers know where her work was situated with respect to prior research.

The data analysis ends when you have found overarching themes and put them in the context of broader theory and answered the question "So what?" Then you write the final report.

11

Sharing the Results

By the end of the data analysis, you have worked out the major themes from the interviews, clarified the concepts, and put together an overarching description or explanation. The last step in the research is to put this information into a report that is convincing, thought provoking, absorbing, vivid, and fresh (cf. Blauner, 1987; Hess, 1989; Van Maanen, 1988). The report communicates in detail what the interviewees described about their lives and experiences so that readers can enter into a world they may never have seen.

To communicate what you have learned, organize the material so that readers can follow the logic of your argument. Write about the core themes and concepts clearly, letting the voices of the interviewees come through at appropriate moments. Excerpts from your interviews help make the report fresh and convincing while drawing the reader along to your conclusions.

ORGANIZING THE MATERIAL

A common way of organizing the report is to open the presentation with a statement of the problem, explain why it is puzzling and important, and then present what you have learned in ways that solve the puzzle. The flow of the report moves the reader toward this solution a piece at a time. The writing should build to a climax, maintaining at least a little drama right up until the end.

To organize the flow of what you write and to ensure that you provide evidence for each theme, first prepare an outline. The outline highlights the main topics, listing the evidence for each one, and puts the topics in order. An outline is not cast in concrete; you can change it as you write to clarify topics or strengthen the logic of the argument.

Most of our writing outlines include four main headings, indicated by capital roman numbers. The first heading is for a statement of the problem. The second heading highlights the importance of the research topic in terms of its policy implications or its impact on theory. The third heading, which introduces the main content of the report, organizes what you have learned by the individual themes or concepts or the steps in your argument. Subheadings under the third heading might describe components of a culture, steps in decision making, or stages in a historical process. In a study of budgeting, one subheading might be the history of the budget crunch, a second how the new budget format was introduced, and the third might be political obstacles that the new budget format encountered. If you have been able to pull the themes together into several overarching themes, these larger themes become subheadings that help organize the presentation. The final heading contains the conclusion.

An outline includes each main heading and the material that explains the subject matter and provides evidence for your argument that you place under each heading. The following is an example of what a writing outline looks like:

   I. The subject: Community development organizations
     A. What are they
     B. Some overall examples of what they do
  II. The importance of community development organizations
     A. They help the poor get jobs
       1. Example 1: Job training and day care
       2. Example 2: Housing and the building trades
     B. They physically redevelop dilapidated communities
       1. Evidence: Summary data on projects
       2. Specific examples, by city
     C. They bring commercial development to neighborhoods that have no shopping

       D. They build affordable housing
          1. Examples of making housing affordable
          2. Summary data from reports of number of homes built
       E. They help recreate a sense of community and community control
          1. Examples from projects done by community development organizations
          2. Quotations from community members on community control

 III. The findings about community development organizations
       A. How community development organizations are formed
       B. How community development organizations are financed
       C. Theories of development that guide community developers
          1. Empowerment for communities and the poor
             a. Example of fighting the banks
             b. Example of how owning a home empowers a poor person
          2. Owning the community from within
             a. Example of how a community supermarket keeps funds in the neighborhood
             b. Example of how a community association obtained and used zoning powers

 IV. Conclusions
       A. Interpretations of theories of community development for community-based development organizations
       B. Implications of the theories of the interviewees on how to bring about changes in communities of the poor

The order in which you present your main findings depends on which of four general patterns of report writing you prefer to use. With one pattern you create a narrative line (organized by time periods) that unravels a problem or process step by step or event by event, building to the conclusion of what happened, why, how, and when.

Another approach is to present the conclusion of why something occurred or failed, and then present step by step how your conclusion was reached. Evaluations and policy reports follow this pattern, almost always presenting the conclusions first and then the evidence for the conclusion. The audience for an evaluation or policy report has little time and less patience for reading lengthy documents, so with this approach important points are made early in the writing.

An analytical presentation, the third pattern, organizes your findings and interpretations in terms of an existing theory from your professional field. For example, in a report on a holistic study of a cultural group, you might organize your data to match existing theories of how cultures hang together. With an analytical presentation you describe the theories or policy alternatives at the beginning of the report and then present what you have learned as it illuminates these theories or policy alternatives. Each major subheading can address a part of the theory or a particular policy proposal. Such writing creates a tension that brings the reader along. Will your data support the accepted theory? Will you knock some well-known perspective off its pedestal?

The fourth approach organizes the writing to show how your findings illustrate the logic of your original design. Suppose that when you designed the research, you assumed that your findings would differ depending on the background characteristics of the interviewees. You reasoned that middle-class individuals would respond differently to a job-retraining program than working-class people, so you did some interviews in each group. Your report would follow this distinction, presenting the results from the working-class and the middle-class interviewees separately. Then, in your conclusion, you discuss whether your expectation that the two groups would respond differently to the program was correct, or if not, how the results differed. Or if you varied the research sites to check out whether a theme you discovered in one setting extends to other settings, you can present the results site by site.

MAKING THE REPORT CONVINCING

Through the writing you are trying to carefully portray the world of your conversational partners while convincing the reader that you accurately recorded and heard the meaning of what your conversational partners said. You do so by presenting descriptions and quotations that are detailed yet easily understood. Further, you verify that each point in your argument flows logically from another and is backed up by evidence.

Portraying the Interviewees' World

The goal of writing is to represent the world of your interviewees accurately, vividly, and convincingly. Using the conversational partners' words helps to provide detail and realism. You will have gathered an overwhelming amount of evidence for each point that you want to make and you cannot use it all, so you have to select from many quotes, examples, and illustrations those that make your case most convincingly.

With secondary parts of your argument you typically use one quote or example, or just summarize the point without quoting it directly. Thus, a series of direct quotes such as, "We really have no problem with the budget office, the director has always been fair with us," could be reported in your paraphrase as, "Several interviewees noted that the department had no problem with the budget office."

For major points in your argument, try to present one or more full quotations or elaborated examples. You want the reader both to understand what the interviewees said and why you reached the conclusions that you did. In one of Irene's books, she argued that agency cutbacks changed the role of the unions. Before the cutbacks, unions had been cooperative with management; afterward, they took a more formal and oppositional posture. To back up this crucial part of her argument, Irene chose an extensive quote from a union activist:

> The union strategy has been to outmanage management. I am less inclined now to try to convince managers and more inclined to state a position. I used to try to help them find a way. Now I am saying, "it's crazy." It's given me an ulcer. I don't trust the assistant secretary, and I don't think the employees do. He hasn't met with the employees. He hardly comes here. We are losing the cooperative relationship. There is no more romance. We are playing by the book. It's a shame. Management loses more than the employees. (I. S. Rubin, 1985, p. 97)

This quote was one among many that made the same point and was chosen because it illustrated the theme most clearly.

In general, when choosing among numerous quotations that illustrate the same point, think about what makes one quotation more convincing than another. First, a convincing quotation speaks directly to the point, leaving little need for the reader to make an inference. Second, the quotations should come from interviewees who are in position to know the answer. A quotation from a student or a professor about the motivations of the university president is not as convincing as what the president said when discussing a particular decision. If you are arguing that a point of view is commonly held, you need to present several quotes from people who represent the variation within the arena. When Herb was arguing that a particular opinion of community developers was widespread, he supported the argument with quotations from developers working in white, black, and Hispanic inner-city neighborhoods; in small cities; and in rural areas (H. J. Rubin, 1994).

Identifying your interviewees also adds credibility to a report. In most cultural interviews, you identify interviewees by position or experiences rather than by name in order to protect them from harm. Disguising names is especially common when studying groups or individuals who are afraid they will be punished for what they tell you. Prisoners, members of street gangs, con artists, hackers, and those practicing unusual sex are rarely identified by name. What you need to demonstrate in your report is that the interviewees know enough to give you firsthand information.

In oral histories and many studies based on elite interviews, the text identifies the speaker because the meaning of the interview depends on who the speaker is. In topical studies more generally, you want to identify interviewees by name and position whenever you can, that is, whenever the interviewees explicitly permit you to mention who they were. Anonymous reports and quotations make weaker evidence than statements that the conversational partners openly claim. "One informant reported" is considerably weaker than "A division manager reported," and both of these are weaker than "Mr. Argentino, the division head, said." If you describe the position that person occupied, you are describing the person's responsibilities and experiences, lending credence to what he or she said. If you name an individual, that person can be found and can confirm or deny your report.

Credibility Through the Logic of the Argument

To make sure your argument is convincing, you should double-check that it is logical and supported by evidence. First, write up a draft of the entire report and make a couple of copies (or even better, have two copies appear on a computer screen side by side). In one copy, delete all quotations and extended examples, leaving only the main arguments. In the second, cross out the thematic arguments, leaving only the detailed quotations and examples. Then place the two drafts side by side, so that you can see the correspondence between each stage in presenting a theme or point in a major argument and the evidence you put forth as its backing. Now ask yourself, do the main points by themselves make a coherent argument? Do they speak to the same theme and flow from one to another? Would reasoned argument based on the main points imply the conclusion that you reached? Then ask yourself whether the detailed evidence speaks to each of the main points. If someone read only the evidence, could he or she reconstruct the major arguments? Are the illustrations clear enough that a reader could come to the same conclusions you did? If any of your answers are no, then keep working on that part of the report until you can answer yes.

Remember though, qualitative reports can offer multiple and sometimes conflicting themes and you can present contrary evidence, as long as you interpret what the contradiction means. Qualitative theory is developed by elaborating and interpreting the unexpected and the apparently contradictory. You don't have to make the argument neater than it is or present the evidence as more one sided than it is. If you have evidence for both sides of an argument, then present and explain it. If, however, you have contradictory evidence for most of your main points, the report is likely to sound incomplete and muddled. You had better get back to the interviewing and see if you can resolve some of these issues.

The Credibility of the Researcher

Another way of convincing the reader that the report is correct is to show that the interviewer is a careful and thoughtful researcher. One way of beginning to establish credibility is to demonstrate the researcher's familiarity with the overall field by putting the study in the context of professional literature or current policy discussions. For instance, in a report on how people reacted to school reform, you can discuss background material such as comparative test scores, recent research on the importance of stimulating young children so their minds grow, and the relative decline of school funding in state budgets.

A researcher gains credibility by getting all the details correct. If you have a wrong name of a place or an erroneous date, anyone who knows about the subject will have a hard time believing the more subtle evidence you present. To avoid radiating carelessness, check your background details. In addition, your writing style should convey precision. For example, if you can, pinpoint dates and amounts exactly, rather than using phrases like "around then," "more or less," or "in the late 1930s." Don't overdo it, however. Suggesting more precision than you could possibly know also stretches credulity. To convince readers of the systematic and logical nature of your research, describe the research design in a confident and straightforward manner. Explain to the reader how you chose the interviewees and gained access to them, and why they were willing to talk with you. Describe the research role that you assumed or negotiated. For example, if you were doing research in a prison, under whose auspices did you enter the cells and how did you earn enough trust to get reliable and open interviews? How do you know, for example, that your interviewees were not pulling the wool over your eyes? Include in this section the details of the data collection, such as how many people you interviewed, how long each session lasted, and how many sessions were spent with each conversational partner. Describe how the interview was recorded. Be sure to include the basics of your design, such as how you varied the conditions or backgrounds of interviewees, the ways in which you tested your themes, and how you did your data analysis.

The tone of your methods discussion should be quietly authoritative. Make sure you do not sound apologetic for not having carried out a quantitative design. If you apologize for having only 10 interviewees or for an inability to generalize because your interviewees were not picked at random, you come across as if you do not understand either the qualitative interview model or the quantitative one.

In short, establishing the credibility of the report has implications for both style and content. The precision of the writing style, the confidence of tone, and the use of evidence including background data suggests that the researcher is careful and thorough, with a mastery of details and control of the facts. The thoroughness of the design, the appropriateness of the choice of interviewees, and the transparency of the methods all contribute to the persuasiveness of the report. The richness of the report further enhances it credibility.

Building in Richness

Good qualitative reports are rich and nuanced. A research narrative is rich when it presents not only the main themes, but also variations and refinements, each illustrated with clear examples. A description of a theme or concept is nuanced when it communicates shades of meaning or varies under different circumstances you can specify.

A nuanced explanation of the concept of empowerment examines the different ways the term is used in the interviews, and then explores the implications of each conceptualization of the term. Can one person help empower someone else? Or do people have to empower themselves? What does it mean to say that homeownership empowers people? How does the empowerment from ownership differ from the empowerment that comes from joining in a protest action?

A rich study keeps on asking and answering questions like when, why, how, and under what circumstances. Rich narratives do not stop with a description of a current quarrel; they investigate what the actors in the present quarrel have learned from previous encounters and how past understandings are influencing the current struggle. The researcher doesn't mark out a single issue and stop there, but examines a research problem in its context, even when the context is complicated.

A rich report provides enough of the context to make themes understandable. For instance, the fiscal stress experienced by Southside City in the mid-1970s (I. S. Rubin, 1982) stemmed from a period more than 20 years earlier when the city replaced a political machine with a city manager but failed to provide the manager with appropriate powers to carry out the job. Without understanding that historical context, the problems experienced in the 1970s were uninterpretable, and so the report included the historic background.

When writing for richness and subtlety, you can use longer passages from your notes that illustrate both major and minor themes and sometimes suggest contradictions. The following passage from an article by Herb illustrates the level of complexity you can communicate in this manner, without losing readability. The African American interviewee is discussing the relationship of his community development organization to city hall.

> The other thing that tends to happen . . . is favoritism. You know, if you are in with the bureaucrats on a particular day, then you might fare well.

If you are on the outs with them, you don't fare so well. . . . At one time, I had $50,000 in city monies, three or four years ago, to do housing. I used to do a lot of money with the city in terms of community development block grants. But over a period of time the city became increasingly more intrusive [slow and careful choice of words] as a result of that relationship. Meaning that they would demand things of me that had nothing to do with the proficiency of the project. Accounting records.

Or they even went so far as to suggest that I put some Caucasians on my board of directors. So they could say "you need to expand your board." I said, "what you mean, expand your board." [They said] "You know, so you got a more diverse representation on your board." Now I got school teachers, I got business owners, I got directors of alternative education programs. I got an accountant. You know, all of them African-American. But in his eye, he didn't see shit. All he saw was a bunch of black folk down there and you need to expand your board. So I said, "what you mean, expand my board." [the city official responded] "Well, you know it is perceived as being very closed corporation and you know a lot of people won't trust that situation, the way it is, so if you expanded it, you know, a little more expertise, and what not." "So you're talking, put some white people on my board?" "Well that would help, you know, that would help." And, I gave him their $50,000 back. (H. J. Rubin, 1993, p. 432)

The complexity of the passage derives from the two related and somewhat antagonistic themes, that the city seemed racist in its dealings with black groups, and that the city was concerned with accounting records. To what extent was the city's demand for better records of how its money was being spent racist? Real life is complex and that complexity can be conveyed in passages such as these.

Not only can quotes develop themes and subthemes simultaneously, but they also give off secondary messages that can either bolster the overall intent of the report or sabotage it. For example, a quote that describes the frustration of the community developer when a project fails might inadvertently convey the idea that the project did not work because the poor in the new homes failed to take care of the property. In the interview, the conversational partner did mention this problem with a new owner, but many more examples discussed problems caused by bankers and other granting agencies. By picking this quote, you inadvertently communicate that the poor themselves are to blame for the problems they face. This unintentional message may not fairly reflect the overall intent of the interviewee, who mentioned this problem as one among many examples. Further, it may directly contradict the overall theme of the report, that the poor are successfully carrying out the projects themselves.

If you don't pay attention, you can convey an incorrect message with the secondary themes raised in longer quotations. If you do pay attention, you can use these secondary points to reinforce core themes. In a study to find out how employees learned to use a new computer program, you might get a variety of answers. Some interviewees might describe the frustration of bad documentation; others describe the fun of mastering something new. But taken together the quotes might include a second and distinct message, that computers are fun, that people help each other learn to use them, and that new software is an occasion for social interaction. You can choose your quotations to intentionally convey this second message.

Sometimes when you read the quotes together, with the explanatory text around them removed, you do not get as strong a secondary message as you want. If that is the case, look for other quotations that make the same main points, but that make the secondary points better. Paying attention to this cumulative message of the quotations can give the report an extra dimension of richness.

Style

Writing styles for qualitative research differ depending in part on the purpose of the report and how you intend to distribute it. Styles vary from formal writing in academic journals to more conversational styles for persuasive pieces in magazines or newsletters.

One element of style is the choice of whose voice dominates the writing. In topical studies that present a version of events as weighed and balanced by the researcher, the researcher's is the dominant voice. You draw your own conclusions by synthesizing the arguments or discussions that many actors have given you, often without quoting them directly or at length. In cultural studies, the voices should be more those of the conversational partners, with greater use of extended quotes and a relatively smaller proportion of the researcher's own interpretations. At the extreme, in oral history reports, the entire presentation might be in the (edited and reordered) words of the conversational partners, with but a brief introduction or transition provided by the researcher.

Some reports, in an effort to sound scientific and unbiased, eliminate the voice of the researcher and try to present the material clinically. But a good qualitative interview is often a product of the interaction of interviewer and interviewee. If the voice of the interviewer drops out of the report completely, the writing misrepresents how the work was done. If the interviews were deeply interactional, with the parties exploring ideas together and coming to a joint conclusion, then the researcher's voice and role should be apparent in the report.

MAKING THE REPORT READABLE

In qualitative research, the writing has to be not only rich and convincing, but also readable. The report should address theoretical and practical issues without pedantry. The writing should be lively; the excitement of learning that you experienced during the project should be conveyed to the reader.

The text should present a comfortable interlacing of example and argument or explanation, in which the examples are vivid and anchor the more abstract arguments in understandable cases. Report writing can be dramatic or powerful, but not flowery or maudlin. The presentation should be balanced, so topics of roughly equal importance in the argument get approximately equal space.

Good writing means not setting up intellectual obstacles for the reader to overcome. The thematic presentation should not be interrupted with lots of methodological quibbles, even if they are technically correct. Don't overwhelm with masses of detail. Pick a few examples that are memorable and make the case clear.

Look over your draft writing and try to tone down any pedantry. Pedantry is an effort to impress by using the trappings of scholarship, often without making the material clear and illustrating it well. Pedantic writing uses too many big words, too many abstract ideas and phrases, and too many references to the literature. Whenever possible use ordinary words, not special technical ones. If you have to use a technical word, make sure it is defined the first time you use it. Eliminate long, complex sentences. If the quotes you use are jumbled, edit them, consonant with accuracy, to make them readable.

Good writing means catching and clarifying ambiguous phrases or sentences and making sure the logic is clear. The writer should always ask him- or herself in reading the drafts, what did I mean here? What was I trying to say? If I were not so steeped in the subject matter, would I be able to follow the discussion? Have I left out steps in the reasoning or in the evidence?

Keep paragraph length moderate—long paragraphs discourage readers. Avoid the passive voice and weak sentence beginnings, such as "there are," that obscure who is responsible. Journals often expect academic writers to use the passive voice, but doing so makes the writing seem distant and dull and removes the analysis from the hand of the author.

Good writing entices readers with an opening that makes them curious and suggests the scope of the report. Sometimes writers present a story or narrative near the beginning of the essay or book, and draw on it again and again throughout the discussion, to suggest and carry the main themes throughout the report. Such a story, narrative, or vivid introduction is a hook that like the cane of the barker at the circus reaches out and brings the reader in, by arousing interest in the subject matter. Hooks come in many patterns, but they have some common characteristics. They are relatively brief, probably no more than a page or two; they are interesting and vivid; and they suggest the content of the book or article or report.

William Gamson (1992) began his book on how ordinary people view politics with an excerpt from his notes written as a play, with the names of the characters and their occupations listed first, and then the dialogue, in which the characters talk about what interests them in the news. This works well as a hook, because it is vivid, has real people speaking, and introduces the topic of the book. Joseph Shapiro (1993) began *No Pity*, a book on the political movement of people with disabilities, with quotes from former poster children describing their experiences as poster children contrasted with the reality of growing up handicapped. These sketches work not only because they involve real people, but because of the symbolism, the economy of meaning, in the contrast between the poster child who is cute and lovable and evokes pity, and the adult who isn't viewed as cute or lovable, but shunned, and who doesn't want pity, but some measure of independent living as a valued member of society. The hook anticipates the tension that the entire rest of the book spells out.

Another approach to designing a hook is to describe a puzzle that might intrigue the reader or describe the stakes involved in a problem. Clarence Lo (1990) in his study of the property tax revolt in California begins with the puzzle: Why did blue-collar homeowners of limited means support a political movement that primarily benefited businesses and the well-to-do? Marilyn P. Davis, in *Mexican Voices/American Dreams* (1990), in her opening hook describes a vibrant Mexican market in Texas. This vivid description suggests the favorable economic impact of Mexican migration on a depressed economy, suggesting the importance of Mexican migration to the United States, the topic of the rest of the volume.

Keeping the Audience in Mind

Researchers write best when they keep the audience in mind. Sometimes they conjure up a single individual whom they know, for whom they write. Doing so reminds the author of how much the reader knows and what types of examples are most likely to engage that reader's interest and suggests how much context the writer needs to communicate and how difficult or abstract the writing can be.

In writing a consultancy report for busy policymakers, the tone should be purposeful and efficient, with no side comments and little theory. You only need a short introduction, because the readers who hired you know the importance of the topic. You focus on the matter that you were assigned to study, including where problems lie and what solutions seem most appropriate.

With academic journal articles, you are often pressed for space, because such pieces are usually restricted to 20 to 40 typewritten pages. That means you have to isolate one or two main themes, boil down the argument, and present solid evidence for each main point. You usually do not have space to develop several subthemes or present contradictions.

Journal articles often require explicit attention to the "So what?" question, requiring a section on why the problem is important and what the theoretical or practical implications of the work are. You also need to include what other academic literature has said on this topic and how your study fits into that literature. In some, but not all, professional journals, longer quotations are acceptable, so that the voice of the interviewees can come through clearly.

In more popular magazines or books, the writer adopts a less formal tone to convey the emotions that interviewees expressed. You may want to select passages from the interviews and put them back to back to let different voices tell the story of a period of time or a way of life. Studs Terkel's books on working (1974), race (1992), and World War II (1984) and Jonathan Kozol's (1991) descriptions of problems in the public schools illustrate this approach.

Writing a whole book allows the most scope, although you might have to search a while to locate a publisher who is comfortable with how you express your argument. In a full book you can develop multiple themes, show how they interrelate, and take advantage of the space to develop subtler points. You can explain a complicated story piece by piece. In narrating what you learned, you might choose to put some passion in your book, because you were moved by what you heard. However, you usually keep the emotion out of your own arguments, allowing it to be suggested by the intensity within the examples and quotations.

In a book you can describe the methodology in full in an appendix, so that it doesn't interrupt the flow of the writing. You can also devote a whole chapter to the theory that you have built from your analysis of the interviews.

HANDLING QUOTATIONS

Quotations from your interviews provide the evidence for the themes and at the same time enable you to evoke the interviewees' world accurately and vividly. But excerpts from the interviews can be difficult for readers to understand. You spent a long time learning the language of the conversational partners and now understand the assumptions that make many of these passages meaningful and interpretable. Most readers won't have had your exposure. Moreover, quotes are not always understandable because many interviewees do not speak grammatically; they interrupt and repeat themselves, they leave sentences dangling and unfinished, and they sometimes change tenses in the middle of a phrase.

How much freedom do you have to change a quote? If the key example was delivered in an ungrammatical way, should you quote it that way? What do you do if a grammatical mistake draws away attention from the key point? What about speech mannerisms, like uhhhns, mmms, and y' knows? What if there is a lot of repetition in a quotation, or if there is an interruption in the middle or a detour in the conversation? More difficult yet, what do you do when some interviewees speak in dialect that others might not understand? What about eliminating text that digresses from the thought at hand?

To improve the grammar, complete the thought, or eliminate dialect can make the text far more readable. But doing so might distort what the person said and impute to him or her too much of your own interpretation. At the very least, such changes alter the flavor of how people talk. Even worse, changing the quotes may destroy the evocative messages that the responses give off.

Researchers differ in their willingness to modify a quote. The two of us will alter a quote, but only in limited way. When we do so, we clearly mark the passages so that the reader can tell the changes apart from the original statement. Sometimes we send a copy of a quotation we are going to use to the interviewee for comment before we use it. If he or she doesn't want us to reproduce the dialect, or wants us to improve the grammar, and we don't want to make the changes, we can withdraw the quotation and find a substitute, or we can summarize the point in our own words, but without quotation marks.

Because space is limited in most reports, we follow the common practice of editing quotations by omitting repetition and comments that have nothing to do with the topic. As long as the meaning is preserved, the words that are quoted were actually said, and you mark the places where you made omissions, this practice is generally acceptable and even advisable. Otherwise your quotes will be too long and hard to follow.

What about editing a quotation for style—is that permissible? This is more dubious. Generally, you want to retain the style of the speaker. If he or she hesitates a lot, especially around difficult questions, those delays are part of the information being conveyed and help readers feel as if they are at the interview watching the conversational partner struggle for coherence to bring an idea to light. On the other hand, reading a lot of uhhs and y' knows is boring and doesn't add much meaning. These throat clearings are normally dropped. A good general strategy is to maintain enough of them to suggest the manner of speech and to indicate any special hesitancy that is necessary to interpreting the meaning.

It can be very tempting to improve the grammar of a particularly important passage to make the meaning clearer, but then you must be careful not to put into quotes words that were not spoken by the conversational partner. On the other hand, sometimes conversational partners are upset to see themselves quoted in ungrammatical English and expect you to clean up what they said. If they approve a corrected version or correct it themselves, we use quotation marks in our reports.

Our basic guideline in deciding when to change a quote is whether we can do it without misrepresenting the meaning of the conversational partner. You can distort what the person said even if you quote each word exactly, if the original quote is muddled and communicates inaccurately. People accidentally drop words they meant to say, and even the most polished of speakers leave sentences unfinished in informal conversation. You can insert missing words in brackets. These words can finish up a thought and make it more grammatical, and the brackets show that the original version was more fragmentary. You can use information that was provided elsewhere in the interview or in your other research to fill in blanks, such as missing names, dates, or titles. The following excerpt from interview notes shows how this looks:

> It was a top down process. [Budget Director] Stockman and OMB determined where [the cuts would be], quickly, and I might say, efficiently. There was not a lot of appeal [from their decision]. Cabinet officers were in sync with the philosophy; it was not a normal policy review. It was almost done by fiat. (I. S. Rubin, 1985, p. 81)

CRITIQUES AND REWRITES: THE FINAL DRAFT

When you have a good clean draft of your report, circulate it for comment among your interviewees, your colleagues, whomever funded your project, and potential book publishers. If you send a manuscript off to a journal, the journal may send the manuscript to "blind" reviewers, that is, people in your field who do not know who wrote the manuscript. You should get back comments from these initial readers. Read these comments carefully, and incorporate the ones that make sense to you into the manuscript as part of the final changes.

If your conversational partners tell you that you got something wrong, you probably want to correct what you have written. If they agree with your facts, but disagree with your interpretations, interview them again to see if what they say is persuasive. If you still disagree with their interpretation, you can keep what you wrote—the interpretations are yours—but you might want to add a footnote to indicate that they disagreed and describe what the interviewee thinks the material means.

If any of your reviewers point out incomplete thoughts or arguments, or language that is ambiguous and hard to follow, take their advice and clean up that portion of the manuscript. If the manuscript is not clear to these readers, if the evidence you present doesn't persuade them, it probably won't convince a more general audience later. After all the time you spent with your data, you can be too close to the manuscript to notice that you have left out background material that readers need to know.

As you receive these reviews, both from your interviewees and from colleagues in the field, read them to discover whether the readers recognize the world and events you have portrayed, whether it seems real and accurate to them. If people from the research arena and others who are familiar with that arena say, "Yes, this is the way it is," then your research is finally complete. Your work has passed its last test.

References

Adler, P. A., Adler, P., Rochford, J., & Burke, E. (1986, January). The politics of participation in field research. *Urban Life, 14*(4), 363-376.

Anderson, K., & Jack, D. C. (1991). Learning to listen: Interview techniques and analyses. In S. B. Gluck & D. Patai (Eds.), *Women's words: The feminist practice of oral history* (pp. 11-26). New York: Routledge & Kegan Paul.

Antaki, C. (Ed.). (1988). *Analyzing everyday explanation.* Newbury Park, CA: Sage.

Antaki, C., & Leudar, I. (1992). Explaining in conversation: Towards an argument model. *European Journal of Social Psychology, 22,* 181-194.

Balshem, M. (1991, February). Cancer, control, and causality: Talking about cancer in a working-class community. *American Ethnologist, 18*(1), 152-172.

Bart, P. (1987, Winter). Seizing the means of reproduction: An illegal feminist abortion collective—how and why it worked. *Qualitative Sociology, 10*(4), 339-357.

Becker, H. S., Geer, B., Hughes, E. C., & Strauss, A. (1961). *Boys in white.* Chicago: University of Chicago Press.

Bellah, R. N., Madsen, R., Sullivan, W. M., Swidler, A., & Tipton, S. (1985). *Habits of the heart: Individualism and commitment in American life.* New York: Harper & Row.

Berger, P., & Luckman, T. (1967). *The social construction of reality: A treatise in the sociology of knowledge and commitment in American life.* Garden City, NY: Anchor.

Blauner, B. (1987, Spring). Problems of editing "first-person" sociology. *Qualitative Sociology, 10*(1), 46-64.

Bowman, B., Bowman, G. W., & Resch, R. C. (1984). Humanizing the research interview: A posthumous analysis of LeRoy Bowman's approach to the interview process. *Quality and Quantity, 18,* 159-171.

Brajuha, M., & Hallowell, L. (1986). Legal intrusion and the politics of fieldwork: The impact of the Brajuha case. *Urban Life, 14,* 454-478.

Braungart, M. M., & Braungart, R. G. (1991, August). The effects of the 1960s political generation on former left- and right-wing youth activist leaders. *Social Problems, 38*(1), 297-315.

Briggs, C. L. (1983). Questions for the ethnographer: A critical examination of the role
    of the interview in fieldwork. *Semiotica, 46*(2/4), 233-261.
Broadhead, R. S., & Fox, K. J. (1990, October). Takin' it to the streets: AIDs outreach as
    ethnography. *Journal of Contemporary Ethnography, 19*(3), 322-348.
Brown, J. D. (1991, July). Preprofessional socialization and identity transformation: The
    case of the professional ex-. *Journal of Contemporary Ethnography, 20*(2), 157-178.
Brown, R. H. (1985). Social reality as narrative text: Interactions, institutions, and polities
    as language. *Current Perspectives in Social Theory, 6,* 17-37.
Cannon, L. W., Higginbotham, E., & Leung, M. (1988, December). Race and class bias
    in qualitative research on women. *Gender and Society, 2*(4), 449-462.
Charmaz, K. (1983). The grounded theory method: An explication and interpretation. In
    Robert Emerson (Ed.), *Contemporary field research* (pp. 109-126). Boston: Little,
    Brown.
Cohen, R. (1991). Women of color in white households: Coping strategies of live-in
    domestic workers. *Qualitative Sociology, 14*(2), 197-215.
Counihan, C. M. (1992). Food rules in the United States: Individualism, control, and
    hierarchy. *Anthropological Quarterly, 65*(2), 55-66.
Davis, M. P. (1990). *Mexican voices/American dreams: An oral history of Mexican
    immigration to the United States.* New York: Henry Holt.
Denzin, N. (1989). *The research act: A theoretical introduction to sociological methods.*
    Englewood Cliffs, NJ: Prentice-Hall.
Devault, M. L. (1990, February). Talking and listening from women's standpoint: Femi-
    nist strategies for interviewing and analysis. *Social Problems, 37*(1), 96-116.
Douglas, J. D. (1985). *Creative interviewing* (Sage Library of Social Research No. 159).
    Beverly Hills, CA: Sage.
Eden, K. (1991). Surviving the welfare system: How AFDC recipients make ends meet
    in Chicago. *Social Problems, 38*(4), 462-473.
Emerson, R. M. (1988). *Contemporary field research: A collection of readings.* Prospect
    Heights, IL: Waveland.
Fantasia, R. (1988). *Cultures of solidarity: Consciousness, action, and contemporary
    American workers.* Berkeley: University of California Press.
Faupel, C. E., & Klockars, C. B. (1987, February). Drugs-crime connections: Elaborations
    from the life histories of hard-core heroin addicts. *Social Problems, 34*(1), 54-68.
Fenno, R. (1978). *Home style: House members in their districts.* Boston: Little, Brown.
Fisher, B. J. (1987, Summer). Illness career descent in institutions for the elderly.
    Qualitative Sociology, 10(2), 132-145.
Forester, J. (1993). *Critical theory: Public policy and planning practice.* Albany: State
    University of New York Press.
Fox, K. J. (1987, October). Real punks and pretenders: The social organization of a
    counterculture. *Journal of Contemporary Ethnography, 16*(3), 344-370.
Frey, J. H., & Fontana, A. (1991). The group interview in social research. *Social Science
    Journal, 28*(2), 175-187.
Friedman, R. (1989, April). Interaction norms as carriers of organizational culture: A
    study of labor negotiations at International Harvester. *Journal of Contemporary
    Ethnography, 18,* 3-29.
Frisch, M. (1990). *A shared authority: Essays on the craft and meaning of oral and public
    history.* Albany: State University of New York Press.
Gagne, P. L. (1992, January). Appalachian women: Violence and social control. *Journal
    of Contemporary Ethnography, 20*(4), 387-415.

Gamson, W. A. (1992). *Talking politics.* New York: Cambridge University Press.

Geertz, C. (1973). Thick description: Toward an interpretive theory of culture. In C. Geertz (Ed.), *The interpretation of cultures* (pp. 3-30). New York: Basic Books.

Glaser, B., & Strauss, A. (1967). *The discovery of grounded theory.* Chicago: Aldine.

Gluck, S. B., & Patai, D. (1991). *Women's words: The feminist practice of oral history.* London: Routledge & Kegan Paul.

Goffman, E. (1959). *The presentation of self in everyday life.* New York: Anchor.

Goldman, A. E., & McDonald, S. S. (1987). *The group depth interview: Principles and practice.* Englewood Cliffs, NJ: Prentice-Hall.

Gorden, D. F. (1987, Fall). Getting close by staying distant: Fieldwork with proselytizing groups. *Qualitative Sociology, 10*(3), 267-287.

Grele, R. J. (1985). *Envelopes of sound: The art of oral history* (2nd ed.). Chicago: Precedent.

Groce, S. B. (1989, Winter 1989). Occupational rhetoric and ideology: A comparison of copy and original music performers. *Qualitative Sociology, 12*(4), 391-410.

Gurney, J. N. (1985, Spring). Not one of the guys: The female researcher in a male-dominated setting. *Qualitative Sociology, 8*(1), 42-61.

Hamabata, M. M. (1986, Winter). Ethnographic boundaries, culture, class, and sexuality in Tokyo. *Qualitative Sociology, 9*(4), 354-371.

Harding, S. (1991). *Whose science? Whose knowledge? Thinking about women's lives.* Ithaca, NY: Cornell University Press.

Heinsler, J. M., Kleinman, S., & Stenross, B. (1990). Making work matter: Satisfied detectives and dissatisfied campus police. *Qualitative Sociology, 13*(3), 235-250.

Helling, I. K. (1988). The life history method: A survey and discussion with Norman K. Denzin. *Studies in Symbolic Interaction, 9,* 211-243.

Hess, D. J. (1989). Teaching ethnographic writing: A review essay. *Anthropology and Education Quarterly, 20,* 163-176.

Hallowell, L. (1985). The outcome of the Brajuha case: Legal implications for sociologists. *Footnotes American Sociological Association, 13*(1), 13.

hooks, b. (1989). *Talking back: Thinking feminist, thinking black.* Boston, MA: South End.

Horowitz, R. (1986, January). Remain an outsider: Membership as a threat to research rapport. *Urban Life, 14*(4), 409-430.

Hubert, H., & Mauss, M. (1964). *Sacrifice: Its nature and function.* Chicago: University of Chicago Press.

Hummel, R. P. (1991, January/February). Stories managers tell: Why they are as valid a science. *Public Administration Review, 51*(1), 31-41.

Hummon, D. M. (1986, Spring). City mouse, country mouse: The persistence of community identity. *Qualitative Sociology, 9*(1), 3-25.

Jankowski, M. S. (1991). *Islands in the street: Gangs and American urban society.* Berkeley: University of California Press.

Karp, D. A. (1985, Spring). Gender, academic careers, and the social psychology of aging. *Qualitative Sociology, 8*(1), 9-28.

Kasinitz, P. (1988, Fall). The gentrifiction of "Boerum Hill": Neighborhood change and conflicts over definition. *Qualitative Sociology, 11*(3), 163-182.

Kleinman, S. (1983, July). Collective matters as individual concerns: Peer culture among graduate students. *Urban Life, 12*(2), 203-225.

Kozol, J. (1991). *Savage inequalities: Children in American's schools.* New York: Crown.

Lee, R. M. (1993). *Doing research on sensitive topics.* Newbury Park, CA: Sage.

Levi-Strauss, C. (1963). *Structural anthropology.* New York: Basic Books.

Lewin, R. G. (1990). *Witnesses to the Holocaust: An oral history.* Boston: Twayne.

Liebow, E. (1967). *Tally's corner: A study of Negro streetcorner men.* Boston: Little, Brown.

Liebow, E. (1993). *Tell them who I am: The lives of homeless women.* New York: Free Press.

Lincoln, Y. S., & Guba, E. G. (1985). *Naturalistic inquiry.* Newbury Park, CA: Sage.

Lipsitz, G. (1988). *A life in the struggle: Ivory Perry and the culture of opposition.* Philadelphia, PA: Temple University Press.

Lo, C. (1990). *Small property, big government: The social origins of the property tax revolt.* Berkeley: University of California Press.

Locke, L. F., Spirduso, W. W., & Silverman, S. J. (1987). *Proposals that work: A guide for planning dissertations and grant proposals.* Newbury Park, CA: Sage.

Lord, G. F., & Price, A. C. (1992, May). Growth ideology in a period of decline: Deindustrialization and restructuring Flint style. *Social Problems, 39*(2), 155-169.

Lozano, W. G., & Foltz, T. G. (1990). Into the darkness: An ethnographic study of witchcraft and death. *Qualitative Sociology, 13*(3), 211-234.

Lummis, T. (1988). *Listening to history: The authenticity of oral evidence.* Totowa, NJ: Barnes & Noble.

Lyman, S., & Scott, M. (1968, February). Accounts. *American Journal of Sociology, 33*(1), 46-62.

MacLeod, J. (1987). *Ain't no makin' it: Leveled aspirations in a low-income neighborhood.* Boulder, CO: Westview.

Maines, D. R. (1993, Spring). Narrative's moment and sociology's phenomena: Toward a narrative sociology. *Sociological Quarterly, 34*(1), 17-38.

Marshall, C., & Rossman, G. (1989). *Designing qualitative research.* Newbury Park, CA: Sage.

Mast, R. H. (1994). *Detroit lives.* Philadelphia, PA: Temple University Press.

McCall, M. M. (1990). The significance of story telling. In N. Denzin (Ed.), *Studies in symbolic interaction* (Vol. 11, pp. 145-161). Greenwich, CO: JAI.

McMahan, E. M. (1989). *Elite oral history discourse: A study of cooperation and coherence.* Tuscaloosa, AL: University of Alabama Press.

Merton, R. K., Fiske, M., & Kendall, P. L. (1990). *The focused interviews: A manual of problems and procedures* (2nd ed.). New York: Free Press.

Miller, G. I. (1987). Observations on police undercover work. *Criminology, 25*(1), 27-46.

Mishler, E. G. (1986). *Research interviewing: Context and narrative.* Cambridge, MA: Harvard University Press.

Moerman, M. (1988). *Talking culture: Ethnography and conversation analysis.* Philadelphia, PA: University of Pennsylvania Press.

Moffatt, M. (1989). *Coming of age in New Jersey: College and American culture.* New Brunswick, NJ: Rutgers University Press.

Morgan, D. L. (1988). *Focus groups as qualitative research* (Qualitative Research Methods Series No. 16). Newbury Park, CA: Sage.

Mumby, D. K. (Ed.). (1993). *Narrative and social control: Critical perspectives* (Sage Annual Review of Communication Research Vol. 21). Newbury Park. CA: Sage.

Myers, J. (1992, October). Nonmainstream body modifications: Genital piercing, branding, burning and cutting. *Journal of Contemporary Ethnography, 21*(3), 267-306.

Neuman, W. L. (1994). *Social research methods: Qualitative and quantitative approaches* (2nd ed.). Boston: Allyn & Bacon.

Oakley, A. (1981). Interviewing women: A contradiction in terms. In H. Roberts (Ed.), *Doing feminist research* (pp. 30-61). London: Routledge & Kegan Paul.

Ochberg, R. (1988). Life stories and the psychosocial construction of careers. *Journal of Personality, 56*(1), 173-204.

Padilla, F. (1992). *The gang as an American enterprise.* New Brunswick, NJ: Rutgers University Press.

Patton, M. Q. (1990). *Qualitative evaluation and research methods* (2nd ed.). Newbury Park, CA: Sage.

Prasad, P. (1991, September). Organization building in a Yale union. *Journal of Applied Behavior Science, 27*(3), 337-355.

Rakove, M. L. (1979). *We don't want nobody nobody sent.* Bloomington: Indiana University Press.

Reinharz, S. (1992). *Feminist methods in social research.* New York: Oxford University Press.

Richardson, L. (1990, April). Narrative and sociology. *Journal of Contemporary Ethnography, 19*(1), 116-135.

Riessman, C. K. (1987, June). When gender is not enough: Women interviewing women. *Gender and Society, 1*(2), 172-207.

Riessman, C. K. (1990). *Divorce talk: Women and men make sense of personal relationships.* New Brunswick, NJ: Rutgers University Press.

Riessman, C. K. (1993). *Narrative analysis* (Qualitative Research Methods Series No. 30). Newbury Park, CA: Sage.

Rubin, H. J. (1973, May). Will and awe: Illustrations of Thai villager dependency upon officials. *Journal of Asian Studies, 32*(3), 425-444.

Rubin, H. J. (1983). *Applied social research.* Columbus, OH: Charles E. Merrill.

Rubin, H. J. (1988a, August). Shoot anything that flies; claim anything that falls: Conversations with economic development practitioners. *Economic Development Quarterly, 2*(3), 236-251.

Rubin, H. J. (1988b, Winter). The Danada Farm: Land acquisition, planning, and politics in suburbia. *Journal of the American Planning Association,* pp. 79-90.

Rubin, H. J. (1993, September/October). Understanding the ethos of community-based development: Ethnographic description for public administration. *Public Administration Review, 53*(5), 428-437.

Rubin, H. J. (1994, August). There aren't going to be any bakeries here if there is no money to afford jellyrolls: The organic theory of community based development. *Social Problems, 41*(3), 401-424.

Rubin, I. S. (1977). Universities in stress: Decision making under conditions of reduced resources. *Social Science Quarterly, 58,* 242-254.

Rubin, I. S. (1982). *Running in the red: The political dynamics of urban fiscal stress.* Albany: State University of New York Press.

Rubin, I. S. (1985). *Shrinking the federal government: The effect of cutbacks on five federal agencies.* New York: Longman.

Rubin, I. S. (1992). Budget reform and political reform: Conclusions from six cities. *Public Administration Review, 52,* 454-466.

Sarbin, T. R. (Ed.). (1986). *Narrative psychology: The storied nature of human conduct.* New York: Praeger.

Schegloff, E. A. (1992, March). Repair after next turn: The last structurally provided defense of intersubjectivity in conversation. *American Journal of Sociology, 97*(5), 1295-1345.

Schein, E. H. (1985). *Organizational culture and leadership*. San Francisco: Jossey-Bass.
Schutz, A. (1967). *The phenomenology of the social world*. Evanston, IL: Northwestern University Press.
Shapiro, J. P. (1993). *No pity*. New York: Times Books.
Siegel, K., Levine, M. P., Brooks, C., & Kern, R. (1989, October). The motives of gay men for taking or not taking the HIV antibody test. *Social Problems, 36*(4), 368-383.
Silverstone, R., Hirsch, E., & Morley, D. (1991, May). Listening to a long conversation: An ethnographic approach to the study of information and communication technologies in the home. *Cultural Studies, 5*(2), 204-227.
Sink, D. W. (1991, September). Focus groups as an approach to outcomes assessment. *American Review of Public Administration, 21*(2), 197-204.
Snow, D. A., & Anderson, L. (1993). *Down on their luck: A study of homeless people*. Berkeley: University of California Press.
Snow, D., Benford, R. D., & Anderson, L. (1986, January). Fieldwork roles and informational yield: A comparison of alternative settings and roles. *Urban Life, 14*(4), 377-408.
Spender, D. (1985). *Man made language* (2nd ed.). London: Routledge & Kegan Paul.
Spradley, J. P. (1979). *The ethnographic interview*. New York: Holt, Rinehart & Winston.
Strauss, A. S. (1987). *Qualitative analysis for social scientists*. Cambridge, UK: Cambridge University Press.
Tannen, D. (1990). *You just don't understand: Women and men in conversation*. New York: Ballantine.
Terkel, S. (1974). *Working: People talk about what they do all day and how they feel about what they do*. New York: Pantheon.
Terkel, S. (1984). *"The good war": An oral history of World War Two*. New York: Pantheon.
Terkel, S. (1992). *Race: How blacks and whites think and feel about the American obsession*. New York: New Press.
Tesch, R. (1990). *Qualitative research: Analysis types and software tools*. New York: Falmer.
Thomas, J. (1993). *Doing critical ethography* (Qualitative Research Methods Series No. 26). Newbury Park, CA: Sage.
Thomas, J., & Marquart, J. (1988). Dirty information and clean conscience: Communication problems in studying "bad guys." In D. R. Maines & C. J. Couch (Eds.), *Communication and social structure* (pp. 81-96). Springfield, IL: Charles C Thomas.
Tixier y Vigil, Y., & Elsasser, N. (1978). The effects of ethnicity of the interviewer on conversation: A study of Chicana women. *International Journal of the Sociology of Language, 17*, 91-102.
Van Maanen, J. (1978). The asshole. In P. K. Manning & J. Van Maanen (Eds.), *Policing* (pp. 221-238). New York: Random House.
Van Maanen, J. (1988). *Tales of the field: On writing ethnography*. Chicago: University of Chicago Press.
Van Maanen, J., & Barley, S. R. (1985). Cultural organization: Fragments of a theory. In P. J. Frost, L. F. Moore, M. R. Louis, C. C. Lundberg, & J. Martin (Eds.), *Organizational culture* (pp. 31-54). Beverly Hills, CA: Sage.
Vellela, T. (1988). *New voices: Student political activism in the '80s and '90s*. Boston: South End.
Walker, K. (1990). Class, work and family in women's lives. *Qualitative Sociology, 13*(4), 297-320.

Watson, L. C., & Watson-Franke, M. B. (1985). *Interpreting life histories: An anthropological inquiry.* New Brunswick, NJ: Rutgers University Press.

Weeks, L. E., & Berman, H. J. (1985). *Shapers of American health care policy: An oral history.* Ann Arbor, MI: Health Administration Press, School of Public Health.

Weitz, R. (1987). The interview as legacy: A social scientist confronts AIDS. *Hastings Center Report, 17*(3), 21-23.

West, P. (1990). The status and validity of accounts obtained at interview: A contrast between two studies of families with a disabled child. *Social Science and Medicine, 30*(11), 1229-1239.

Wharton, C. (1987, Summer). Establishing shelters for battered women: Local manifestations of a social movement. *Qualitative Sociology, 10*(2), 146-163.

Whyte, W. F. (1955). *Street corner society.* Chicago: University of Chicago Press.

Wiggington, E. (1992). *Refuse to stand silently by: An oral history of grass roots social activism in America 1921-1964.* New York: Anchor.

Williams, C. (1992, August). The glass escalator: Hidden advantages for men in the "female" professions. *Social Problems, 39*(3), 253-267.

Yanow, D. (1992). Supermarkets and culture clash: The epistemological role of metaphors in administrative practice. *American Review of Public Administration, 22*(2), 89-110.

Youth of the Rural Organizing and Cultural Center. (1991). *Minds stayed on freedom: The civil rights struggle in the rural south: An oral history.* Boulder, CO: Westview.

Author Index

Subject Index

Emphasis, nonverbal cues to, 7
Employers, topic choice and, 49
Empowerment, feminist research and, 36
Ethical obligations, 39-40, 93-101
Ethnic barriers, interviewing across, 111-
    113
Ethnic identity, topics developing out
    of, 50
Evaluation, of projects and programs, 4,
    6, 27, 206-208
Evaluation interviews, 6, 27, 30
    report and, 259
    truth and, 224
Events, 3
    building theory and, 57
    chronology of, 204
    coding, 251
    daily, 168, 179-180
    examples describing, 24
    firsthand descriptions of, 80-81
    follow-up questions and, 146, 156
    historical, 17
    history of, 203
    iconic, 187-188
    interpretive approach and, 34-35
    main questions and, 146, 147
    minitours and, 188-189
    narrative and, 24
    oral histories and, 6, 27, 31
    ordinary, 168, 169-171, 179-180
    positivists and, 33
    probes and, 208-210
    record of, 84
    slowly evolving, 51
    taken-for-granted, 170
    topical interviews and, 6, 28, 29
    versions of, 87, 88, 209, 212-214, 215-
       218
Evidence, probes and, 146, 150, 210, 211
Examples, 24, 39, 40
    building theory from, 56
    cultural interviews and, 28
    culture and, 175
    details and, 80
    emerging theory and, 60
    follow-up questions and, 151, 192, 212
    grand tour questions and, 180

probes and, 146, 184-185, 208
in report, 261
vivid, 80-81
Excerpts, in report, 271
Excuse, account and, 25
Expectations:
    choices and, 170
    front and, 25
    mutual, 6
Experience probes, 210-211
Experiences:
    building theory from, 56
    common, 22
    context and, 9-10
    cultural interviews and, 6
    cultural premises and, 176
    learning about, 2
    others benefiting from, 170-171
    reflecting on, 104
    shared, 1-16, 132
    topics growing out of, 50
Explanations, 4, 40
    building theory and, 57
    contradictions and, 89, 216
    follow-up questions and, 153-154
    probes and, 208
    report and, 268
    themes and, 234
    winnowing, 46
    for worldview, 24
Explanatory concepts, 229-231

Factions, choosing interviewees and, 68-69
Facts, 134
    positivist model and, 32
    probes and, 209
    topical interviews and, 196
Falsehood, 223-225
Feelings:
    feminist research and, 37
    learning about, 2
Feminist model of critical social
    research, 32, 35-38, 39
Flexible research design, 43, 44-46, 56
Focused format, 5
Focus groups, 27-28, 139-140

About the Authors

Herbert J. Rubin is Professor of Sociology at Northern Illinois University. He received his bachelor's degree in Mathematics from Harvard University, his master's degree in Mathematics from Rensselaer Polytechnic Institute, and his Ph.D. from MIT in Political Science. He is author of *Applied Social Research* and (with Irene Rubin) *Community Organizing and Development.* He has written articles based on in-depth interviewing that explore rural development in Thailand, suburban land-use fights, cooperative housing, economic development, and community development, as well as a monograph, *The Dynamics of Development in Rural Thailand.* His current project on community-based development involves several years spent interviewing hundreds of people who work to renew hope in the inner city.

Irene S. Rubin is Professor of Public Administration at Northern Illinois University in DeKalb, Illinois. She received her bachelor's degree from Barnard College in Oriental Studies in 1967, her master's degree in East Asian Studies from Harvard in 1969, and her Ph.D. in Sociology from the University of Chicago in 1977. Her books based upon interview data include *The Politics of Retrenchment* (with Charles Levine and George Wolohojian), *Running in the Red,* and *Shrinking the Federal Government.* She has also published many articles based on in-depth interviews. She is currently editor of the journal *Public Budgeting and Finance.*

The authors undertake their research independently and on different topics and have consequently developed distinct interviewing styles. By talking with one another, reading each other's interview transcripts, and on occasion, watching each other interview, they have learned to respect a variety of interviewing styles that result from differences in topics, settings, and personalities. Both authors teach qualitative interviewing at Northern Illinois University. Their students have read chapters from the manuscript and contributed to the final presentation by asking questions and demanding clarifications.